_Pour ...

Avec toute mon affection fraternelle

Noël 1948.   Buffalo.

Lucien

# FOOTLOOSE IN FRANCE

(Jean Manzon)

# *Footloose*
# IN FRANCE

## by Horace Sutton

WITH PHOTOGRAPHS MOSTLY BY
THE AUTHOR

RINEHART & COMPANY, INC.
NEW YORK · TORONTO

*The first is for*
WALTER
*who in his short life was,*
*in so many things, first himself.*

# FOREWORD

IN the old days, the guidebooks used to speak a language laden with naves, clerestories, flamboyant windows, and trefoil-headed triforiums. I, for one, got the idea that travelers were an estoteric lot who jabbered in their own patois as soda-jerks, hash-slingers, mahjong-players, or Texans do. Sometime afterwards I discovered that travelers were everybody, and that travel is a recreation like going to the theater or listening to the radio. As in the case of the lives of the demi-mondes of historical novels, travel ought to make good reading as well as being fun to do.

This travel book reports the story of post-war France, and it presumes that you are not seeking an intermediate course in architectural planning. It is also practical. Francophiles can read it by the fireside in Cicero Falls. People looking for trouble abroad can learn where to find it. Schoolteachers from McCool Junction, Nebraska, on their first trips to France should be able to use it as a Bible.

Although one man's name is listed on the jacket, this is not, I hasten to say, a one-man show. In the first place, there is Philippe de Croisset, who arranged to have the facilities of the French National Tourist Office, of which he is North American agent general, placed at my disposal in France. A vote, too, in favor of George Tremel and Mme. Angele Levesque of the same organization, for planning the itinerary and providing background material; to J. B. Verlot and Henri LeMasson of the French National Railroads; to the ladies and gentlemen of Air France, particularly Ellis Reed in New York, Alex Belanco in Paris, and Leon Garnier in Corsica. And, in the order of their appearance, to the following Frenchmen in the four corners of France who showed me the land: Jean Thesmar in Paris; George Afrossimow in the suburbs; Paul Enault and Professor V. A. Priout in Normandy; Andrée Moussard, Jean Herbert and the Countess de Kermerec in Brittany; Roland Audemard in the valley of the Loire; Robert Riquelme in the Basque country; Commandant Prat in Provence; Pierre Van Overschee in Corsica; M. Viers and Mme. Berthe Pourriere on the Riviera; Mlle. Suzanne Helft throughout the Alps; Commandant Henri Charrier and M. Ph. Collot in Burgundy, and Edmond Lechten in Alsace.

The hotel and restaurant listings in this book are abridged from the famed *Guide Michelin,* and are reprinted through the courtesy of the Michelin Tire Company, publishers of maps and regional handbooks of France—and manufacturers, incidentally, of some pretty good tires. I am particularly indebted to Daniel Barcet, Chef des Services de Tourisme Michelin, for his co-operation, especially in making available the advance proofs of the new *Guide Michelin* for inclusion here.

Unless otherwise credited, the pictures were taken by me on a Rolleiflex camera, with a Schneider Xenar 3.5 lens, in post-war France, and were finished by the Leco studios in New York.

Somewhere along here there should be a word for Bill Raney, Executive Editor of Rinehart and Company, who helped me immeasurably in the preparation of this book—until he got the wanderlust somewhere in the middle of the eleventh chapter and took off for Europe himself. Also for Mike Dann and Nancy Waring who, as friends, advised, listened, read, suggested, cajoled, sympathized, humored, indulged, and tolerated beyond the call of friendship. I should also like to thank Norman Reader, Public Information Director of the French National Tourist Office, who started the whole thing one day by making a careless statement. "Why don't you write a book on France?" he said. H. S.

# CONTENTS

# THE FACTS OF LIFE

L. Viguier

# 1. THE FACTS OF LIFE
## ... in France

◇◇◇◇◇◇◇◇◇◇◇◇◇◇◇◇◇◇◇◇◇◇◇◇◇◇◇◇◇◇◇◇◇◇◇◇◇◇◇◇◇◇◇◇◇◇◇◇◇◇◇

FRANCE is alive and kicking. It is alive mainly through the efforts of its friendly neighbors, the Americans and the Britons, and in most quarters the debt is clearly recognized. It is kicking because after interminable years of war and occupation and liberation it has, in a way, failed to find the rosy future or the bright new tomorrow.

It kicks because the very existence, for a Frenchman, has been incredibly expensive. It kicks because in the first years following the liberation, its economic system became ensnarled in a hopeless entanglement never known in the worst days of the war. Because at the bakery one bought brown bread, at the polls one became involved with red politics, and to exist one had to buy in the black market.

Withal, only some of these pigments will color the life of the post-war tourist in France. It can be flatly stated that conditions for travelers are not nearly so bad as a daily session with the United States press over the past few years may have indicated. The first people who went to France after the war were fraught with stark impressions of rib-lean children and famine-bare restaurants, and took with them incredible stocks of canned meat, jars of vegetables, cartons of biscuits, jellies, chocolates, and bottles of potables. It amused French hotel owners, who stood ready to offer meat and fish

· 5 ·

in ample quantity, vegetables, salads, a fair supply of pretty good pastry, eggs, coffee, and, in most places, a medium amount of sugar.

Some restaurants and cafés serve an ersatz coffee known as *café national,* which although national, and often hot, is neither coffee nor drinkable. Most every place, however, serves *café filtré,* which is about the same brew that the French served for coffee before the war. Coffee grounds are placed in a silver receptacle, then flooded with hot water, and the whole contraption is placed on top of an ordinary cup. That's the way it comes to you. The coffee drips through a sieve, and, in a process not unakin to the Chinese method of water torture, gives you a cold cup of coffee in slightly less than twelve minutes.

This, mind you, is not just a post-war inconvenience. In the old, lush twenties, Americans used to carry a can of G. Washington's. Now everyone takes along a jar of instant coffee.

There are a few places where sugar is not available, especially on railroad trains, in small cafés, and in scattered cities. It is quite the thing to keep a small tin of sugar cubes in purse or pocket, and, even in elegant society, to offer to use your own.

Travelers may bring in a fair load of cigarettes—five cartons when we checked last, but you might inquire. French regulations change as often as the legislature. At any rate, the cartons you bring in must be carried in hand luggage and declared. Bringing in cigarettes in trunks or other hold baggage may be subject to a mighty substantial fine. If you are a smoker, bring the limit. Americans will find French cigarettes as strong as Mexican stogies, and American cigarettes are four or five times the domestic price.

The jack and master of all trades in a French hotel is the *concierge,* which means "janitor"—and which he really is not at all. A *concierge* corresponds more closely to a bell-captain, but he will also give you your key, find stamps for your mail, get you tickets for the theater, see that your laundry is sent out, and—what is most important—he will, more than likely, speak English. He can, also, cut the red tape spun by French officialdom. Visitors as well as citizens are required to have bread tickets, and while all restaurants do not demand them, there are some which do, and still others which are downright adamant about it. Travelers in France will be given a temporary supply of coupons immediately upon arrival at customs. When these are gone, the *concierge* can usually get the book renewed without your appearance at the city hall.

Every French hotel is required by law to have its guests fill out a police information form, when registering. The blank demands the usual vital information, including the point of origin of the trip, the destination, citizenship, purpose of travel, and passport number, about twenty questions in all.

Most hotels, and a great many restaurants, add ten, twelve, or fifteen per cent to every bill as a customary service charge. The process is extremely disagreeable to most Americans, who prefer to do their tipping on a merit basis, but the hotel owners say the policy was instituted by the trade unions. In some resorts a fifteen per cent service charge will automatically be added to your hotel bill.

In spite of this system, it will still be necessary to scatter tips like a Kansas farmer with a bag of seed. For porters, figure a base of ten cents per bag, and then add a little more, depending on the weight and distance. In spite of the fact that you are paying a service charge anyway, it is going to be very difficult to dismiss a bell-boy who has brought up your mail, or has had your suit pressed, with nothing more than a big, broad smile. Usherettes in the theaters rely on your tips, cab drivers expect ten per cent, and it is against the rule, but socially required, to give tour guides one or two hundred francs.

French hotel rooms are ordinarily a good deal larger than the miserly *boîtes* into which we cram our transients in the States. Naturally enough, they are fitted with French windows—distinctly a feast-

or-famine contrivance which allows huge gusts of air into your room, or none at all. There are practically no new hotels in France, and the *décor* is usually a slightly shabby version of some distinguished period. Marble clocks, ceiling to floor drapes, quilted walls, gilded furniture, and an outside terrace, may go with the most modest accommodations.

Every hotel of consequence supplies toilet tissue, perhaps not always the kind associated in American advertisements with plump, smiling, contented, unpsychotic babies—but paper just the same. Such public places as office buildings, depots, museums, and railroad trains will be found without. The international set has long since learned to bring along a package of flat-packed tissues from home, and to have some on hand when abroad in the land.

Don't expect hotels to have cute, little, guest-size bars of soap all over the bathrooms; as a matter of fact, don't expect any soap at all —and that goes for even the best hotels. You can bring in all you want short of making it look like a commercial importation.

The most violent Francophobe would have to admit that, if nothing else, the French are probably the best cooks in the world. They have a faculty for hanging enough trappings on a dinner to make ham and eggs look like a banquet. The practice of the culinary art is a respected profession in France for which one serves an apprenticeship, and because of which one commands respect.

The few restaurants in France which make a practice of hiring all-purpose waitresses, after the American method, are decidedly less expensive. Restaurant prices got so high for awhile that all eating places were required by law to post their menus outside the establishment. Every dining room, regardless of class, was also required to serve and advertise a fixed-price dinner for about thirty or forty francs. The result was that places comparable to the Waldorf, or the Pump Room, in the United States, were offering a thirty-cent meal consisting of cabbage and potatoes.

It became quite *au fait*, if one was on a budget, to shop for menus as one shopped for a new handbag or a new tie. The list prices, however, are often misleading. A great many restaurants charge a *couvert*, an addition to the check paid by each guest allegedly for the privilege of getting a tablecloth, napkin, and bread (if you have ration tickets). Add to this an automatic fifteen per cent for service and a two per cent tax; it looks big in francs but it isn't many dollars. GI's in France after the war, who tried to live on the government's $65 a month allowance, always claimed the French added to the check every number they could think of, including the date. That's why, they said, it was always more expensive to eat at the end of the month than at the beginning.

The French eat a breakfast that would starve a bird, and a lunch that would choke a horse. The ordinary breakfast is known as the *petit déjeuner*, which could be literally translated into "little lunch." If you take it all it will consist of bread, jam, and coffee, and sometimes butter. The old croissant and brioche breakfast is all but extinct, except on transcontinental flights of Air France. In most good hotels you can get eggs, sometimes fried in vegetable oil, and bacon which seems to be like bacon anywhere. Since a cup of coffee spiked with hot milk suffices for most Frenchmen, there are very few places open at breakfast time. It seems easiest in the long run to order breakfast brought to your hotel room, and be done with it. If you go downstairs to the dining room in the morning you are likely to find the waiter in shirt sleeves, the chairs on the table, and the evil eye upon you. This condition does not hold for most of Paris, where a number of restaurants serve American breakfasts—a bit of intelligence which will be dealt with anon.

Lunch in France is a ceremony that begins sharply and ceremoniously at twelve, and ends at two. Every shop and every office is closed, and it is impossible to accomplish any business—a situation which soup-and-sandwich Americans will find it less ulcerating to accept without a fight. Many people travel home for the noon meal, which in a restaurant might consist of hors d'oeuvres, wine, fish, and meat, potatoes, vegetable, cheese, pastry, coffee, and liqueur. It may turn out that each dish—let alone each course—will be served individually. First the meat, then the potatoes, then the vegetable, and so forth. One of the neatest tricks of any French holiday is to arrange for dessert and coffee to arrive at the same time. The most logical way is, of course, to ask for it that way. Usually the idea will seem so preposterous to the waiter that he figures he has misunderstood, and he thoughtfully waits until the last morsel of cake has gone drily down the hatch before appearing with the coffee. Cheer up—if it's *café filtré*, in twelve minutes it's yours.

The Frenchman drinks wine before, during, after, above, and beyond every meal. Some French workers start with a white wine eye-opener first thing in the morning. Nearly every district of France produces some kind of *vin du pays*—some white, some red, some rose, some sweet, some dry. White wine goes with fish or poultry, red wine with meat or roasts, and champagne with dessert. Three or four wines may go with each meal. The Frenchman seldom gets drunk, in spite of the fact that he puts the stuff away as we do water.

A lot of foreigners in France have often wondered whether there was a direct relationship between the amount of liquid swallowed daily by every Frenchman, and the necessity for keeping their toilets right out there in the open, handy as the corner newsstand. Some pompous old American biddies who used to come before the war got themselves habitually into a frenzy over the vulgarity of open-air *pissoirs*. That never bothered a Frenchman, who thinks nothing of asking a lady to wait a minute while he steps behind the screen.

There is also some sort of French law that prohibits the use of regular rest rooms, as we know them, in public places. Especially in the provinces, many cafés, swimming pools, and railway stations provide turkish toilets, tiled but decidedly primitive contrivances which will make an awful lot of Americans awfully homesick.

Not every hotel in France has a bath in every room. What is more, a room with a bath may be just that. The bath will consist of a bathtub, a washstand, and a *bidet,* but the toilet may be out in the hall. The barest sanitary facilities will include a washstand and a *bidet* behind a screen. This *bidet* business is a rather serious proposition with the French, and in the order of necessity it comes before a toilet any day. Michelin's guide tenderly translates *bidet* into *sitzbath.* Actually, it is a European device for feminine hygiene which resembles a toilet bowl without a seat. The Hotel Californie in Paris—and there may be others—has some rooms which contain *bidets* on wheels.

When they do put in an honest-to-goodness bathroom, it's as ornate as Versailles. Sometimes the bathrooms are cavernous and contain double washstands, cabinet toilets, and pipes for heating towels, but seldom will you find a shower. A suitable consultation with the chambermaid may produce a huge terrycloth bathrobe affair in place of a bathtowel, if you so desire.

As you must have realized by now, French habits, customs, manners, and morals, differ rather widely from what goes at home. Regarding this fact, many United States visitors will, from time to time, be extremely glad, utterly annoyed, completely outraged, absolutely charmed, and pre-eminently interested.

Some of the old *politesse*—what we in the States knew as "the grand European manner"—has disappeared following the realities of war. Still, Frenchmen lift their hats clean off their heads as a greeting, a process which must involve a point of integral honor, because sometimes the one being greeted is two blocks past at the height of the gesture, and most certainly never looks back. On the slightest recognition, a Frenchman will bow, and most certainly, if you are the guest, he will make a four-star production of shoving you through the door first. At the drop of a pinky a Frenchman shakes hands, lightly and daintily, but with everyone in sight. Ladies are expected to proffer their hands first, likewise upperclass men in cases of employer-employee or master-servant relationships. Upon entering an office, a board meeting, or a party, you shake hands with everyone; with good friends a left-hand waggle will suffice. In any case, don't leave anybody out, or the omitted one will trundle home brooding over what in hell it was he said the other day that made you angry.

As André Maurois so needlessly explained, the French are mature about sex. You'll find the maturity expressed in the Paris shows, which are bare and bawdy, in the bold approach of prostitutes who might just as well be asking for the time. More on this later. The maturity is also expressed in the frank approach of women in all social spheres which is quite unlike the characteristic well-should-I or well-shouldn't-I vacillations of the ladies here at home, the Kinsey report be damned. A French lad and a French girl in love have eyes only for each other. You may think it's a disgusting display, a fortunate exhibition, or ain't France romantic! Locally they think it's lovely. After a while you may, too.

### ◆§ How to Get There

Even Finian McLonergan, the sage Broadway philosopher, had something to say about passports. "How do you expect to get in a free country without one?" he asked.

France is free again, but you still need a passport to get there. An American citizen, native-born or naturalized, may apply for a passport before a clerk of a Federal court or a state court authorized to naturalize aliens, or before an agent of the Department of State. Passport agents of the State Department can be found in New York in the Subtreasury Building, and on the mezzanine of the International Building in Rockefeller Center. There is an office at 100 McAllister Street in San Francisco, and people handy to Washington may file directly with the passport division of the State Department.

The first passports ever issued were carried by envoys of the old Roman emperors to identify the diplomats as legal recipients of aid and comfort in their travels. Modern passports, as we know them, were originally devised to cut down on spy traffic, but before World War I tourists could travel through England, France, Germany, Italy, Spain, Holland, Belgium and most of the rest of the world without them. Nowadays, although every country's Justice Department is aware that any international spy who wants a passport knows where to get one, here is what the honest American citizen still needs for permission to get out of the country:

1. Two photographs, full face, against a light background, printed on thin paper, size three inches square or 2½ x 2½.

2. $10.

3. For native-born citizens, a birth certificate or old passport.

4. For naturalized citizens, naturalization papers.

5. One form describing yourself and the purpose of your trip.

6. If traveling on pleasure, proof of return passage.

7. If traveling on business, a letter written by your employer, addressed to the Secretary of State, describing the purpose of the trip, the destination, and the expected duration of the stay.

8. One witness who has known you two years, who is a United States citizen, who will appear with you in person to file your application.

An experienced travel agent will, in many cases, be glad to relieve you of the details of filing your passport application. In any event, your petition for the document must be sent to Washington, and the clearing process takes two to three weeks. In emergency instances, however, passports have been obtained in a few hours.

Armed with a passport, you are now eligible to try for the visa which is demanded by the French government. To obtain the visa you must present yourself, one photograph, $4.31, and your passport, at any French consulate. Special visas are also issued for students, business people, and persons stopping in France in transit. The visa is an imprint stamped in your passport.

French consuls authorized to issue visas in the United States are located at the following addresses:

610 Fifth Avenue
New York, N.Y.

690 Market Street
San Francisco, Calif.

919 North Michigan Avenue
Chicago, Ill.

712 International Building
New Orleans, La.

448 South Hill Street
Los Angeles, Calif.

178 Beacon Street
Boston, Mass.

2129 Wyoming Avenue, N.W.
Washington, D.C.

There is no limit on the amount of American money you may bring into France, nor are there any restrictions on denominations of bills. It is against the local ground rules, however, to take in more than 4,000 francs.

Even though what was once the black market has since become the "free market," travelers entering France are required to declare all their money. Every once in a while somebody gets searched, and the excuse that the offender didn't think travelers' checks counted as money has long since been overworked. Dollars can be exchanged for francs at any bank, at certain depots, and at many big Paris hotels which have been licensed by the government for such purpose. Each exchange is recorded in your passport, and when you leave the country the sum you have in cash, the amount you have exchanged, and the original amount you had when you arrived, are all supposed to tally.

The United States Government requires that all persons entering the country, its own citizens included, shall be able to show certificates of smallpox vaccination not over three years old. This is a strict regu-

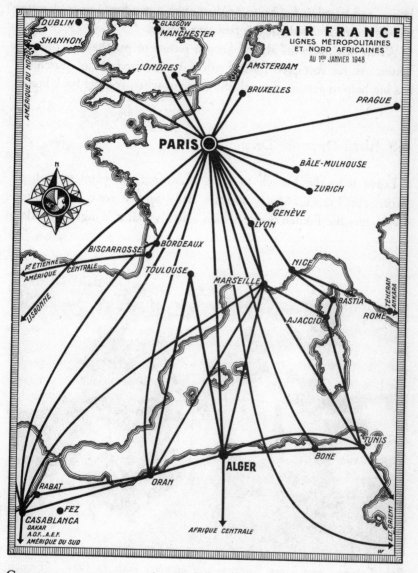

CONTINENTAL ROUTES OF AIR FRANCE.

lation, and travelers failing to produce such a certificate upon re-entry will be required to submit to a new vaccination.

When buying items abroad keep a record of purchases — or even better, ask for receipted bills of sale. An itemized list of purchases is a big help in getting through the customs when you get back home.

### ᦉ *Asleep Over the Deep*

Leave it to the French to have discovered the painless path to Paris. Air France, which operates daily service from the United States, flies the French way — which is to say that it brings to aviation

*Bob Topping and Lana Turner—the painless path to Paris.* (French National Tourist Office—Chadel)

a maximum of comfort and the absolute quintessence of luxury. The French have opened their own magnificent building in New York, they have painted the insides of their aircraft in soft pastel colors, and they have put aboard a cuisine that remains unrivaled in the air.

Twice a week, Air France flies the Golden Comet, non-stop Constellation sleeper service, direct from New York to Paris. Only 18 passengers are taken aboard the Golden Comet, and there is a $125 extra charge for the berth, $150 if two sleep in the same compartment. The regular fare to Paris is $370. The Golden Comet roars out of New York about seven p.m., and the doors are hardly closed when the steward serves an *apéritif*, vermouth or Dubonnet. Then begins the famous 440-mile meal. Paté maison, lobster salad, and breast of chicken with mushrooms, truffles, and rice. A split of Mumm's Cordon Rouge is popped open for every passenger, and the bottle is slipped into a special compartment. Asparagus is served as a separate course, followed by grapes, apples, and an assortment of cheeses. Ice cream covered with chocolate sauce and topped with a cherry ends the 440-mile meal, so called because when you have eaten it you are already 440 miles nearer Paris.

The berths, both upper and lower, are broad and spacious, about twice the size of Pullman accommodations. Unless you are an extremely restless sleeper, it is quite convenient to take an overnight case into the berth. The beds are soft, the flight is smooth, and all you hear is the quiet, even hum of the engines, a mere purr compared with the rattle of a railroad. You fly into the dawn, and eight hours later comes the knock of the steward — coffee and brioche in bed. Paris in forty minutes. There is just time to dress and shave in the modernistic men's room, which holds four at a time. It has adequate shaving mirrors, wash basins, and an electric shaver. The ladies' room is decorated with cream-colored furniture trimmed in pink, has dressing tables, offers Kleenex, band-aids, towels, and soap.

By the time you are dressed, the signs flash on ordering passengers

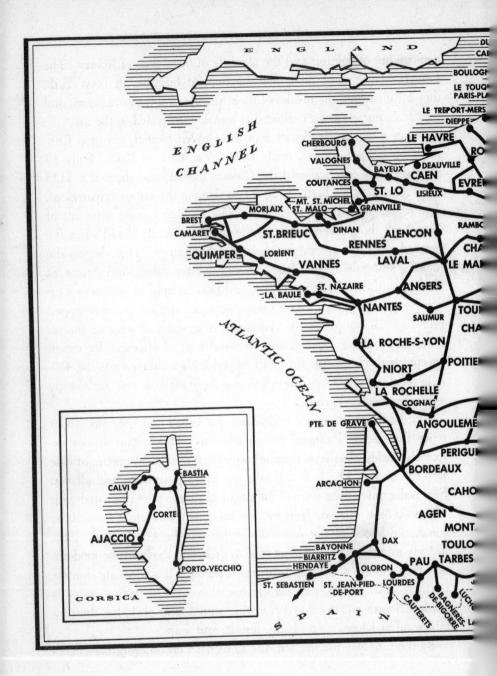

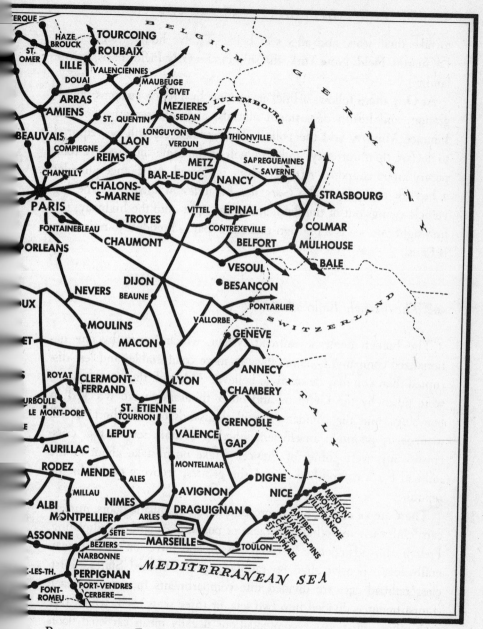

ROUTES OF THE FRENCH NATIONAL RAILROADS

to take their seats, and affix seat belts. Twelve hours after leaving LaGuardia Field, New York, the ship circles Orly Field, Paris, before landing.

At Orly there follows a brief inspection by French customs, immigration, and health department officials, and representatives of the Finance Ministry and the police. Here passengers will be required to declare their currency, and they will at the same time receive temporary ration coupons. After everyone is cleared, Air France provides a bus for the ride to the *Gare des Invalides* in town. As the big vehicle swings out of the field, and turns right onto the highway, the first sight you see is a big sign that says "Bar — Freddy's Joint." This is Paris!

## The French Railroads

The French domestic railroad system, which is run by one nationalized company, is more efficient, more comfortable, and less disrupted than you may be ready to believe. Although thousands of cars were taken by the Germans and other thousands were wrecked in bombings, and the company is still thousands of cars short, it still manages to maintain an efficient schedule of train service that crisscrosses into every corner of France. Make no mistake about it, the railroad has accomplished one of the greatest recovery efforts in the republic.

There are, of course, few fluorescent lights, automatic doors, nursery cars, club cars, and other gimcracks of post-war American railroading. French railroads operate in three classes, and travel on them is generally less expensive than on railroads in the United States. First-class railroad cars are divided into compartments for six, and each compartment is divided into two sets, of three seats each, which face each other. First-class accommodations usually mean carpeted floors

*French Railroads—"more efficient, more comfortable, and less disrupted than you might be ready to believe. . . ."*

and upholstered seats. Second-class quarters, designed to accommodate eight per compartment, are usually wood and leather. Third-class space amounts to hard, wood benches, ten persons to a compartment. Whatever the class, the continental compartment system strips from a traveler the private anonymity of being alone in a carful of people. It forces him into company with passengers he never saw before, submits him to their constant scrutiny, scrambles his knees freely with theirs, subjects him at close range to their habits, idiosyncrasies, thoughts, conjectures, and snoring.

Railroad travelers must present their tickets when going through the gate to the train. During the trip the ticket is controlled again by a conductor who habitually announces his arrival by knocking on the glass of the compartment with his ticket punch. When debarking it is again necessary to show your ticket as you leave the station. If you are traveling with suitcase, overnight bag, typewriter, and briefcase, and you can't find a porter, you may find yourself unloading a string of epithets at French efficiency every time you have to unload your bags to show your ticket.

Eating and sleeping on French trains is a process pretty well controlled by an organization similar to the Pullman Company in the United States. It is known, rather grandly, as the Compagnie Internationale des Wagon-Lits et des Grands Express Européens. Hours before each mealtime, the dining-car steward comes around with slips of paper, yours for the taking. The slips bear numbers indicating the seating at which you are entitled to eat. The sooner you take a slip the lower your number, and the earlier you eat. A waiter comes through the cars tinkling a little bell to announce each sitting. Meals are both basic and standard aboard the cars of the Wagon-Lits people. There is only one meal from which to choose, à la boarding house. Either you eat it or you don't. You cannot substitute — simply because there are no substitutions — although you can omit, and you can supplement from a long list of wines, beers, cakes, extra desserts, and liqueurs. When you take something extra the waiter-in-charge-of-supplements makes a small chalk mark on the table. At the end of the meal the steward comes around with a cash box, adds up all

*First class sleeping car—second class has two berths.* (French National Railroads)

## Charting the Course for France

| By Air | Route | Time† | Minimum Cost | Type Aircraft |
|---|---|---|---|---|
| Air France | New York—Gander Shannon—Paris | 16 Hours | $370 | Constellation |
| | New York—Paris Non-stop | 12-14 Hours | $370 plus $125 for Berth * | Constellation "Golden Comet" |
| American Overseas Airlines | New York—Shannon—London. Change to British European Airways for Paris | 16 Hours | $370 | Constellation to London DC-3 to Paris |
| Trans World Airlines | New York—Gander Shannon—Paris | 15.40 Hours | $370 | Constellations |
| Pan-American World Airways | New York—London Non-stop. Change to Panair Do Brasil for Paris | 14.45 Hours | $370 | Constellations to London |
| | New York—Lisbon via Azores. Change to Panair Do Brasil for Paris | 20.25 Hours | $370 | Constellations to Lisbon |
| British Overseas Airways Corp. | New York—Gander Shannon—London Change to British European Airways for Paris | 16 Hours | $370 | Constellations to London Vikings to Paris |
| Sabena Belgian Airlines | New York—Gander—Shannon —Brussels—Paris | 16 Hours | $374 | DC-6 to Brussels DC-4 to Paris |
| KLM Royal Dutch Airlines | New York—Gander—Prestwick —Amsterdam—Paris | 20.50 Hours | $370 | Constellations to Amsterdam DC-3's to Paris |

* $150 for berth if occupied by two persons  † Elapsed scheduled flying time, not including station waits

| By Sea | Ship | Route | Time | Minimum Cost‡ | |
|---|---|---|---|---|---|
| French Line | De Grasse | New York—Southampton—Le Havre | 9 days | 1st Class | $265 |
| | | | | Cabin Class | $180 |
| Cunard White Star Line | Queen Mary | New York—Cherbourg | 5 days | 1st Class | $375 |
| | | | | 2nd | $232.50 |
| | | | | 3rd | $170 |
| | Queen Elizabeth | New York—Cherbourg | 5 days | 1st Class | $375 |
| | | | | 2nd | $232.50 |
| | | | | 3rd | $170 |
| United States Lines | America | New York—Cobh—Cherbourg | 6 days | 1st Class | $335 |
| | | | | 2nd | $217.50 |
| | | | | 3rd | $165 |
| | Washington | New York—Cobh—Le Havre | 7 days | One-Class | $185 |
| Holland-American Line | Nieuw Amsterdam | New York—Southampton—Le Havre | 7 days | 1st Class | $325 |
| | | | | 2nd | $215 |
| | | | | 3rd | $165 |

‡ Passengers debarking at French ports add the following extra charge for port tax:
1st Class, $6.50; 2nd Class, $4.50; 3rd Class, $3.00

the potsy scores with the cost of your basic meal, and that's your check. From bell tinkle to cash box takes about an hour and a half.

There are two ways to sleep aboard a French train: one is to engage a *couchette*, and the other is to take a regular berth. *Couchettes* are nothing more than three seats, or one-half of a compartment with the arm rests removed. There are four *couchettes* (two upper and two lower) in first class, six in second class, and tickets are purchased from the French Railroads (Société Nationale des Chemins de Fer). You can rent blankets and pillows on board. Regular sleeping berths are found only in sleeping cars operated by the Wagon-Lits Co., and except for the general informality and the fact that all berths are enclosed in compartments, things are about the same as they are with the Pullman Company. First-class accommodations are private, but second-class cabins are equipped for two passengers.

A man I know, on his first trip to France, had reservations from Paris to Mégève, and was assigned to a lower in a closed compartment that had two berths. Nobody arrived to claim the upper until two minutes before the train departed, when a handsome, blonde lady opened the door and walked in. Our man spoke no French and the lady no English, and so the fellow was left to his unilingual thoughts. By means of sign language the lady conveyed her intended departure from the train by 5 A.M. She thereby won the right to his lower berth, he gallantly taking the upper. "Those things will happen in France," said the fellow — who happens to be a laconic sort, anyway.

Most of the French National Railroad system operates under steam, although a general program for electrification is under way. On short runs the railroad uses something called the "Autorail," which is a one-class, motor-driven, modern-looking train. "Autorails" are clean and fast, and used a great deal by country people who travel with bundles of vegetables, shopping bags loaded with wine, pots full of plants, and live ducks.

The French railroads also maintain a network of bus transportation, principally in Corsica and on the Grenoble-Riviera run, two services which are outlined in the chapters on those regions.

### ᴥ§ France by Sea

The gay old French Line, once renowned for the finest food and service on the Atlantic, for its celebrity-studded passenger lists, and for its fine ships, suffered heavily from the war and a consistent run of bad luck. Of its once great fleet, the *Normandie* burned at her New York pier in 1942, the *Paris* sank at Le Havre, and the *Champlain* fell prey to a magnetic mine dropped during the night by a German plane, before the French armistice. The German steamship *Europa,* which once held the blue ribbon of the Atlantic, was awarded to France after the war as part of German reparations. She was renamed *Liberté,* but before she could be placed in service she broke from her moorings at Le Havre, ran afoul of the sunken *Paris,* and sank. The *Ile de France,* which survived the war, is being refitted and will carry 521 first-class passengers, 634 in cabin class, and 292 in tourist class, all in completely refurnished surroundings. The *Liberté,* afloat again, is also being readied for service.

Meanwhile, the French Line is maintaining the "longest gangplank in the world" with the *de Grasse,* which carries 711 passengers in two classes, and two small ships, the *Wisconsin* and the *Oregon,* which, respectively, carry 57 and 75 passengers. The *de Grasse,* which takes nine days to plow from New York to Le Havre, spent most of its pre-war North American service on the West Indies cruise run. For passage to France the *de Grasse* now charges $265 first-class, and $180 cabin-class, the only two classes on the ship, but there is no guarantee of a private stateroom, even in first-class accommodations. In the old days, the French chefs used to claim they could whip up anything at sea from "quail under glass" to reindeer. The larder isn't quite that well stocked aboard the *de Grasse* these days, although the food is substantial and excellently prepared. The best thing that can be said for the *de Grasse,* is, of course, that as the only major French boat in service it is staffed with the cream of the personnel from the fine old French Line ships.

For the time being, at least, the Atlantic crown seems to be shared by the Queens of the Cunard White Star Line, which between them maintain weekly service, New York to Cherbourg.

The French National Railroads maintains special boat trains from the docksides of Le Havre and Cherbourg to Paris. Passengers clear customs upon debarking, then cross the quays to the waiting trains. The trip from Le Havre takes three hours, costs $4 for first-class seats, $2.75 for second-class. Everybody ends up at the Gare St. Lazare — which, as anybody knows, is hardly a row of sidewalk tables away from the Café de la Paix.

### ◆§ How to Eat in French

French menus, like French foods, are done up under truffles of terminology, seasoned with a sea of adjectival sauces. The epicurean result is superb, but for the curious and/or uninitiated who want to know what they're eating, there follows a glossary of French menu terms. A typical menu listing might read *Le Coq au Vin à la Bourguignonne,* which means chicken cooked in wine the-way-they-make-it-in-Burgundy. The glossary includes basic food expressions, but it does not list methods of preparation. That would take a book in itself.

| | |
|---|---|
| abat | giblets |
| abricots | apricots |
| agneau | lamb |

| | |
|---|---|
| alose | shad |
| aloyau | sirloin |
| amandes | almonds |
| ananas | pineapples |
| anchois | anchovies |
| anguille | eel |
| artichauts | artichokes |
| asperges | asparagus |
| aubergines | egg plant |
| avoine | oats |
| bananes | bananas |
| barbue | brill (fish) |
| becasse | woodcock |
| becassine | snipe |
| beignets | fritters |
| beurre | butter |
| blé | wheat |
| boeuf | beef |
| bouilli de boeuf | boiled beef |
| brochet | pike |
| brochette | skewered |
| cabillaud | scrod |
| caille | quail |
| canard sauvage | wild duck |
| caneton | duckling |
| carottes | carrots |
| carpe | carp |
| carre d'agneau | rack of lamb |
| carre de mouton | rack of mutton |
| carre de porc | rack of pork |
| carre de veau | rack of veal |
| celeri | celery |

| | |
|---|---|
| cepes | mushrooms (French) |
| cerises | cherries |
| champignons | mushrooms |
| chataignes | chestnuts |
| chateaubriand | steak |
| chevreuil | venison |
| chicoree | chicory |
| choucroute | sauerkraut |
| chou fleur | cauliflower |
| chou rouge | red cabbage |
| chou vert | cabbage |
| choux de Bruxelles | Brussels sprouts |
| clovisses | clams |
| concombres | cucumbers |
| coq | chicken |
| coq de bruyere | grouse |
| coquillages | shellfish |
| côtes d'agneau | lamb chops |
| côtes de mouton | mutton chops |
| côtes de porc | pork chops |
| côtes de veau | veal chops |
| courgettes | small squash |
| crêpes | pancakes |
| cresson | watercress |
| crevettes | shrimp |
| croustades | tartlets |
| cuissot de veau | leg of veal |
| dattes | dates |
| ecrevisses | crawfish |
| endives | endives |
| épaule d'agneau | shoulder of lamb |
| épaule de mouton | shoulder of mutton |

| | |
|---|---|
| épaule de veau | shoulder of veal |
| eperlans | smelts |
| épinards | spinach |
| escalopes | veal steak (scallopini) |
| estragon | tarragon (seasoning) |
| esturgeon | sturgeon |
| faisan | pheasant |
| farine | flour |
| faux-filet | joint of beef |
| fenouil | fennel |
| fèves | lima beans |
| figues | figs |
| filet de boeuf | fillet of beef |
| flageolets | kidney beans |
| foie | liver |
| foie gras | goose liver |
| fraises | strawberries |
| framboises | raspberries |
| gelinotte | hazel grouse |
| gigot d'agneau | leg of lamb |
| gigot de mouton | leg of mutton |
| glace | ice cream |
| glace naturelle | sherbet |
| goujon | whitebait |
| graisse | lard |
| grille | broiled |
| grives | field fare (game) |
| groseilles | currants |
| groseilles à maquereau | gooseberries |
| haddock | haddock |
| hareng | herring |
| haricots verts | string beans |

| | |
|---|---|
| homard | lobster |
| huîtres | oysters |
| laitue | lettuce |
| langouste | crawfish |
| lapin | rabbit |
| lavaret | lavaret (fish) |
| lentilles | lentils |
| lièvre | hare |
| limande | flounder |
| mais | corn |
| mandarines | tangerines |
| maquereau | mackerel |
| marrons | chestnuts |
| mauviette | lark |
| melon | melon |
| melon d'eau | watermelon |
| merlan | whiting |
| merle | blackbird |
| mirtylles | blueberries |
| morilles | sponge mushrooms |
| morue | codfish |
| moules | mussels |
| navets | turnips |
| nèfles | medlars (European) |
| noisettes | hazelnuts |
| noix | walnuts |
| oie | goose |
| oignons | onions |
| oranges | oranges |
| ortolan | ortolan (bird) |
| oseille | soup greens |
| ours | bear |

| | |
|---|---|
| oursins | sea urchins |
| peches | peaches |
| perche | perch |
| perdreau | young partridge |
| petit pois | peas |
| pigeon | squab |
| piments | peppers |
| pintade | guinea hen |
| pluviers | plover (bird) |
| poires | pears |
| poivre | pepper |
| poivrons | peppercorns |
| pommes | apples |
| pommes de terre | potatoes |
| pomplamous | grapefruit |
| potiron | pumpkin |
| poularde | capon |
| poulet | chicken |
| poussin | spring chicken |
| prunes | plums |
| radis | radishes |
| raie | skate |
| raifort | horseradish |
| raisins | grapes |
| reine-claude | green gages (plums) |
| ris de veau | sweetbreads |
| rissolée | browned |
| rognon | kidney |
| rôti | roast |
| rouget | red mullet |
| salade | salad |
| sanglier | wild boar |

| | |
|---|---|
| sarcelle | widgeon (wild duck) |
| sardines | sardines |
| sauce | gravy |
| saumon | salmon |
| sauté d'agneau | lamb sauté |
| sauté de boeuf | beef sauté |
| sauté de mouton | mutton sauté |
| sauté de veau | veal sauté |
| semoule | semolina |
| sole | sole |
| tête de veau | calves head |
| thon | tuna |
| timbale | timbale (pie) |
| tomates | tomatoes |
| topinambours | Jerusalem artichokes (sweet potato) |
| tournedos | steak (fillet) |
| truffle | type of mushroom |
| truite | trout |
| turbot | turbot (fish) |

## The Cathedrals of France After World War II

ABBEVILLE (*Saint Vulfran*)—*Damage*: fairly heavy.

ALBI—*Damage*: none.

ALENCON—*Damage*: slight, glass shattered, vaults cracked and mullions split.

AMIENS—*Damage*: slight. *Repairs in hand*: gable, Maccabean Chapel, roof.

ANGERS—*Damage*: fairly heavy to front of building. *Stained Glass*: partially replaced.

ANGOULEME—*Damage*: none.

AUCH—*Damage*: none.

AUXERRE—*Damage*: mainly to stained glass. *Repairs in hand*: roof of south aisle.

BAYEUX—*Damage*: none.

BAYONNE—*Damage*: none.

BEAUVAIS—*Damage*: fairly heavy, mainly to choir stalls, now restored.

BLOIS—*Damage*: fairly heavy.

BOURGES—*Damage*: none. *Stained Glass*: Partially replaced.

CAEN (*Saint Etienne*)—*Damage*: considerable.

CAEN (*La Trinité*)—*Damage*: fairly heavy. *Repairs in hand*: general consolidation and temporary re-roofing.

CAEN (*Saint Gilles*)—*Damage*: very considerable.

CAHORS—*Damage*: none.

CARCASSONNE—*Damage*: none.

CHALONS-SUR-MARNE—*Damage*: fairly heavy, mainly to stained glass.

CHARTRES—*Damage*: slight. *Repairs in hand*: roof and south spire. *Stained Glass*: partially replaced.

CLERMONT-FERRAND—*Damage*: none.

COUTANCES—*Damage*: considerable to lantern turret and south portal; temporarily closed for repairs.

DOL—*Damage*: none.

EVREUX—*Damage*: considerable.

LAON—*Damage*: slight, mainly to front of building.

LIMOGES—*Damage*: none.

LISIEUX—*Damage*: slight, mainly to lantern turret and roof; some shattering of windows.

LE MANS—*Damage*: slight damage to windows and roof.

METZ—*Damage*: none.

MOULINS—*Damage*: none.

NANTES—*Damage*: considerable, particularly to roof, vaults and apse. *Repairs in hand*: partial reconstruction of four bays.

NEVERS—*Damage*: considerable, particularly to vaults, timber and apse. *Repairs in hand*: south-east roof and transept and timberwork.

ORLEANS—*Damage*: fairly considerable, particularly to cupola, belfry and west façade. *Repairs in hand*: roof, canopies, south tower and High Altar.

PARIS—*Damage*: none. *Stained Glass*: old glass replaced.

PERIGUEUX—*Damage*: none.

POITIERS—*Damage*: none.

LE PUY—*Damage*: none.

REIMS—*Damage*: none.

RENNES—*Damage*: slight, mainly to ceilings and south aisle. *Repairs in hand*: roof.

ROUEN—*Damage*: serious, particularly to south aisle and Saint Romain tower. *Repairs in hand*: temporary roofing, pending completion of roof reconstruction, stone dressings, framework of roof, and vaults.

SAINT-DIE—*Damage*: very serious, building partly destroyed. *Repairs in hand*: cloisters, west façade, south tower.

SAINT-LO—*Damage*: very serious, particularly to roof, vaults and spire. *Repairs in hand*: arrangement of a temporary church.

SAINT-MALO—*Damage*: very serious, particularly to spire, vaults, cross-struts and south roof. *Repairs in hand*: arrangement of a temporary church.

SAINT-OMER—*Damage*: slight. *Repairs in hand*: framework of belfry, restoration of cloisters.

SENLIS—*Damage*: none.

SENS—*Damage*: none.

SOISSONS—*Damage*: slight.

STRASBOURG—*Damage*: fairly considerable. *Repairs in hand*: vaults, lantern turret and crypt. Stained glass back in place.

TOULOUSE—*Damage*: none.

TOURS—*Damage*: slight, mainly to nave upper windows. *Repairs in hand*: general consolidation and re-roofing of north aisle.

TROYES—*Damage*: slight, mainly to roofing, ridge ornaments, mullions, façade and vaults.

PARIS

The Eiffel Tower—"too many tipsy soldiers teetered too close. . . ."

*Ray Milland and wife at the coutourier's—Berlitz French . . . and . . .
the Paris Herald.*

# 2. PARIS

◇◇◇◇◇◇◇◇◇◇◇◇◇◇◇◇◇◇◇◇◇◇◇◇◇◇◇◇◇◇◇◇◇◇◇◇◇◇◇◇◇◇◇◇◇◇◇◇

PARIS, "City of Light," is still shining, although perhaps not quite so brightly as it shone in those gay tourist days before the war. If the light danced then, perhaps you may say it flickers now. Slowly the city is regaining its strong, assertive brilliance. Yet one recognizes the lack of certainty about the future, the disappointment with the present, the fatigue from the past. That much must be admitted. Life is free, but life is also expensive, sometimes a little hungry, and always a little threadbare.

But Paris is 2,000 years old. It has seen kings and emperors, beggars and poets, revolutionists and foreign armies. It has been built by some of the world's greatest powers, flavored by some of the fondest of romanticists. It has outlived them all.

Tourists who remember Paris with a forlorn nostalgia may be assured that the city lives, breathes, even sings. It seems to be emerging from its unhappy decade with a new sense of practicality, patterned not a little after a first-hand look at American initiative, methods of operation, and success.

The city's traffic is teeming. Everything that has wheels, rolls. Anything without power is pushed. The Champs Elysées, the Concorde, the Place de l'Opéra are jammed nightly with a mélange of jeeps, Citroens, go-carts, push-carts, bicycles, carriages, wagons, crumbling cabs, brassy new American cars. A handsome lady in a derby hat and riding coat rides magnificently up the avenues in an

· 39 ·

open carriage, and solicits fares. A mustachioed cab driver still steers his ancient red-and-black Renault; he is as uncommunicative, as horn-happy, as malcontent as ever.

Americans are streaming into Paris almost as they did before the war. You see them crowding the hotel lobbies, buying the Paris edition of the New York *Herald Tribune* at the kiosks and carrying it about town like a badge of nationality. You see them in the shops, you hear them talking their Berlitz French, telling a barber how they want their "horses" cut when they mean their "hair," announcing to the world how "passionate" they are when they mean how "warm." Already the students are back, a thousand or more, living this time on the sixty-five-dollars-a-month GI Bill of Rights, and becoming more bearded and more bereted by the minute. The tourist tours are operating again, and, come spring, the buds burst on the Tuileries trees, old tousled men fish in the Seine, the book stalls open on the Left Bank, the tables go out along the Champs Elysées which becomes one great big long open-air café. The air is sweet, the crowds walk slowly, and — just like that! — a pretty French girl impulsively turns her head and kisses the cheek of her man. Paris is nearly Paris again. It's very plain to see.

Nearly all the travelers in Europe — to say very little of those going elsewhere in France — must stop in Paris. It is a center for travel as well as for fashion, chic, beauty, and the arts. Travelers' welfare groups abound in Paris, and after getting a thorough rejuvenation from the hordes of GIs, WACs, nurses, and civilian aids we sent over during the war, they are operating at full steam, and are schooled perhaps better than ever before in American ways. Not the least of these organizations is the Commissariat General au Tourisme, the government's own bureau at 8 Avenue de l'Opéra. The Paris bureau is headquarters for the far-flung offices which have branches, under the name French National Tourist Office, in London, Montreal, New York, Chicago, and San Francisco. The whole first floor of the

"... come spring, the buds burst on the Tuileries trees, old tousled men fish in the Seine ... the book stalls open on the Left Bank ... Paris is nearly Paris again. ..."

Commissariat's headquarters is given over to those end-products of all the worldwide branch offices, the people who finally have arrived for a holiday in Paris.

To travelers in Paris the Commissariat is all things; it answers questions, solves problems, obtains items that are unobtainable, acts as unofficial lawyer, counselor, confessor, bureau of missing persons, lost and found, ticket broker, translator, and general all-around Aladdin. Kingpin of this clearing house for wayfarers is Jean Thesmar, a tall, thin gentleman with a brush mustache who got his baptism of tourist trouble-shooting in the days following the liberation when there were more khaki-clad Americans in Paris than there were Parisians.

Thesmar developed quite a reputation with the American Army. Tickets for the Folies Bergère, tours of the city, and addresses of good restaurants were easy, he says. One day, however, a huge but unhappy GI presented himself. Tours and girlie shows held no interest for him. He had one hobby: fire engines. Thesmar thought a minute, then reached for the telephone. Soon he had the fire chief of the City of Paris on the wire, and they went into earnest consultation. The chief agreed to meet the GI, and — the way Thesmar tells it — they got along fine from the first minute. They talked about fires and engines, and ladders and fire dogs, the way the boys do around the fire house when things get dull. The GI and the chief met for several days, and spent hours in pleasant discussion before the soldier's leave was up. The chief thought he ought to give his friend a send-off, so as a farewell party he mobilized three hundred firemen, set a practice building ablaze and called out every piece of equipment down to the last pulmotor. Then he gave the GI a fire helmet suitably inscribed from the Fire Department of the City of Paris. The soldier went back to the front an everlasting friend of France, and the helmet went on display in a New York bank.

*". . . in the gay old twenties . . . nightclubbers . . . and onion soup. . . ."*
(French National Tourist Office)

Another soldier came in one morning. The usual tourist haunts
didn't interest him, either. He wanted a skeleton. Could Mr. Thesmar help? Sure, said Mr. T., did the gentleman want a male or a
female? The GI said that wasn't important, just so he had a skeleton.
The next morning Thesmar had the bones ready and waiting. The
only hitch was, there was a slight charge. Thesmar is apologizing

about it to this day. "I was unable," he says, with a hopeless shrug, "to buy skeletons on general expenses."

With this kind of preparation, Thesmar was ready and waiting for the dignitaries and celebrities who flock to Paris in normal times. He says he seems to have the most trouble with Indians and Egyptians. Once a prominent Egyptian who was married to a beautiful woman some twenty years his junior had to send his wife to Tours. Gasoline was in short supply, but he prevailed upon Thesmar to get a car, and make the necessary arrangements. Thesmar decided to use his own official car, and notified the lady. At the last minute a Canadian newspaper man who also wanted to go to Tours turned up, and Thesmar sent him along with the beautiful lady. When the Egyptian found out that an unattached man accompanied his unchaperoned wife, he considered his wife dishonored, set off an international ruckus, and finally challenged the Canadian to a duel.

When the Big Four conference was held in Paris just after the war, many commodities were extremely hard to find in France. At the very head of the shortage list was, of course, soap. And Thesmar's office was asked to find not just soap, but soap that had been manufactured without animal fat. It was wanted by an Indian delegate whose religion forbade him to use soap made with pig grease.

Another Indian, the Honorable Sir Khizar Hayat Khan from the Punjab, who wore a huge turban, needed some starch to keep his headdress in shape. Thesmar put eleven assistants on eleven telephones and scoured all of France for starch, which had been unobtainable for six years. In a little village 600 kilometers from Paris some starch was finally found. It was sent by car to Lyon, flown to Paris, and delivered to the potentate as if the breathless Thesmar had been keeping a piece in the bottom drawer of his desk all along.

When Ludwig Bemelmans was in Paris doing some stories for *Holiday* he was taken in hand by the tourist office. He never forgot the efficient and magic touch of Thesmar's Paris bureau. While traveling through Austria some weeks later, Bemelmans ran out of gas, at a place called Lech am Arlberg. He tried to buy some, but found he was out of ration tickets. He looked up the black-market sources, but none of them had any gas left. Finally, in desperation he wired Thesmar in Paris, signing his plea "Col. Bemelmans." The wire was received at six o'clock one Saturday evening, just as the office was closing. Nonetheless, Thesmar went into action, and immediately radioed General Bethouart, the French High Commissioner in Austria. First thing the next morning an army truck pulled up in front of Bemelmans' hotel; it was loaded with gas for which the driver would accept no payment. What's more, he had an invitation for Colonel Bemelmans to join the general for dinner. The writer was overcome. Some time later he sent Thesmar a thank-you note in which he said:

> I must make it clear, before I shall be unmasked as an imposter, that my title of colonel comes from a friendship with one of the governors of Kentucky and is purely decorative in the fashion in which American politicians permit themselves to be addressed as "honorable". . .

Diplomats always seem to have peculiar requests, Thesmar says. The wife of Herbert Evatt, Australian delegate to the United Nations, once wanted to visit Paris at night by boat. There were no boats available at the time, so Thesmar enlisted the city's fireboat. The Evatts set sail on the Seine aboard the fireboat with all the streams playing.

A Brazilian minister asked to visit several Paris museums, the Arabian mosque, the prison of the Conciergerie, alone, at night, after they had been closed to the public. A Chinese came in looking for a Serbian language teacher with a Chinese background. One visitor habitually took olive oil as a purgative; he couldn't find any in Paris, and appealed to Thesmar. The tourist office found some oil at a church supply company which kept it on hand for Notre Dame, where olive oil is used in the celebration of mass.

One of the first American visitors after the war reported that she had just seen a bicycle ad in a subway, and the man in the picture looked exactly like her third husband. Perhaps, she thought, Thesmar could help her get a copy of the ad. She wanted to send it to her first husband to let him know how well she was doing now.

Thesmar accomplished his most recent feat for a foreign visitor who was trying to find the address of a Paris policeman he used to know twenty years ago. Thesmar found the cop all right. He was living at Blidah, in Algeria.

Thesmar says he meets each odd request with a note of challenge. He likes the direct ways of the Americans, and he is looking forward to the great waves of United States tourists who will come to France now that things are nearly normal again. After all, he says, it took an American to throw him for a loss. One day after the war, a Yankee officer came in and told Thesmar his outfit was in urgent need of a pretty girl with blonde hair and green eyes who knew bird calls. It was the only request that ever "stumped the expert."

The Commissariat will, upon request, organize complete trips for official groups visiting France. Delegations and conventions are usually afforded an official welcome by L'Accueil de Paris, the city's official greeting agency. One Edric Loliée, a patent-leather-looking gentleman with a happy sense of humor, functions as a Parisian Grover Whalen. In his office Loliée keeps eleven miniature national flags. The flag of the group he is greeting at the moment is placed on his desk during the ceremonies. In one week M. Loliée's office extended official Paris greetings to twenty Swiss magicians, forty Swedish architects, six Chilean journalists, forty seniors from Smith, fifteen Brazilian engineers, twenty-two Czech trade unionists, twenty members of a United States hockey team, and a band of Boy Scouts from Oran. All told, L'Accueil de Paris greets about ten thousand persons a year. Each group is taken on a free tour of the city hall, called *L'Hôtel de Ville*, then assembled in a café for a drink. The head of the delegation gets an etching, in the name of the Prefect of the Seine.

The tour of the Hôtel de Ville begins with the Arcades Salon, which has magnificent chandeliers, gilded walls, and great paintings. One painting depicts the entry of Louis XI into Paris on August 30, 1461, a day when wine fountains were erected in the city's streets. In the Prefect's drawing room, Louis XVI is shown receiving the colors of the city of Paris, red and blue. To these colors he added his own color, white, and so the flag of France became red, white and blue. Three medals hang in the same salon, the Croix de Guerre with Palm, the red Legion of Honor awarded to the city by Clemenceau, and the new green and black Medaille de la Libération given to Paris by de Gaulle. A marble table stands nearby, where distinguished guests traditionally sign the book of gold. Among many others, the book holds the signatures of Generals Eisenhower, Patton, and Montgomery, and the King and Queen of England.

Opening from the Prefect's salon is a dining hall in which the Big Four — Byrnes, Bevin, Bidault, and Molotov — were feted. A mirror twenty feet high still bears a bullet hole made in 1944 when the FFI held the Hôtel de Ville, and the Germans were storming it from the outside. Looking from a window in the room, guests are always shown the Church of St. Gervais, where a shell from a German Big Bertha made a direct hit on Good Friday, 1918. More than two hundred and fifty in the congregation were killed or wounded.

Whenever an official celebration is held in the Hôtel de Ville, the brilliant gold and mirrored *décor* is further enhanced with banks of flowers and potted palms. The famous Republican Guards, in spotless white breeches, blue coats, and gold helmets plumed with red feathers, line the stairways. Said an irreverent visitor who saw the spectacle once: "Who are they, the Salvation Army?"

Americans who develop problems in Paris always call at the embassy, which is located in a big white building at 2 Avenue Gabriel, near the Concorde. Our diplomatic personnel has become very weary listening to mink-draped compatriots who come bustling in with petty problems, demanding, "Well, what's my embassy for, anyway?"

Actually, the embassy is for a lot of things. In the matter of private cars, American business will obtain gasoline rations at the embassy. But tourists — who, incidentally, are entitled to a comfortable gas ration considerably over what is allotted to the French — must apply to the Office de Repartition du Petrole et Carburants, 3 Rue Paul Cézanne, telephone number, BALzac 50-32. For a French driver's license, an American needs (1) a United States driver's license from his home state; (2) three photos; (3) a certificate of domicile, from his concierge, which has been legalized by the Paris police; (4) one request for a driver's license written in French on a *papier timbre,* a special legal paper which is bought at most tobacco shops for twenty francs. When all this legal hocus-pocus has been assembled it must be presented in person to the Prefecture of Police. If the French procedure has not dissuaded the foreigner from ever riding in, much less driving, a car, and he should decide to buy an automobile in France, this is what he's in for:

He must obtain a gray card from the Prefecture of Police by presenting (1) an inspection sheet which gives all the facts and figures about the car (available at all car agencies); (2) an ownership certificate (a duplicate of the bill of sale will do); (3) a certificate of *laisser passer* from the French customs. The Automobile Club of France, 8 Place Vendôme, will give you aid and comfort — and you'll probably need it.

A welfare department is operated by the embassy for the benefit of Americans who get themselves into dire straits abroad. Some people run out of money, lose it, or are robbed. The easiest solution is to have travelers' checks transferred from the United States to the Paris office of American Express. Embassy personnel often find themselves digging deeply into their own pockets to help a fellow countryman. The American Aid Society at 67 Avenue Raymond Poincaré was established by Ambassador Herrick as a voluntary welfare group, and is equipped to offer food, money, and interim aid to any American in trouble in France. The only thing needed is a validating letter from a kind and understanding lady named Adele Dix who is Vice Consul in charge of the Welfare Department.

Besides finding themselves short of cash, Americans also have a habit of losing their passports, a rather serious happenstance. The favorite way of losing a passport, the embassy reports, is for the document to slip out of the inside pocket and fall into the water when the holder is leaning over one of the bridges of the Seine to see how the river boats fold their smokestacks. Three losses in that manner were reported in one summer. At least one of the three persons peeled off his clothes and dived in after the document. Passport losers, besides being severely admonished, are required to report their losses to the police, execute an affidavit describing the circumstances of the loss, and await a report which must be cleared in Washington before another passport will be issued.

Americans who break French law are liable to the penalties which may be exacted by a French court. The most common offense is trying to run the customs with undeclared monies. All the embassy can do in such cases is provide the arrested American with a selected list of American lawyers who maintain offices in Paris.

Every American who stays in France for a prolonged period should register at the nearest consulate. No fee is charged, but two photos are necessary. If you plan to stay over three months, it is necessary to make a trip outside the boundary of France and re-enter, or else to apply for a French identity card at the Prefecture of Police.

Veterans' problems, the embassy wishes it known, are the worry of the Veterans' Administration which in Paris has offices on the Avenue d'Iéna. There are times, however, when a veteran's case comes through diplomatic channels, and the embassy personnel is obliged to make its own investigation. Such a case happened recently. It involved some young Americans studying in Paris on the GI Bill of Rights, who found themselves slipping more and more into the web of Parisian Left Bank life. A mother of one such lad who lived in Lubbock, Texas, began to get pretty worried when her son failed to write her for a couple of months. She finally spoke to her mayor, a kindly soul who sympathized and passed the word on to the governor. From the executive mansion in Austin the governor sent a letter to one of the senators in Washington. The senator dictated a note to the State Department, and pretty soon the anxiety of the lady in Lubbock crackled out across the Atlantic cable and reached the American Embassy in Paris. The case history was bucked down through channels until it reached one of the vice consuls in charge of rounding up stray students. The first thing the embassy man did was to call the Veterans' Administration and find out where the boy was studying. Then he called the college, and found out where his quarry lived. Then he hopped into the Métro and rode over to the Left Bank, climbed around among the narrow alleys for awhile, and finally found the tumbledown building where the lad was living. He climbed the creaky stairs, past piles of garbage, while cats scurried from under his feet. Finally he found himself in front of the apartment. He knocked. The door was opened by a bearded man who wore a greasy beret and a broad-striped shirt. Inside, beyond the piles of dirty clothes, the embassy man saw two other men, similarly outfitted, stirring a mess of onions over a one-burner stove. He cleared his throat and said:

"Are any of you gentlemen Americans?"

"Why, yes," replied one of the onion stirrers, "I'm American."

"Do you happen to be from Texas?" asked the man from the embassy. Yes, said the other American, he was from Texas.

"Is your name, by any chance, John Jones?" continued the diplomat.

"... he climbed around among the narrow alleys ... and finally found the tumbledown building ... 'Are you from Texas?' he said. ..." (French National Tourist Office)

"Why, yes," said the Texan, with some surprise, "I'm John Jones."

"Well, goddammit, Jones," the vice consul exploded, "why don't you write your mother?"

An enormous amount of mail flows into the embassy — not all of it American either — a fact which may be indicative of our new-found world position. Not a few of the letters recently have been from broken-hearted French girls who still pine for certain long-departed American soldiers. France is full of the species. Many of them are looking for the fathers of their children, others just have unforgettable memories.

Hundreds of school-children write letters that read like this one, that came in a short time ago:

> Dear Sir: Will you please send me some stamps from your country. I recieved your address from my scout master of Boy Scout Troop 136 of wich I am a member. . . .

One stamp-saver recently offered to do business on a barter basis. "I am a young South African girl," the letter said; "if you could please send me some stamps of France, enclosed are a few pressed silver leaves which I hope you will like. Silver leaves are evergreen flowering trees bearing their seeds in bright silver cones. . . . I could send you more leaves. . . ."

Then there was the staff sergeant in Shanghai who wanted a French motorcycle license plate to add to his collection of motorcycle license plates. And from Missouri a woman wrote asking about "a man named Rogers who lives with an old woman twenty kilometers outside of Paris. Will you find out his first name and address, as I have some important spy information for him."

The embassy's favorite letter, however, came from a Frenchman in Paris. "I am seventy-two years old," the note said in effect, "and I have just fathered two infant children. Would the United States government consider taking care of the children? I am now too feeble to work."

Both the American Veterans Committee and the American Legion have chapters in Paris. The Legion, with more time to work than the infant A.V.C., rents a whole building known as Pershing Hall, around the corner from the Hotel George V. To members it offers

45-franc cognac, a soda fountain, a snack bar called the "Dugout," and lots of pictures from World War I. Recruiting officers man the reception desk, and recently one of them was signing up members with this handy slogan: "Remember, boys, in case of war with Russia this will be the only place in Paris where you'll be able to get American ice cream."

Next-of-kin coming to France to visit the graves of war dead are advised to contact the Quartermaster General, Memorial Division, Washington 25, D.C., before departure from the States, to determine whether the cemetery they plan to visit is open. The permanent American cemeteries in France will be St. Laurent, in Normandy; St. James, near Mont St. Michel; St. Avold, below Metz; Epinal, an hour and a half drive south of Nancy; and Draguignan, fifty miles from Nice. The American Graves Registration Command, at 31 Rue Vernet, maintains complete information concerning all American graves in the European and Mediterranean theaters excepting those in Italy and Africa. It also operates a visitors' bureau which has travel information concerning the cemeteries. The building is located at the corner of the Rue Pressburg and the Champs Elysées; telephone BALzac 5400.

There are ten-year-old children in Holland who have heard about Brooklyn, and people in Burma who know all about Flatbush — and it's that way with Paris. No other city east of Brooklyn has ever achieved such renown. Nearly everyone who has wandered outside the city limits of Weehawken knows a little bit about the place. Everyone has heard about the Left Bank and the Right Bank, and the Seine is perhaps one of the best known bodies of water in the world.

Paris has twenty *arrondissements,* or districts. Fourteen are on the right bank of the Seine, and six on the left. The river flows for some seven miles through the city, forming two islands, the Ile St. Louis, and the Ile de la Cité. Thirty-two bridges connect the river banks and the islands with the mainland. All told, there are some five million Parisians living in an area of thirty square miles. Unlike New York or Washington or Chicago, Paris hardly ever is very hot or extremely cold. Café-sitting goes on into late fall, the horse racing in the Bois de Boulogne through late winter. The temperate weather of Paris is also an incentive for chic ladies to stroll along the boulevards during most of the year, a fact which has helped to make Paris the fashion capital of the world, according to a minority opinion.

The best way to learn Paris is to relax and be a tourist. Take the regular automobile sightseeing trips offered by the hundreds of travel bureaus. Although it is not generally known, all the trips are the same, the prices are standard; as a matter of fact, the cars are pooled among the travel agencies, all of which belong to a co-operative association. The morning tour is advertised as the "Modern City," and the afternoon trip as the "Historic City." Actually, each is a mixture of both modernity and history. There are other trips called "Paris at Night," which include visits to four nightclubs and a sip of champagne, and other full-day excursions to Versailles, Chantilly, and Fontainebleau.

The morning tour starts at the opera house, which measures 11,000 square meters and is the largest in the world. Designed by Charles Garnier, from whose drawing board came also the Monte Carlo Casino, the Paris Opéra was completed in 1875. It took over ten years to build, and is said to reflect the prosperity of the nation under Napoléon III. Most of the space is taken up with such frippery as the monumental staircase and the magnificent marble decorations. The theater itself seats only 2,200. The opera is ensconced at the Place de l'Opéra, at the head of the Avenue de l'Opéra, the only avenue in Paris without trees. It was planned that way to permit an unimpaired view of M. Garnier's architectural work.

The Opéra square is the heart of the city's bustle and the center of the *grands boulevards,* which at one time exemplified Parisian life.

Here were the great cafés, the newspaper offices, and the *boulevardiers*. Today the Opéra, while ancient and sweet with memories, is tackier than the more refined Champs Elysées with which it competes for attention.

A five-minute walk from the Opéra is the Madeleine Church, begun by Louis XV in 1764, and finally altered and modified as a memorial to his troops by Napoléon. Over a hundred yards long, it looks quite like a Greek temple, is nonetheless a Catholic church, one of the smartest, in fact, for elegant Paris weddings.

Two blocks away from the Madeleine, down the Rue Royale, is the vast Place de la Concorde, where in 1793 and 1794 the guillotine of the revolutionists accounted for nearly 3,000 victims. (There is not a trace of this carnage, I might add, the exact spot having long since been covered with a monument to the city of Brest.) Seven other monuments around the square are dedicated to the other principal towns in France, and in the center is an obelisk from the temple of Rameses II, a big gun in Egypt in 1300 B.C. Looking at them clockwise, the four sides of the Place de la Concorde are flanked by the Tuileries Gardens, the Seine, the beginning of the Champs Elysées, and a number of buildings which include the offices of the Guaranty Trust Co., Time Inc., and the American embassy. The embassy building, a handsome white affair staffed by United States Marines, was built to match the home of Baron Rothschild on the other side of the square.

The route up the magnificent, broad, tree-bordered Champs Elysées has known the tread of many a victorious army and the shuffle of many Sunday afternoon strollers. It stretches for over a mile; the first part, as far as the Rond Point, is bordered by gardens, the rest by shops, cafés, and theaters. The Champs ends at the Place d'Etoile in the very center of which is the Arch of Triumph.

The largest triumphal arch in the world, it was planned by Napoléon as a modest memorial to himself and his armies. On the sides of the monument are the names of a hundred and ninety-six battles and three hundred and eighty-six generals who fought in them. Among the battles mentioned are those with Spain, Italy, Germany, Russia, Austria, and Holland, which made nearly a clean sweep for Europe. The names of those generals killed in battle are underlined. At the street level rests an Unknown Soldier's grave, with an eternal light. Military men in uniform traditionally salute the grave, and civilian gentlemen are expected to remove their hats. One hundred stone pillars surround the arch, representing the hundred days after Napoléon's return from Elba. An elevator takes one to the top of the Arch.

The Place de l'Etoile is so called because an even dozen avenues fan out from the Arch, forming an *étoile,* or star. The avenues concerned are the Champs Elysées, Avenue Marceau, Avenue d'Iéna, Avenue Kleber, Avenue Victor Hugo, Avenue Foch, Avenue de la Grande Armée (really a continuation of the Champs Elysées leading to Neuilly and the suburbs), Avenue Carnot, Avenue MacMahon, Avenue Wagram, Avenue Hoche, and Avenue Friedland. Of all of these the Avenue Foch, a hundred yards from side to side, is the widest and smartest residential boulevard. The first three buildings on the avenue were once the headquarters of the Gestapo. A bizarre pink house is owned by the Duchess of Talleyrand, who was first Anna Gould of New York, and then Countess Boni de Castellane, before becoming a duchess, and among the neighbors are Vanderbilts, Renaults, and Mohammed Ali of Egypt. The Avenue Foch leads directly into the Bois de Boulogne, a two-thousand acre park on the edge of Paris, filled with trees, lakes, two racetracks (Auteuil and Longchamps), and some elegant restaurants. Among them are the Pré-Catelan and Les Cascades.

Traditional tours always swing back from the Bois by way of Avenue Henri Martin, another smart residential section which leads to the Palais de Chaillot at the Place de Trocadéro. On the site of the village of Chaillot, Napoléon once began a palace. It was never completed, and in 1823 the Trocadéro was built on the palace foundations. The old Trocadéro was destroyed in 1937 to make way for the Palais de Chaillot which was built for the World Exposition of that year. In its broad wings are an anthropological museum, a library, a maritime museum containing models of old sailboats and modern steamships, a museum of arts, folklore, photography and the motion picture, and a theater which seats 3,500. Atop the theater is the terrace on which Hitler strutted for the newsreels and gazed upon the Eiffel Tower just across the Seine.

Just beyond the Trocadéro gardens and the illuminated fountains of the Chaillot palace is the Bridge d'Iéna, and beyond that, on the left bank, the Eiffel Tower. There are three floors to the Eiffel Tower, serviced by elevators which resemble a funicular railroad. Ten thousand sightseers can stand in the Eiffel Tower at one time; it takes 1,800 steps to get to the top; it was completed in 1889, and — if you've a mind for figures — it was built of 12,000 pieces of metal put together with 2,500,000 bolts, a fact I'd like to see somebody dispute. There is a restaurant halfway up the tower which was opened as a GI nightclub after the liberation, and then quickly closed. Too many tipsy soldiers teetered too close to the tower's railings.

The Champ de Mars Park separated the tower from the Ecole Militaire, an academy for staff officers established by Louis XV and Mme. Pompadour. Among its illustrious officer candidates was Napoléon Bonaparte, who studied and received his commission there. The building was the scene of a battle royal in August, 1944, and the walls wear the pockmarks of rifle fire as proudly as a Heidelberg student wears his dueling scar.

Next door, the Hôtel des Invalides is, of course, not a hotel but a tomb for some of the most illustrious of France's military dead. In a sunken plaza on the main floor lies the tomb of Napoléon, sealed in a great, red granite sarcophagus, sculptured from a block of Finnish marble which was a gift from Czar Nicholas I. Around the tomb are twelve statues, each representing one of Napoléon's great victories. According to some stories, the architect designed the sunken well so that all who came to view the remains of the emperor would be obliged to lean over the stone railing and bow.

Small chapels surround the tomb. In a white and black marble tomb lies Joseph Bonaparte, King of Spain. Marshal Foch is buried beneath eight life-size figures of poilus who are depicted carrying the general's body. A soft, blue light from the stained glass windows of the chapel falls with eternal sadness on the shoulders of the bearers.

Here are the tombs of Napoléon's ablest generals — Duroc, who died in Russia, and Bertrand, who accompanied him to St. Helena. The last chapel in the circle contains the remains of Jerome Bonaparte, King of Westphalia. In the center of the same chapel is the body of Napoléon's son by Marie Louise of Austria, proclaimed King of Rome, who died near Vienna at the age of twenty-one. His remains were removed to Paris by Hitler's express order at Christmas time, 1940, in an effort calculated to win French collaboration.

One wall of the Hôtel des Invalides is devoted to a reproduction of the main altar of St. Peter's in Rome. The stained-glass windows give an apparition of continuous sunlight, a representation of the glory of Napoléon. Inscribed in the tomb is the emperor's last wish: "I desire that my ashes remain on the banks of the Seine among the French people I loved so well." Some say the phraseology is indicative that Bonaparte, who was born in Corsica, never considered himself a Frenchman.

Leaving the Hôtel des Invalides, the morning tour returns to the right bank across the Concorde Bridge, which was built of stones from the Bastille. Swinging through the Place de la Concorde again, it turns down the Rue de Rivoli, with its arcaded sidewalks, and then over to the Place Vendôme, an octagonal ring of smart establishments. Charvet occupies No. 8, the Ritz Hotel No. 15, Schiaparelli No. 21.

The Rue de Rivoli—"traffic is teeming . . . everything that has wheels rolls
. . . anything without power is pushed."

*In the Place Vendôme—Charvet, Coty, the Ritz, Schiaparelli, Van Cleef
and Arpels, and Chopin.*

Van Cleef and Arpels, the jewelers, are in the square, so is the Ministry of Justice, and Chopin lived and also died in the house at No. 12. The famous Vendôme column in the center of the square was erected in 1810 by Napoléon and was constructed from 1,200 captured guns which were melted and recast. Atop the column is a statue of Bonaparte dressed as a Roman emperor.

Directly off the Place Vendôme is the world-famous Rue de la Paix, a two-block thoroughfare lined with the elegant shops of Mappin and Webb, Paquin, Cartier, and Dunhill. At the far end is the Opéra square, again, and the end of the morning's tour.

Old Historic Paris, the afternoon trip, begins at the Opéra and swings briefly past the Bibliothèque Nationale, the national library which has 5,000,000 books and 2,500,000 engravings, and is said to be the richest in the world. Every French publisher is required to send to the library two copies of every work printed.

Nearby is the central market, Les Halles, often called "the stomach of Paris," where produce that comes in from the farms is redistributed for retail sale. In those gay old twenties and thirties, nightclubbers still in evening dress traditionally invaded the market in the early morning hours for a bowl of hot onion soup, a French way of saying Alka Seltzer.

Everybody has heard of the Louvre, but nobody knows where the name comes from. Suffice it to say that it comprises a great bank of buildings on the bank of the Seine, at the far end of the Tuileries. First built as a fortress by King Philip Augustus as long ago as 1204, the Louvre was made over into a royal residence by Charles V, who used to journey to the Louvre to go wolf hunting. For four hundred years the palace was altered, developed, and expanded. Finally, it was completed under Napoléon III in 1857.

In 1791, two years after the French Revolution began, the Louvre was established as a museum. During the 18th century the Palace of the Tuileries, connecting the two great wings of the Louvre, served

"*Along the Champs Elysées . . . the air is sweet, the crowds walk slowly, and a pretty French girl impulsively kisses her man. . . .*" (French National Tourist Office)

as a royal residence. The building was destroyed during the Revolution of the Commune following the war of 1870. Today the courtyard is known as Carrousel Square, and in the center a small arch of triumph commemorates the victory at Austerlitz. Looking through the small arch it is possible to see past the obelisk at the Place de la Concorde, all the way to the Arch of Triumph at the Place de l'Etoile.

There are some sixteen miles of galleries of the Louvre. During the war 4,000 pictures were sent to the chateaus in the country for safe-keeping. All the works are back now and can be seen six days a week, every day but Tuesday. Said one post-war visitor to the Louvre recently, "Well, we've seen the Venus de Milo, and, frankly, she looks better in her pictures."

From the Louvre the tour of Historic Paris follows the Seine, lined with the famous bookstalls which have become a trademark of Paris, crossing via the Pont Neuf to the Ile de la Cité, called "the cradle of Paris." Here Paris had its beginning in a small village called Lutetia, which was the home of river boatmen known as "les Parisii." They lived on the island because they thought it was easier to defend, but some of Julius Caesar's men captured the village, any-way. The Romans held Lutetia and developed it until 500 A.D., when the city became known as Paris.

On the island today is the Palace of Justice, which has seen, through the ages, the trials of persons who have offended France, from Marie Antoinette through Pétain and Laval. Here, too, is the Prefecture de Police, and, on the far end of the isle, the famous Cathedral of Notre Dame. The site on which the cathedral now stands has a long history. Under the choir loft searchers found, in the 18th century, a Roman monument dedicated to Jupiter; it was erected by Tiberius. The construction of the cathedral itself was not begun until 1160, and was not completed until 1197. The towers were erected some years afterwards. Napoléon was crowned in Notre Dame in 1804—or, as some historians prefer to have it, he crowned himself, inasmuch as he took the headpiece in his own hands and placed it on his head. Then, with his own hands, he crowned Josephine. In the same hallowed walls, General de Gaulle was fired upon immediately following the liberation, and here, too, are held the burial ceremonies for France's great; among them was the late General Leclerc. Stained-glass windows in brilliant hues made from certain metallic oxides still beam colors on the interior of Notre Dame. The secret oriental process was lost in the 14th century and has never been duplicated. A number of red hats hang inside the church; they belonged to cardinals of France who have died. There is a saying that until their red hats fall, the souls of the late cardinals remain on earth.

Crossing from the Ile de la Cité to the left bank of the Seine, the tour enters the famed Latin Quarter, so-called because in the old days the students of the city's universities, which are centered there, all spoke Latin. The main artery of the Latin Quarter is the Boulevard St. Michel, referred to in the local sophomoria as the *Bull-mish*. Most famous building just off the *Bull-mish* is the Sorbonne, founded by a 13th-century chaplain named Robert de Sorbon. The Sorbonne developed largely through the efforts of Cardinal Richelieu in the early 17th century, and the great cardinal is now buried in the university's chapel. Next door sits the Cluny Museum, on what is believed to be the site of the Roman governor's house. It is considered a gem of 15th-century architecture.

On the other side of the boulevard is the Luxembourg Palace, an extravaganza in Italian renaissance style built in the early 17th century as a home for Queen Marie de Medici, mother of Louis XIII. During the Revolution, the palace became a prison which held, among other inmates, a lady named Josephine who was later to become the wife of Napoléon. The Petit Luxembourg, a building nearby, is the residence of the president of the Senate, and the gardens are a popular breath of greenery for Parisians who live among the literary cafés and the dingy streets of the Latin Quarter.

On the way to Montmartre, back across the right bank, the afternoon tour stops at the Places des Vosges, a residential square built by Henri IV, and so named because the province of the Vosges was the first in the land to pay its taxes. It was once a smart residential section, and among its tenants were Madame de Sévigné in No. 1,

Victor Hugo in No. 6, Rachel the actress in No. 13, and Richelieu at No. 23. There is a stop, too, at the Place de la Bastille, the site of what was once a fortress, and later a famous prison. It is now an open square. The prison was stormed and destroyed on July 14, 1789, which became Bastille Day, a holiday since greeted with the same pyrotechnic exuberance we reserve for the Fourth of July. An outline of the famous walls still remains in the square, which is just three miles, along the extension of the Rue de Rivoli, from the Place de la Concorde where the guillotine was operating during those bloody Revolution years.

Montmartre sits high on a hill overlooking Paris, and is reached by a funicular railroad. It is, in a way, an awful lot like Greenwich Village in New York, being informal, folksy, full of night clubs, artists, and the people who come to watch the Bohemians. The Sacré Coeur church, a big piece of Byzantine architecture, sits on top of the Montmartre hill, and has become a sort of symbol of the section. It was almost ruined at one point during the war, when an aircraft of alleged Allied markings dropped thirteeen bombs all along the edge of the church. Nobody has ever found out the reason, but, at any rate, to commemorate the event a plan showing just where the bombs fell has been erected in the building.

The highest house on the highest hill in Montmartre is owned by a not-so-starving artist named Louis Icarte, who also has a place in New York. The inside is just what you might expect of Monmartre, only a bit plushier. Paintings of voluptuous and naked blondes in various poses are all over the studio—leaning against some stuffed lions, lounging over a chair in a negligee, holding the leash of a pair of fluffy dogs. There is a mirrored and spotlighted podium for the ladies who pose for this art, and on the other side of the room, behind the suburban flavor of a papier-mache hedgerow, stands a green and yellow bar. From the bar stools it's easy to see the Sacré Coeur, the Eiffel Tower, and sometimes, on a clear day, Notre Dame.

Not far away from M. Icarte's place is an old gray house in which Renoir lived, about 1875. It overlooks the last vineyard of Paris, from which the people of Montmartre extract a harvest each September. The grapes are sold at an auction which becomes an annual festival. In the Theater square, where the bistros put out their tables under the trees in summer, performers play an open-air benefit, and the talent is the best in France.

Two old windmills still stand in Montmartre. One has become a cabaret, and the other, known as the Moulin de la Galette, dates from the 13th century. At one point in his career, Renoir painted at the Moulin de la Galette every day, commuting from the old gray house over the vineyard.

A number of small industries flourish in Montmartre, among them the Poterie du Vieux Montmartre, a small ceramic works which has indeed caught the spirit of the section. A handful of artists create all manner of gay ribaldry which they have designed on vases, plates, and statuettes. A set of eight luncheon plates, for example, depicts the romance of a young swain who meets a fair lady on the first dish, and lands up in bed with her on the serving platter. Another item sings the glory of Montmartre wine, which in legend is supposed to have four times the liquid generative effect of any other beverage outside of Milwaukee beer. There are flagons, jugs, pitchers, and plates all finished in the tender motif of old sailors' songs. The store closes in the summer, but an equal selection of this clay pornographia is available at the summer-time branch located at Belle Ile, Finistère, in Brittany.

There are three principal means of getting around Paris aside from proceeding afoot, a pleasant if primitive method in itself. The taxicabs, which have been immortalized in story and in such music as Gershwin's "An American in Paris," are pre-war holdovers held together with spare parts and hope. They park in the middle of avenues like the Champs Elysées, are habitually short of gas, and will

*Montmartre sits high on a hill . . . and is reached by funicular railroad . . .
on a clear day you can see Notre Dame. . . .*

agree to take you as a passenger only if your destination proves economical from a point of view of gas expenditure and profitable from
the anticipated meter reading. Reading a Paris taxi meter is no less
complicated than the theory of relativity. Some cabbies have new
meters and charge just what the apparatus says. Others have not

been able to buy new equipment, and the cost of the trip is divined from the meter reading plus an added charge figured on a table of accelerated rates. Cab drivers are not averse to charging you double and triple fares no matter what the meter reads, especially in the early morning hours when taxis are hard to find. It's a sound economical idea to hold a parley with the driver first.

A fairly efficient bus system operates on a strictly first-come, first-served basis. Prospective bus passengers are expected to obtain a priority ticket from an automatic device located at each bus stop. Each ticket bears a number, and passengers mount according to the number they hold.

The simplest and fastest way to get around Paris is, all things considered, the subway, locally known as the *Métro*. A Métro map looks not unlike a set of strangulated intestines, and if you've an aptitude for operating a Chinese abacus the rest is easy. First take note of your point of origin, then find the station nearest to your destination. On the map, follow the continuation of the line *present location-destination* to the end of the run, and take note of the name of the last station. That name becomes your *direction*. Look for the sign that says Direction So-and-so, get into the train, and ride to your station.

To avoid spending an unlooked for vacation in Barcelona or some other suburban point, we shall have a simple exercise in how to keep from getting lost on the Métro. Repeat after me: We are now at the Arch of Triumph, and we wish to go to the American embassy. On the Métro map which is reprinted on pages 70-71, take note of the station called Etoile, which is right at the Arch. Since the American embassy is at the Place Concorde, the Concorde station becomes our destination. By following the line Etoile-Concorde on the map to the very end of its run, we find the name of the last station to be Chateau de Vincennes. At the Etoile station, therefore, we would follow the signs that say Direction: Chateau de Vincennes, board the train, and

*The Métro—"if you've an aptitude for operating a Chinese abacus, the rest is easy. . . ."*

get off at Concorde. If, woe betide, your destination does not lie on a direct line from your point of origin, you can change *directions* at any *station de correspondance* (transfer point), always taking note and following the signs of your new *direction*. To travel from the Etoile to the Invalides, for example, take Direction: Chateau de Vincennes as far as Concorde. At Concorde change to Direction Balard, and get off at Invalides.

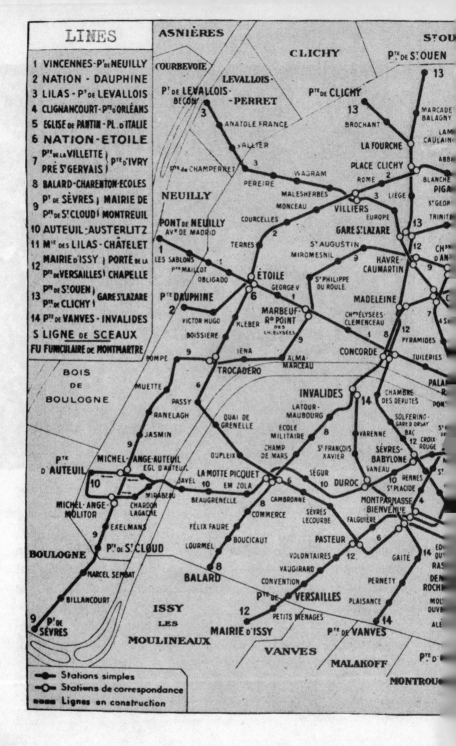

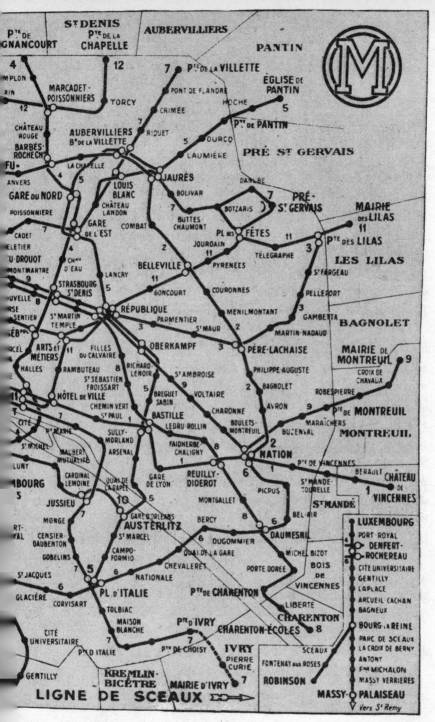

The Paris Metro

The Métro fare is less than a nickel. The cars come in red, yellow, and baby blue. Tickets are purchased upon entering the subway, and punched by an attendant at the gate to the platform. One-time, two-time, and whole books of tickets are available, and there is no extra charge for making a transfer. The station gates close automatically before the arrival of each train, a process which will be completely frustrating to Americans in the habit of catching the 8:15 from South Norwalk by a cat's whisker. The doors close automatically, but they must be opened manually by the passengers. Some subway cars leave certain seats which are reserved in this priority: (1) Incapacitated war veterans; (2) persons injured on the job; (3) the blind and the infirm; (4) pregnant women. The two newest station names on the Paris Métro are Stalingrad and Franklin D. Roosevelt, both presumably subject to change at a turn in events.

In choosing a place to stay in Paris, from among the hundreds of hotels in the city, consider cost, location, and reputation. The man to advise you is your travel agent, and travelers will do well to make reservations in advance. Cook's and American Express both have large offices in Paris, to serve you in case of arrival in the city without a room, and in an emergency the Commissariat General au Tourisme at 8 Avenue de l'Opéra will answer an S.O.S. any day of the week, Sundays included. There are a number of terminals in the city and the one at which you arrive depends upon your point of origin. Passengers coming from Le Havre wind up at the Gare St. Lazare, near the Opéra. Passengers coming by air are deposited at the Gare des Invalides, just across the Seine from the Concorde.

In the bustling Opéra section are big, transient hotels like the 600-room Grand, and the smaller Scribe, across the street. They are generally like big hotels anywhere, and can hardly be classified as typically French. They are moderately priced and handy.

There are a half dozen of the fine old Paris hotels known all over the world, of which the newest (1929), gayest, and most elegant, is

In the "quietly extravagant" Hotel Georges V, your "initials in pistachio. . . ."

probably the George V. To its modern, quietly extravagant layout in the Champs Elysées section flock the movie stars, the potentates and well-to-do Americans. Famous feet, from those of Hermann Goering to those of Rita Hayworth, have sluffed through its rich, puffy carpets. The chi-chi crowd that gathers in its cocktail lounge at tea-time probably generates the most elegant, the most international chit-chat in the world. The combination of scents develop the viscosity of a pea-soup fog, easily capable of anesthetizing a regiment.

Running this gilded three-ring circus is a youngish, multilingual, ebullient gentleman named Max Blouet who remembers names with the facility of Mr. Chips, and delights in offering unlooked-for personal fripperies. An American publisher who was stopping at the George V recently gave a little farewell party in the hotel for some of his Paris friends. He decided to go the whole hog and ordered a baked Alaska. "Four waiters pushed in the thing on a wagon," he explained when he returned to New York, "and, holy gee, my initials were painted on the sides in pistachio!"

Probably there is not much initial-decorating going on at the famed old Crillon, a sedate dowager among Paris hotels which traces its ancestry to the Duc de Crillon, who built the place as a private residence in 1750. It was confiscated by the revolutionists in 1789, but didn't become a hotel until 1909. Sitting on the Place de la Concorde, in the very shadow of the American embassy, the Crillon has always been a favorite with diplomats. One upstairs suite bears a plaque indicating that President Wilson, E. M. House, J. C. Smuts, Baron Makino of Japan, and Wellington Koo of China met there to draft the original plan of the League of Nations, from February 3 to April 11, 1919.

The guest book of the hotel contains a now invaluable collection of signatures, among the most recent of which are those of James F. Byrnes, Tom Connally, Alfred Duff Cooper, and Ernest Bevin. Andrew Carnegie signed on July 2, 1913, and the following June saw

Teddy Roosevelt and Alice Longworth. "Black Jack" Pershing was there on June 13, 1917, and from then on he always spent two or three months a year at the hotel, staying in Suite 547' and 549. The book lists Winston Churchill, Pétain, and Aristide Briand. Nungesser was there in 1918, Richard E. Byrd in 1927, Jimmy Walker wrote that he had a nice stay in September, 1927, and Charles A. Lindbergh registered in on November 1, 1933.

Down the street, under the arcaded sidewalks of the Rue de Rivoli, is the old Hotel Meurice which is rather reminiscent in a lace-collar, potted-palm way of the ancient elegance of the Plaza in New York.

> HOTEL MEURICE, Rue de Rivoli and Rue St. Honoré, at Paris.—MEURICE begs to express his gratitude to the English who have honoured him with their patronage, of which he solicits a continuance, assuring them no effort on his part shall be wanting to merit their kind support. He has added four new suites of apartments, facing the Tuilerie Gardens, in one of which he can make 30 beds, if required; smaller suites, down to a single bed, at three francs per night. The price of every article is fixed and moderate. Printed particulars are in every room. Meurice flatters himself no Hotel in Europe is better regulated or calculated to afford every comfort to the English, whose habits and customs have been his constant aim to study, and he trusts, by a continuance of their favours, he will ever merit their approbation.

The Meurice, which likes to call itself the "Hotel of Kings," was advertising for the British trade in the *Morning Chronicle* of London as long ago as April 21, 1819. The King of the Belgians spent his honeymoon at the hotel, and among the other monarchs who have been guests are George of Greece, Carol of Rumania, Alfonso of Spain, and Christian X of Denmark.

One W. Pegler castigated the place in the New York *World-Telegram* of October 30, 1935, and Lucius Beebe eulogized it in the New York *Herald-Tribune* of June 20, 1936, sounding a note of consistency for both gentlemen. The hotel was headquarters for E. Berry Wall, a gay dog who sent out his Christmas cards from the place in 1939. Before the next Christmas rolled around, Wall was forced to relinquish his command post in favor of the German military government, who likewise established headquarters in the hotel, posting sentries front and back and requiring every member of the hotel staff to carry an *ausweis*.

When liberation appeared imminent in 1944, the German officers elected to defend the hotel, despite the management's protestations. Leclerc's troops attacked by the Rivioli street entrance, and killed one Nazi die-hard who had barricaded himself behind some sandbags on the *entresol*. In the midst of the fight a shell fired from the direction of the Concorde burst through a Rivoli side window, crossed the lushly draped dining room, barely missed decapitating a headwaiter, crashed through a screen, bounced off the buffet, splintered the cashier's desk, and embedded itself in the kitchen. The shell failed to explode, and no one was hurt.

Things have quieted down considerably since those harrowing days. The staid Meurice has redecorated some of its suites, but its famous old elevator hasn't been touched. It is still fitted with sedan chairs covered with tapestries, curtains on the windows, and glass doors decorated with green and gold. The thing runs just as well as it did when it was installed in 1907—and for all I know it is still carrying the same passengers.

The Chinese are long on laundries, Irishmen make fine cops, but leave a Frenchman to his own devices and he'll open a restaurant. Most of the Chez Pierres, Chateaubriands, and Maison Henris that populate the earth had their beginnings in Paris. There are, I am glad to report, a few French restaurants left in Paris, more perhaps than you'll get to try on a visit. They vary in price, size, and quality, quite as they might anywhere else. Best known and most expensive is La Tour d'Argent, where pressed duck is the specialty. Every bird has been numbered since the place started in business somewhere in the Middle Ages, and it is exciting competition to see which shall be the higher figure, the serial number of your duck or your check.

The Perigord on the Rond Point has a glassed-in terrace and is pleasant for lunch. For a glittering evening Maxim's is nearly as good as ever, with formal clothes obligatory Friday nights.

A small French restaurant charging nominal prices may very well serve fine food. Don't let the façade fool you. Swapping Paris restaurants is a favorite sport of foreigners abroad, and these addresses, obtained just that way, are offered in good faith but with no guarantees: Les Marroniers, Boulevard Arago, corner of the Rue de la Glacière; La Grenouille, Rue des Grands Augustins; La Chevrotine, 10 Rue Gustave-Flaubert; Chez Pierre, 125 Rue de Tocqueville. On the medium expensive side are the small but pleasant Windsor at 68 Rue Pierre-Charron, near the Champs Elysées, famous old Fouquets on the Champs itself, and the Relais de la Belle Aurore, 6 Rue Gomboust, which calls its customers *citoyens* and serves fine food amid a mélange of revolutionary trappings. Chez Mercier is a big low-price, hustle-bustle place at 13 Rue Lincoln, and if you like things Russian try the Auberge d'Armaille. You can go bilingual at a French chop-suey emporium known as the Canton Etoile. Kin Long's, a similar establishment at 58 Rue Monsieur-le-Prince, insists, however, that his Cantonese specialties are "100 per cent Chinese." The Flambaum at 37 Rue Faubourg Montmartre has Jewish dishes, and a spot known as the Petit Rancho, 5 Rue de Metz, bills itself as a "Yiddish cabaret" with a "Tel-Aviv Orchestra." Au Petit Coteau, 161 Faubourg St. Honoré, announces that it is the "cutest Italian-French restaurant in Paris" — if you can believe that kind of talk. As for Czech dishes, the closest you can get to Prague these days is Chez Louis, 14 Rue Lincoln. There are several pseudo-American places around, notably the chain of Pam-Pams, which are decorated in bright yellow and green, play scratchy old American jazz records, and operate on a semi-snack basis. The menu is a collection piece listing among the "Specialties Pam-Pam, Chaud," an item called the "Old Pappy" which is described as "saucisse, oeuf poêle, pommes Pont-Neuf."

*At the Café de la Paix, "a bacon and egg breakfast . . . and . . . baby whisky. . . ."*

Among the "plats rapides" is an American importation known at the Pam-Pam as "Le Chicken Hash." Harry's New York Bar ("Just tell the cab driver Sank Roo Doe Noo") is still in business, still serving pretty good beer and Gallicized hot dogs. One of the newest of the American-type restaurants is Le Hamburger at 19 Rue d'Antin, near the Opéra. It offers a club breakfast, hamburgers, cheeseburgers, American coffee, and gooey soda-fountain desserts. The famous old Café de la Paix, smack in the middle of the Opéra, serves a bacon and egg breakfast, but not before 10 A.M. Other Café de la Paix attractions, according to the menu, include something called a "hot infusion," and a beverage known as "baby whisky." Search me!

Tea is served at Louis Sherry's at the Rond Point of the Champs Elysées, and at Rumpelmayer's on the Rue de Rivoli, which has ice cream sodas and therefore many American patrons.

If you get lonesome in Paris there is an escort service at 78 Champs Elysées that specializes in escorting people who don't speak French. Telephone number, Elysées 48-91.

The Paris edition of the New York *Herald Tribune,* usually a four- to eight-page sheet, is on the stands everywhere every morning except Saturday. Around the Concorde it is hawked with more alacrity than the French papers. *Time* and *Newsweek* both publish European editions which come out Saturdays, and an emasculated version of *Life* is printed every two weeks. Such ordinary United States fare as *The Saturday Evening Post, Collier's,* and the women's magazines are all available in Paris about one month late. French newspapers are two or four pages, which is normal. They give a smattering of the news, and occasionally run serial stories like "Mademoiselle Fanny," which was "Fanny by Gaslight" before it went native. Some English-language books are available in the big book stores like Brentano's, and there are any number of French and translated American novels and non-fiction available in soft covers. "Alice au Pays Merveilleux" is still going strong.

Most of the films shown in Paris are American, and you can find them listed in *Une Semaine de Paris* and *Parisian Weekly Information,* two amusement magazines like *Cue* in New York. American films are either presented in English with French subtitles, or otherwise a new soundtrack is dubbed in after the film arrives in France. Sometimes the titles are direct translations, and sometimes they are given a new meaning altogether. "The Best Years Of Our Lives" became simply "Les Plus Belles Années de Nôtre Vie." "The Hitler Gang" was shown as "Hitler et Sa Clique." "Mr. District Attorney" came out as "J'Accuse Cette Femme." "Now, Voyager" went under the French monicker of "Une Femme Cherche Son Destin." Errol

*"After dark . . . loose ladies on the make and gentlemen on the loose. . . ."*
(French National Tourist Office—Romess)

Flynn's epic known as "They Died With Their Boots On" became "La Charge Fantastique." What Hollywood chose to call "Along Came Jones" the French named "Le Grand Bill." "The Jolson Story" was a great Paris hit as "Le Roman d'Al Jolson," and a rundown house over in Montmartre which shows Westerns recently advertised a six-gun feature called "Les Mousquetaires de la Far West."

The next time you see Paris, chances are her heart will once more be light and gay. Paris after dark is gay, exciting, and uninhibited. Along the Carré section of the Champs Elysées, the by-play begins between loose ladies on the make and gentlemen on the loose. In Place Pigalle—christened "Pig Alley" by our troops—petite demoiselles will take you by the arm, and offer to show you things you never saw before. If it's raining they trip out under bright little parasols. If business is bad they offer to throw themselves in as a bonus, and if you should still remain unconvinced they will guarantee to serve drinks during the performance. Most night-club doormen also act as official agents for these spectacles *a la française,* and usually they extract a middleman's fee.

Biggest tourist attraction in Paris is the famed Folies Bergère, a big, loud, bawdy burlesque that goes on every night and Sunday, Monday, and holiday afternoons. A continuous review in two acts and about thirty scenes, the Folies Bergère counts on elaborate staging, magnificent costumes, and bare bosoms. The singing and dancing are decidedly second-rate, but as far as the skits go, nothing like them has been seen on this side of the Atlantic outside of a stag dinner. Tickets for the Folies are available at the box office or at any of the travel agencies, most of which double as ticket brokers. A harsh carnival atmosphere pervades the Folies, and there is no avoiding feeling like a yokel in a sucker trap. There is a charge for checking your coat, and if you don't give a tip to the checkroom girl, on top of the charge, she'll ask you for it. There is a charge for a program, and if you don't tip the program girl you'll be asked again. Naked dolls and novelties that perform in the bump-and-grind technique are on sale at inflated prices. The girl that sells them will want a tip, too. At intermission time a daring, enticing interim spectacle is offered downstairs—at an extra fee, of course. It turns out to be a stable for ancient Folies girls who bend their creaking hips and shake their sagging stomachs to the screeching of a played-out recording of a played-out tune. After ten minutes of this, the front doors are slammed shut and guarded by a pair of Paris gendarmes. Then the time-worn seductresses clamber over the seats, open the back doors, now the only avenue of escape, and stand there with tambourine in hand waiting for a handout. If you visit a rest room don't pass up the lady who takes a position midway between the men's room and the ladies' room and collects donations from both sides. Also, don't forget the usherette who shows you to your seat. She gets a tip, too. That's custom.

As traditionally French as a kiss of the hand, if not as genteel, the old can-can is still being ground out daily at the Bal Tabarin, 36 Rue Victor-Masse in Pigalle. There is a nominal entrance fee, and the show, which starts at 9:30, can be seen from the floor tables or the bar. Tabarin is huge, sparsely decorated, and features a large dance floor which doubles as a stage. The show alternates with dance sets played by capable, brassy bands. Aside from the can-can, the Tabarin's show, in the accepted manner, goes in for bizarre stage effects, bad dancing, good costuming, and extravagant tableaus. Lofty ideas earthily displayed is the Tabarin technique. One night they may have Justice, naked as a babe, but considerably more developed, slide right out of the ceiling on a gigantic scale. The next night it may be a snake—bare and feminine version—which slithers down to earth on a simulated vine. Such exotica as "The Garden of Eden" and "The Origin of the Aztecs" provide the themes—but no matter what the show, Earl Wilson would certainly harvest himself a bumper crop. A distinctly dowdy assortment of house-planted hostesses who order nothing but champagne inhabit the bar, and on your way out, should you want it or not, the doorman at Tabarin is likely to extend some plain and fancy neighborhood addresses where men are invited to see some plain and fancy biological exhibitions.

In Pigalle proper (a misleading statement if I ever wrote one) there are perhaps fifty nightclubs cramming next to each other as they are on West 52nd Street in New York. Every place has a doorman who acts as a barker, and all the doormen of all the clubs are dressed alike, as if they had bought up the war surplus officers' uniforms from the French navy. Up among the hills of Montmartre are a handful of combination nightclubs and restaurants, among them Chez Ma Cousine, Le Vieux Châlet, which has a pleasant garden, A la Bonne Franquette, and Sur les Toits de Paris, easily spotted by its big Montmartre windmill. A La Mère Catherine, which has gingham tablecloths, low-beamed ceilings, old paintings, old plates, an old piano, and a garden in the back, first opened for business in 1793. Nearby are La Cremaillère, La Mairie du Vieux Montmartre, and Le Coucou. Most famous of all is the Lapin Agile, which, because of its renown, seems to have developed a staginess about being quaint. It was, a long time ago, a restaurant famous for its lapin—rabbit. An artist named Gile popularized the place among his painter friends; soon it became known as the Lapin à Gile, and finally, through usage, as the Lapin Agile, or the "Nimble Rabbit." Today the place is just as old and creaky as you would suspect it to be. Patrons are seated on backless benches, and there is virtually continuous entertainment from some remarkably good voices featuring such sweet madrigals as the saga of the eighty chausseurs who went hunting, and before the day was done every last man had seduced a willing, if overtaxed, marquise. Everybody is expected to join in the sing, and it is also a house rule that no one enter or leave while a song is being sung. No cover, no minimum, you can order what you want, and, incidentally, you pay on the honor system on your way out.

Intellectual dives, where you can trap the bearded thinker in his habitat, vary in Paris with the quixotic moods of the intellectuals. Wherever Sartre should choose to hang his hat one night may, on the next, be the rage of the city. Among those hangouts in current favor is La Rose Rouge, 53 Rue de la Harpe, where talented performers, whose hearts are still in the smoky lowlands, appear nightly in a den so small they must rush onstage from the toilet. An international, unshaven, unscrubbed assortment of artists, writers, and hangers-on cram the hardwood benches of the Rose Rouge nightly, 'neath the cubist paintings and the voodoo heads that hang on the dirty, yellow walls. Said a St. Louis girl dressed in navy blue sweater, navy blue slacks, uncombed hair and unpainted face who had turned painter and existentialist, "Oh, I couldn't explain existentialism; only Sartre himself can do that." Nonetheless, she loved the existentialist life and was in fact thrilled over the way she had been greeted by a French lady only the night before: "Vous êtes formidable! Vous êtes merveilleuse! Vous apportez les pantalons!"

Said another existentialist of existentialism: "It cannot be defined in the crass surroundings of an ordinary café." I have it on good existentialist authority, however, that the post-war fad is on its way out. Advanced Parisian thinkers already are embracing a new culture. The new group is known as Les Animalists. Perhaps you will be unable to tell an existentialist from an animalist, but, anyway, you'll find both categories at the famous Tabou, Le Mephisto, and the Caveau des Oubliettes, a Latin Quarter cellar once less profitably, if more appropriately, used as a dungeon.

If you prefer breathing space and elbow room, there are a number of nightclubs in Paris that are big, brassy, and loud in the Broadway manner. Perhaps the biggest, if not the brassiest, of these is the Lido at 78 Champs Elysées, which is done up in red drapes, yellow walls, and a blue ceiling, and offers two dance bands which provide continuous music. A once-nightly vaudeville show goes on at 11:30, offering typical vaudeville talent in the Laurel and Hardy tradition.

Along the same lines is Les Ambassadeurs at 3 Avenue Gabriel, near the American embassy. As at the Lido, Les Ambassadeurs serves expensive dinners, and restricts beverage orders to champagne. A sort of flimsy *décor* is achieved with curtains, lattice work, and potted palms. An American ice show played Les Ambassadeurs for some six months—an indication of what type of entertainment you can expect to find.

Among the quietly elegant spots is the Club des Champs Elysées, at 15 Avenue Montaigne, which has tea and dinner dancing and sedate entertainment. Plushy and intimate, with brown suede walls and impeccable service, the Champs Elysées gets single act talent like the Nicholas Brothers and Lena Horne. Friday night is formal.

Paris has a type of nightclub unknown in the United States, or, as far as I know, in the world. It seems to be the very personification of the French understanding for romance and their indulgence in good living. These clubs are small, exquisitely furnished, candle-lit, and brightened with fresh flowers. A large orchestra, virtually all violins, plays both classical and popular music. At the end of each set, the violinists descend from the bandstand, scatter all over the room, and play at the tables.

Monseigneur at 94 Rue d'Amsterdam, in Montmartre, is that kind of place. Every night except Sunday, beginning at 9:30, Monseigneur's symphonic orchestra plays the classics and soft popular music until 11 P.M. Then it goes into a schedule: from 11 P.M. until 2, gypsy music; from 2 until 3, popular numbers; then gypsy music from 3 to 3:30; popular until 4, then gypsy airs until 6. As long as customers sit at the red-covered tables amid the flowers and the candelabras sipping champagne at 2,500 francs a bottle, Monseigneur stays open, if necessary until noon.

In the same rich vein is Le Drap d'Or at 58 Rue Bassano, one of the most lavish nightclubs in the world. The decorative theme of the club, which opened in 1946, is taken from the meeting between the rival French and English armies under François I and Henry VIII at Pas de Calais. Instead of using force, the two armies tried to outdo each other with displays of luxury. According to the legend, the French showed up with a complete set of gold camping equipment, including the tents. Things are just about that lush at Le Drap d'Or now. The ceiling is an exact copy of the one in the study of François I at Blois, one of the chateaus of the Loire. The *boudoir d'amour* of François I is also reproduced, and the chimney is a copy of one at Chenonceaux. The bar is a reproduction of an old-style canopied bed from an unnamed somebody else's *chambre d'amour*. A twenty-four piece orchestra, half of which is violins, performs separately or in ensemble from the dinner hour until morning. Guests like Robert Taylor, Barbara Stanwyck, Marlene Dietrich, Sonja Henie, Secretary George Marshall on his way to Moscow, and a handful of Indian princes, have stopped by to gape at the splendor of Le Drap d'Or, and to sip champagne, as do all the guests, from silver goblets encrusted with the seals of François and Henry.

An American who was lapping up the luxury and taking in the spectacle of the Drap d'Or's twenty-four wandering musicians who played first on the bandstand, then on the dance floor, in the corridors, at the tables, in the bar—in fact, everywhere but in the kitchen—exclaimed, "Well, you can just imagine what Petrillo would have to say about *that!*"

The famous old Boeuf Sur Le Toit, which has moved more times than Annie, is still doing business, I am happy to say—this time at 34 Rue du Colisée. Always a hangout for French and American artists and performers, the Boeuf was an incubator for Jean Sablon, Charles Trenet, Hildegarde, and Josephine Baker. Two New York nightclubs, the Ruban Bleu and the Blue Angel, both in the Parisian motif, are offshoots of the original Boeuf.

After a wartime residence in a wing of the Hotel George V, the bawdy old Boeuf is now happily established in its own building, where it makes merry on three different levels. There is a dance floor on the main floor, newly redecorated with four Cocteau drawings on glass. The cabaret on the second floor, called the Constellation, is a bit more *intime,* certainly more exclusive, and features some pretty funny exponents of dirty double talk who shuttle back and forth between the Boeuf and the two unofficial affiliates in New York. One such artiste is a lady known as Morgane who, longer ago than I can remember, gave up counting the years and started tallying the wrinkles. In a fine Hennessy baritone Morgane sings, talks, mugs, and horses her way through numbers like "I Love to Sew," which will be funnier if you know French—and I don't mean the kind every high-school sophomore should understand.

In a little corner of its new quarters the Boeuf runs a semi-private bar which gets the artists, writers, designers, couturiers, and those who have been friends of the house for years. Well-known artists may doodle on the tablecloth, as a tip. Sketches by Jean Cocteau, a sort of over-age Orson Welles, are known to have been sold by waiters for several thousand francs. In this atmosphere, what is probably Paris' greatest concentration of successfully creative talent gathers in small groups to discuss their newest enterprises. Somebody always has a new play, a new act, a new collection, or a new book about to come out. But nobody ever says "Good luck!" In the superstitious creative set, to say good luck means bad luck, so everybody offers best wishes by just saying *merde*.

If you're really out on the town, one of the few places open in Paris for an early morning snack is the Club Paris des Champs Elysées. Not to be confused with the Club des Champs Elysées, the Club Paris is in the basement of the Elysées Park Hotel, near the Rond Point. It serves bacon and eggs, cheese sandwiches, welsh rarebit, and society piano music to a sophisticated crowd. All à la carte, and not expensive.

Whether you're out to see the Gay Paree or the Paris of arts and letters, the Paris of chic luxury or a student Bohemia, you'll find every mood, every nuance, every environment all crammed into one bubbling city. Paris is a world, somebody said once, and nobody has found that more true than American tourists, from Ben Franklin to George Marshall.

The first time I saw Paris I had ridden for eleven hours in the back end of an army truck over tank-torn roads, through the cobble-stoned streets of endless French villages that smelled of charcoal fires and horse dung. I was sick and I was tired and cold, and had I felt better I would have been hungry. I was in no mood to meet anybody. But Paris won me over. A perfume seemed to fill the air—it was pulsating, exciting. This was what was different from London or

Sioux City, from Chicago or Madrid. This was what a school teacher in Conshohocken saved up for fifteen years to have a look at. This was where an Italian poet, and a Swedish artist, and a Scotch philosopher, and an unknown nobody chose to live. This is the city for whom men cry when she is captive. Paris has a personality—perhaps in its rooftops, in its three-globe street lamps, its broad avenues, and trees, and cafés, and cops, and bridges, and monuments, and shops, and garrets, and history. Whatever else Paris may be, certainly it is a handsome lady with a past that an awful lot of people would travel a long way to see. Standing on a balcony of the Hotel Meurice at twilight one day, watching the long shadows fall across the broad Concorde, and the dusk settle like down around the big iron feet of the Eiffel Tower, one American explained it for everybody: "Dammit, he whispered, "it just gets ya."

## ✑ *Vichy*

Once noted as a spa, Vichy became infamous as the wartime capital of France. Although the name in peacetime years was virtually synomous for bottled table water, "Vichy," in the turbulent war era, became another word for "collaborationist." France immediately after the war was a land alive with recriminations, and to understand who wore the true badge of loyalty it is necessary to be familiar with the political intrigues of those days.

When France collapsed in 1940, the Germans divided France into three parts. First there was a *"zone interdite,"* a buffer strip strictly administered by the Germans which ran from the sea, at Dunkirk, along France's northern border, through Alsace. Then a line was established running roughly from a point outside of Pau, in the Pyrenees, north and east, skirting Angoulême, Tours, then eastward through Moulins, Châlons-sur-Saône, across the bottom of

*". . . a handsome lady with a past that an awful lot of people would travel a long way to see. . . ."*

Burgundy to the *zone interdite*. All the territory above that line was occupied by German forces. The rest of the country, unoccupied but administered by a French so-called collaborationist government, was headed by Pétain. The capital of the unoccupied state was Vichy.

Many Frenchmen were undecided whether to support the Pétain regime or reject it as a collaborationist. The American government, however, in order to maintain a North African consulate for the flow of intelligence information, elected to recognize the Vichy government, and sent Admiral William D. Leahy over as first ambassador. For a number of Frenchmen sitting on the fence, the apparent support of the American government was enough reassurance for them, and they joined the Vichy cause. Many have since been denounced as traitors.

In November, 1942, American forces invaded North Africa, and the Germans occupied all of France; Vichy became the capital of the entire country. With American support of the Vichy government now withdrawn, and the Germans initiating their forced-labor program in France, hundreds of Frenchmen drifted out of sight and joined the maquis. Many of those who remained in Vichy were branded as collaborationists and were later tried, but the recriminations against those who went free will go on for years.

Vichy today has been cleared of its government officials, traitorous or otherwise. Its more than forty hotels, including the fashionable Majestic, are open again during the long May-to-October season, and the waters are still recommended by the best doctors for the treatment of liver disorders. The city, some 200 miles south of Paris, has three casinos, two open-air swimming pools, an eighteen-hole golf course, and several excellent restaurants, including the Chantecler and the Alhambra. It has also a number of landmarks it never had before the war, and a distasteful name which it will take a lot of years to live down.

# ENVIRONS
# OF PARIS

*Versailles—"Marie Antoinette refused to co-operate. . . ."*

# 3. THE ENVIRONS OF PARIS

◇◇◇◇◇◇◇◇◇◇◇◇◇◇◇◇◇◇◇◇◇◇◇◇◇◇◇◇◇◇◇◇◇◇◇◇◇◇◇◇◇◇◇◇◇◇◇◇◇◇

## ~§ Versailles

One of the most elaborate residences in the entire world, Versailles was built by Louis XIV, restored by Louis Philippe, and maintained for many years by donations from the Rockefellers. On the outskirts of Paris, Versailles can be reached by a forty-minute train trip and a short street-car ride, or, easier still, by taking one of the prepared half-day tours of the Paris travel agencies which operate daily throughout the year.

Louis XIII originally maintained a hunting lodge at Versailles. His son, Louis XIV, visiting the chateau and gardens of one of his ministers near Melun, conceived the idea of a royal residence at Versailles—a notion which cost the French people a formidable wad of francs, and Louis XVI his head. Louis XIV established the seat of the government at Versailles after the Treaty of Njimegen in 1699. After his demise, in 1715, Louis XV took over and added a few new wings and a theater.

Magnificent murals still look down on visitors to the chapel at Versailles, and stained glass bearing the royal family's initials are still intact. During the time of Louis XIV, who used to proclaim "I am the state," the congregation was required to turn their backs on the altar and face the king and queen. In 1939, when the King and Queen of England visited Versailles, a re-enactment of those 18th-century days took place, with George and Elizabeth standing in for Louis and his queen, and members of the Comédie Francaise playing the role of the courtiers.

In the Abundant Salon, the public, which was paying the taxes to support such royal frippery as Versailles, was periodically invited to join in an open feast. No invitation was required, and all were welcome except monks, beggars, and dogs. Besides starting Versailles, Louis XIV also originated the Gobelin tapestry factory in Paris. Some Gobelin pieces which went to the chateaus of the Loire during the occupation are now back in place. In the Apollo Salon, so called because Louis fancied himself as the Sun King, His Extravagant Highness held court, and three hooks that upheld the canopy over the throne are still in view.

The Peace Treaty of Versailles was signed in the Hall of Mirrors at Versailles, June 29, 1919, an occasion which brought as much fame to the place as any of Louis' escapades. The hall is 240 feet long, and is lined with seventeen mirrors which face seventeen windows on the opposite wall. Inside this opulent corridor King George VI of England once gave a luncheon. All the waiters were dressed in the costume of the court, and the food was catered by the Larue Restaurant, which is located opposite the Madeleine Church. Larue has since been dubbed "the king of the cooks and the cook of the kings."

Around the corner of the Hall of Mirrors is the bedroom of the queens of France where some nineteen princes and princesses were, according to a state law, born in public view. Until Marie Antoinette refused to co-operate, any citizen had the right to watch a royal birth— assuming that he got to the royal bedchamber early enough to find a place. On the 6th of October, 1789, Swiss Guards defended this same bedroom against a mob that had marched down from Paris hot on the trail of Louis XVI and his wife. Marie Antoinette escaped through a small door, joined the king in his bedroom, and presently they both appeared on a balcony and addressed the crowd. In an ironic speech Louis promised never to return to Versailles. He never did. In January, 1793, he was beheaded in the Concorde square, to be followed by Marie Antoinette in October.

Most of the beautiful furniture of Versailles was sold during the Revolution. The mob wanted to raze the entire palace, but the people of Versailles intervened, perhaps with an idea of its future tourist attraction. Tour guides traditionally leave Versailles by the same staircase used by the revolutionists in 1789.

Somehow, France has found funds to maintain the fine gardens of Versailles, which took 30,000 workmen seven years to build. An artificial lake and intricate fountains stretch as far as the eye can see. There was no local water supply sufficient to feed the fountains in the 18th century, and every drop was pumped, as it is today, all the way from the Seine.

## La Malmaison

Malmaison was bought by Josephine Bonaparte, and became Napoléon's home when he was First Consul. After his divorce from Josephine he gave her Malmaison; later, he married Marie Louise of Austria. Napoléon was essentially a modest individual in his private life, and historians like to compare the opulence of Versailles with the simplicity of the chateau of Malmaison.

Visits to Malmaison are usually incorporated with tours of Versailles. The ordinary half-day Versailles trip is stretched to a full day, with a morning stop at Malmaison and lunch near the palace.

## Fontainebleau

The standard tour of Fontainebleau is a full-day trip, which takes a route past Orly Field to Barbizon, the artists' center. Here Millet lived amid poverty and eleven children, turning out masterpieces like "The Gleaners" and "The Man with the Hoe." Among the other painters of the Barbizon school, which took its name from a nearby village, were Corot, Rousseau, Diaz, Dupré, Jacques, and Harpignies. Instead of adopting the pedestrian method of painting a central subject, the Barbizon painters took their paints and their canvasses to the woodlands, and sought inspiration in nature.

After lunch at a country inn, the tour proceeds through the forest of Fontainebleau, 42,000 acres in extent and 63 miles in circumference, once a hunting ground of kings. The chateau of Fontainebleau was originally a 12th-century fortress and was reconstructed by François I, in the 16th century, into an Italian renaissance residence. Under the patronage of François I, Leonardo da Vinci went to France, where he later died, and some of his finest works are still in the Louvre.

Fontainebleau became a favorite residence of Napoléon, and much of the furnishings from the days when he lived there with Josephine are still in the rooms. Napoléon announced his divorce of Josephine at Fontainebleau, and it was there, on April 11, 1814, that he formally abdicated. The courtyard in which he bid farewell to his guard was ever afterwards known as La Cour des Adieux.

### ✑ Chantilly

The chateau of Chantilly is built in the middle of an artificial lake, and dates from the 9th century. It was damaged by the revolutionists of 1789, and again by those of 1870. Restored in the late 19th century, the chateau is now a museum containing a collection of paintings of the French school of the 17th, 18th and 19th centuries, and works by Flemish and Italian masters.

Once, during a banquet being given in honor of Louis XIV at Chantilly, a celebrated cook named Vatel, who now seems clearly to have been neurotic, was afraid there would not be enough fish to go around. He worried himself into such a state that he committed suicide before the dinner started. All over France today, hundreds of restaurants have called themselves Au Grand Vatel, in honor of the nervous chef of Chantilly.

## ◄§ Reims

Always popular with tourists for its famous cathedral and for its champagnes, Reims was given an even greater place in history by Dwight D. Eisenhower of Abilene, Kansas. Reims' biggest attraction today is the little red school house, once Eisenhower's headquarters, where the Germans signed the surrender that ended World War II in Europe. Every map and chart in what was at the time the SHAEF war room has been kept exactly as it was on May 7, 1945, the day the European war ended. Reims' great cathedral was untouched by this war, and tourists may visit its grand interior where the kings of France were traditionally crowned until the Emperor Napoléon altered the custom and ordered his own coronation at Notre Dame.

"Champagne" is more than a gay, elegant wine. It is, as well, the name for that generally unfertile industrial section of France stretching between Paris and Belgium. Chalôns is the capital of Champagne, but Reims is the headquarters for tourists and wine. The city is on the afternoon half of a full-day conducted tour operated by the Paris travel bureaus. (In the morning the route follows the one taken by the French taxicab army in 1914, stopping at the American World War I cemetery at Belleau Wood, and at the battlefield at Chateau Thierry. Later in the day a stop is made at the Armistice monument in Compiègne Forest. The famous railroad car, scene of the 1918 German surrender and the French capitulation in 1940, was removed by the Nazis, and later was destroyed.)

Although champagne is manufactured in New York State, in California, and was made, before the war, in Germany, champagne the wine was originally discovered in Champagne, the province which still produces the best in the world. According to an ancient and unreliable legend, the discovery of the sparkling wine is ascribed to a monk named Dom Perignon who was in charge of the Abbey of Hautvillers. Champagne, before the discovery, turned out a rather ordinary dry white wine. Vintners found, however, that the introduction of sugar into dry white wine caused a secondary fermentation which produces the sparkling quality. The best champagnes today are made from a blend of black and white grapes which have ripened all season in the chalky fields of Champagne. The chalk imparts a dry flavor to real champagne, which takes at least four years to manufacture.

Champagne is honeycombed with over a hundred miles of wine cellars tunneled out of underground chalk deposits. During the first World War, when the heaviest fighting took place in the Marne area, the entire population of Reims went underground and lived in the cellars. In these tunnels the champagne is slowly aged and ripened. For the first three months each bottle is set in a rack, neck down, and given a quarter turn every day. After the sediment settles against the cork and the wine becomes clear, the cork is allowed to pop out of the bottle carrying the residue with it. The bottle is capped again, and then sugar is added, the amount varying according to the country to which the lot will be exported. Experts classify the quality of champagne according to its degree of dryness. America gets the dryest and therefore the best, South America the sweetest, and the French themselves, a demi-sec.

Among the world-famous labels of French champagne are Lanson, Clicquot-Ponsardin, Heidsieck-Monopole, Moët et Chandon, Mumm, Pommery, Roederer, Charles Heidsieck, Piper Heidsieck, Pol Roger, Mercier, Krug, and a dozen others. They all flow from the fountainhead of Reims and nearby Epernay.

## ✤§ Chartres

The famous cathedral at Chartres came through the war with a few bullet holes from sniper fire, but otherwise it remains intact. It has long had the reputation of being the most beautiful Gothic cathedral in the world, and as the war approached the center of France again in 1944, the stained glass was removed, and the statues and entrances were sand-bagged. In their attempt to blow up a nearby bridge, the retreating Germans destroyed the Porte Guillaume, part of the ramparts of the city, but the cathedral building nearby was not disturbed. An American officer in a hurry to pursue the attack nevertheless was loath to leave Chartres without having seen the cathedral. GI trucks drove straight up to the church entrance, soldiers removed the sandbags, and Chartres became one of the first of France's great cathedrals to reopen.

Today it can be reached on a full-day tour which leaves Paris at 10 a.m., travels via St. Germain and Mantes to the chateau at Anet which Henry II gave Diane de Poitiers. Chartres, the art city of France, is old and quaint, its ancient houses nestling up to the very sides of the majestic cathedral. Originally built in 1020, the cathedral was burned and rebuilt later on a Roman base. Among the hundreds of statues is one of the Black Virgin which since the 14th century has drawn pilgrimages of devout Catholics, particularly sterile women. Chartres is probably the oldest pilgrimage place in France, and its church was once known as the Cathedral of the Virgin.

# NORMANDY

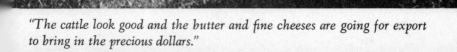

"The cattle look good and the butter and fine cheeses are going for export to bring in the precious dollars."

"... the Vikings in the ninth century and the Allies in the twentieth. ..."

# 4. NORMANDY

NORMANDY is a rich, green, fertile, farming land, historically bracketed by the invasion of the Vikings in the ninth century and the Allies in the twentieth. It still bears souvenirs of both events. At Dives-sur-Mer, where William the Conqueror gathered his boats for his invasion of England, one can lunch at L'Hostellerie Guillaume le Conquerant, a magnificent garden restaurant believed to be about 1,000 years old. The only thing that has changed is the price. Before the recent war a meal there cost about 150 francs; it runs about 1,500 francs now.

The broad Normandy fields, which are not unlike those of the American Midwest, were churned into a morass of mud by the heavy tread of the liberating army in 1944, but most have since been leveled, re-seeded, de-mined. In 1947 Normandy produced its first bumper post-war harvest. The cattle look good, and the butter and fine cheeses of the province are going for export to bring in precious dollars. From Normandy's unending rows of apple trees come, each fall, the juices for cider and Calvados, a local brandy which American soldiers likened to kerosene and used for lighting lanterns and lightening the outlook. One can still see, here and there, the remains of German trucks and American tanks, rotted and rusted, as misshappen by time as by war. Much of the debris is rudely marked "Vendu," sold, for scrap to a Paris firm. The war is done, and there are no souvenirs. From a German block house on the Atlantic wall a white streamer flutters in

*Normandy shipyard—"Day-Day was the memory of a lifetime."*

the wind. It says, "Ambre Solaire Pour Brunir La Peau" — "Use Ambre Sun Lotion to Tan the Skin."

The farmland has done well, but the tiny Normandy villages that found history in that summer of 1944 are still struggling to get on their feet. Some of them will limp for twenty years. In the minds of the stolid, stoical Normans who think a lot and say little, the invasion will remain the most vivid memory of a lifetime. It is referred to locally as "Day-Day." At St. Lô, which American forces captured on July 17, 1944, after a furious battle, the once bustling main street simply doesn't exist. In the residential section, called La Place de Beaux Regardes (Fair View), not a house stands. Everywhere there

*St. Lô—"the clink of mason's hammers is the sound of France."*

are neat piles of stone blocks which were once houses. In some sections of the city one hears the clink of mason's hammers, which is the sound of France rebuilding. But the process is slow, and often it is necessary to use the old blocks. Some new modernistic stores have been built, and old stone buildings, partly damaged, have been patched with brick, like an old pair of pants. Signs point the way to United States cemeteries, and one road through town is marked with the red, white and blue stanchions which commemorate the "Road of Liberty" through which the American Army scorched its way to victory. From a tree, which somehow escaped unharmed, a child rocks back and forth in a swing. And because there is no longer any bell because there is no longer a belfry, the terrible siren still screams twice a day in St. Lô, once at noon and again at six o'clock.

Normandy's biggest and flashiest resort is Dèauville, at the mouth of the Seine, opposite Le Havre, and just a few hours from Paris. A popular watering place for the English before the war, Deauville has reopened its three big hotels and its five smaller ones to a post-war trade predominantly French. It would like to welcome Americans, and there is no reason why it shouldn't. The season stretches from June to September, with plenty of space available in June and July. The ultra-fashionable season for a Deauville visit is the first three weeks in August, where, for those who find it so, to be seen at the resort is a must. Newest hotel in Deauville is the du Golf, which was built in 1929, the last year of any construction of consequence in France. During the war it was taken over for the headquarters of the German Luftwaffe for France. Upon his return from five years' captivity in Germany, Manager Maurice Foucret found the doorway of the finest suite unaccountably wider, the toilet seat in the W.C. as big as a barrel head. Inquiry revealed that the rooms had been occupied by Field Marshal Sperrle, a man as fat as Goering and twice as pompous. M. Foucret also found his hotel tenanted by some 1,200 American GIs, a fraction of the pen and pencil brigade of the United States Headquarters, Normandy Base Section, to whom Deauville became as sweet as home.

All that is over now. The Hôtel du Golf has been completely redecorated, and offers spacious double rooms with immense baths. On the terraces that flank the hotel, guests can follow the golfers on the front lawn, sit on a summer's night and watch the beacons of Le Havre flicker across the water. For this pleasure the du Golf has been charging its guests three times the 1939 price level, and it seeks to raise the ante to four times. Rooms under the three-time rate cost 1,145 francs for two. Meals are a flat 400 francs, wine not included. Similar prices exist at Deauville's two other large hotels, the Royal,

"And because there is no longer any bell because there is no longer a belfry, the terrible siren still screams twice a day in St. Lô."

and the Normandie, which is run with excellent taste by M. H. Mailier. The Normandie is under the same management as the ·Deauville Casino which has gambling, dancing, a restaurant, a movie theater and a playhouse. There are excellent tennis courts in Deauville, and in addition to the 18-hole course at the du Golf, a nine-hole course for women is also being readied. There are two racetracks; polo has been started for the first time, and plans are going ahead for the rebuilding of the yacht club which was mined and destroyed by the Germans. The Aga Khan and many another celebrity have villas by the seaside; there is twice-a-day air service during the season from Croydon Airport in London and once-a-day service from Brussels. All the best Paris stores have branches at Deauville, the representation including Printemps, Hermes, Patou, Van Cleef and Arpels and Jeanne Lanvin. A Marquise de Sévigné chocolate shop is doing business in a cement bunker once occupied by the German Wehrmacht.

Some effort has been expended to establish Deauville as a center for trips to the Normandy landing beaches and cemeteries. It has also been argued that the gaiety of Deauville is not in keeping with the solemnity that should be accorded a visit to the battlefields. Certainly, Deauville will be out of keeping for those who seek to visit relatives buried in nearby military cemeteries. So far, next of kin have been staying in small, but oft-times excellent seaside resorts that line the whole Normandy coast. A typical one is the Hôtel du Centre, at Duc-sur-Mer. The British landings were made near Riva Bella, Courseilles and Ver Plage, places known now as Sword Beach, Juno Beach, and Gold Beach, the code names used in the original military plans. Many British families therefore seek accommodations at Caen, which is central but badly battered. As a retired Caen professor said, "You can't make an omelet without breaking eggs. Unfortunately, in the battle of Normandy we were the eggs, but on the whole the omelet was pretty good." Although the historic

*Hotel du Golf, Deauville—"in the W.C. The seat was as big as a barrel-head."* (French National Tourist Office)

*Caen—"you can't make an omelet without breaking eggs . . . and we were the eggs."*

city is a shambles, the people seem to take their fortune with cold logic, and harbor no grudge against the Allies whose bombs crushed their homes and killed their neighbors. Just before their liberation on the 9th of July, 2,000 citizens of Caen were weathering the bombardment by lying on the straw-covered floor of the Cathedral of St. Etienne. Suddenly, someone spotted two Canadians and shouted, "Les voila!" The people of Caen rose, free men, from the floor, and hoisted the Canadians on their shoulders. A rousing cheer echoed through the Cathedral of St. Etienne, loud enough, they say, to stir the bones of William the Conqueror, who is buried there. To this day Caen has not forgotten. Its chapter of a cultural club called

France-Grand Bretagne-Les Etats Unis has been organized to help to locate British and American graves, find accommodations for visiting relatives, and, even in the face of severe shortages, to conduct them to cemeteries by motorcar.

Near Caen is the city of Lisieux, which is, like Lourdes, one of the great religious centers of France, and which was also crushed during the invasion. The famous ancient houses that had survived so much turbulent history fell finally before twentieth-century weapons. Despite the destruction, the annual pilgrimage held every third of October is still being made to the shrine of St. Thérèse, who is remembered because she said, in effect, "I want to pass my time in heaven by doing good deeds on earth." Her exact words are inscribed in French in St. Patrick's Cathedral in New York City. A Carmelite nun, St. Thérèse died of tuberculosis in 1897 at twenty-four. She had come from the rose country of Normandy, loved the flower, and roses are associated to this day with her and with the miracles with which her shrine is credited. As a pilgrimage city, Lisieux has much of the same tourist flavor as Lourdes. The hotel situation cannot compare with the accommodations available in the southern city, however. About the best available is the three-star, forty-five room Hôtel Espérance.

Rouen, the museum city on the Seine, was badly hit in 1940 and again in 1944. Work is going ahead on the restoration of the cathedral, which was seriously damaged, and in spite of the destruction the city still retains tremendous historical interest in the story of Joan of Arc, who has been canonized, and is now St. Joan. Joan was captured at Compiègne by the Duke of Burgundy on May 23, 1431. She was forthwith sold to the English by the Count of Luxembourg, and tried before a church tribunal as a fifteenth-century war criminal. As the voices had told her, Joan was condemned to die, and on May 30, 1431, she was burned alive at the stake in the old marketplace in Rouen. The question whether her execution day should be commemorated in France was long the subject of debate between royalists who were against the idea, and the liberal forces who were in favor of it. After World War II, a leftist government was swept into power, and the question was decided. May 30 is now a national holiday.

Although it had been years in the preparation, the invasion came suddenly to the people of Normandy. Following a tremendous aerial bombardment and parachute droppings during the night, on June 6, 1944, invasion craft of the Allied armies put ashore along the Normandy coast, from the Orne River opposite Caen all the way up to the Cotentin peninsula. As the attackers saw the picture, the British held the left flank and the Americans the right. The extreme eastern landing was successfully effected by British troops at Sword Beach, now officially called Colleville-Montgomery Plage. A tablet honoring Montgomery and the first Allied soldiers who fell there has been erected a few yards from the beach, just facing a huge bunker which dates from another war in the seventeenth century. A few kilometers to the west, a simultaneous British landing was accomplished at the oyster center of Courseilles, on what was known on June 6 as Juno Beach. Old ships purposely sunk to form a harbor still lie in the sea. A tablet at Courseilles notes that General de Gaulle himself accomplished a successful personal landing on the beach on June 14, coming ashore quite without the invitation of Montgomery, the area commander. Since some of the local lawmakers installed by the Germans had been inclined to nod toward Vichy, Monty feared de Gaulle's presence might touch off a minor civil war. The Briton had made every effort to keep de Gaulle from the beaches, and when he heard that the Frenchman had landed, Monty is reputed to have blown his British top. Intelligence personnel were dispatched to the area (a) to find de Gaulle, and (b) to determine what he was up to. The intelligence people searched all over, and finally turned up Le Grand Charlie taking an evening repast over at the Lion d'Or. He

*The landing beaches—"beyond the surf . . . a late-arriving vulture. . . ."*

had already installed a few new mayors here and there without revolutionary effect, and intelligence was able to report to a much calmed Montgomery that the situation was well in hand.

The beaches chosen for British landings were excellent for invasion. They led to broad expanses of flat land, and the troops gained their objectives quickly, and advanced four to five miles. There are some remnants of radar, artillery, and tank equipment still lying about. On the ramparts above Port Winston, used as a supply port, a German bunker, later taken over by the Allies, still bears the inscription, "Harry's Mansions."

A short way up the coastline, the Americans landing at Omaha Beach ran into trouble and tragedy. To the 29th United States Division was assigned the mission of effecting a landing on a beach commanded by a steep cliff. Near the heights a German division, engaging in practice maneuvers, was immediately pressed into action. It deployed on the cliff and rained fire on the unprotected 29th as it poured from its invasion barges. While the American 4th Division was doing well up the line at Utah Beach, by sunset the troops at Omaha were still under German artillery fire.

Omaha Beach is desolate now, quiet except for the chug of a cement mixer pouring concrete for a new road that will run along the battlefield. An oversimplified monument notes that here American troops made a landing. The pattern of the broad, clean sand is broken only by the hulk of a battered landing craft, a few chunks of twisted iron—metal guts spewed from a wounded ship. The surf comes in easily, slips onto the sand, and falls back, washing away the vestiges of the event, the heel prints, the face prints, the sweat, the gore, as a wet rag, in a twinkling, sweeps away a priceless formula chalked on a blackboard. Beyond the surf a salvage tug puffs among a score of sunken ships, like a late-arriving vulture picking clean the bones before surrendering the carcass to the sea. Such is Omaha Beach today.

Late in 1947 the Graves Registration Section of the United States Army began the grisly task of exhuming bodies of dead soldiers whose next of kin requested their reburial in the United States. Elaborate precautions were taken to finish the job in privacy. Cemeteries that faced on roads were hidden behind high, cloth screens. Road barriers were built, sentry boxes installed, and armed guards posted at entrances. French labor was recruited to do the digging, but it was decreed that only American hands should touch American bodies. A complete staff of undertakers and burial experts was imported from the States. When everything was ready, a few colonels visited each temporary cemetery, conducted a brief service, and officially closed the area. The bodies of those soldiers who were to remain buried in France were conveyed to permanent military cemeteries. Before the shifting of American military dead, local French families had been in the habit of adopting American graves, keeping the grass trimmed and the plots decorated with flowers. The French completely ignored German graves in the same cemetery. "Grass got so bad in the enemy section," said one American guard, "we finally had to cut it ourselves."

It was also customary in the early post-war period for French communities to send plaques of tribute to American cemeteries. On the honor board of one cemetery, crowded with French plaques, was one simple hand-lettered sign which said, "In Loving Memory of Our Boy." It was signed by his parents and sent from a small town in West Virginia. Some of the tablets sent by the French read:

A Ses Liberateurs
La Commune de St. Germain du Pert
Reconnaissante

A La Mémoire des Soldats Americains
La Commune de la Cambe Reconnaissante
30 Mai 1945

Les Medailles Militaire
du Canton d'Isigny

Souvenir à nos amis Americains offert
par les ouvriers de Grand Camp

Just below Avranches, and hanging onto Normandy only by a technicality, is Mont St. Michel, prime sightseeing attraction in France, and believed to be the second most popular in the world next to Niagara Falls. Mont St. Michel is a tiny rock, perhaps two kilometers in circumference, sitting in the middle of the Bay of Mont St. Michel in the Channel. During most of the year the rock is isolated in the center of a great expanse of sand flats and is connected to the mainland by a solitary road. The big event of each springtime is the Grand Marée, when the tide comes rolling in at about ten miles an hour, surrounding the rock with water and often flooding the rock's one tiny, cobblestoned street.

Mont St. Michel was founded in the eighth century by monks who built an abbey there. The Benedictine monks, who took over in 966, found the original building too small, destroyed it, and started on another. The main section of the Abbey is called the Marvel, a modernistic structure the way time is figured at Mont St. Michel. It was started in 1203 and is called the Marvel because it was completed only twenty-five years later. The Marvel comprises four buildings containing 100 rooms. In the monks' dining room, a plain, square chamber, one can see only two windows from the entrance, but there are sixty visible from the interior, a local architectural trick of the thirteenth century. On the roof of the Marvel are over 700 arches all sculptured differently, and some partly destroyed during the French Revolution. The monks originally had a garden blooming among the arches, but the water seeped through on to the friars below, and they had to abandon that idea. Still in evidence on the roof is a stone bench where every Thursday the monks held a foot-washing ceremony, the seniors washing the juniors.

In 1811, Napoléon took over Mont St. Michel as a prison, and one can still see the dungeons and also a great, covered wheel with built-in treadway by which food was pulled up from the kitchens to the tower cells. All told, Mont St. Michel was burned thirteen times—ten times by lightning, twice by war, and once by the prisoners themselves. After 1863 the prison was closed and the abbey was restored.

Today Mont St. Michel is a jumble of hotels and shops, one plastered on top of the other, and the whole pile crowned with the abbey. There are seven hotels in all, and they are moderately priced. Le Poulard is the best, and its cuisine is noted for a huge, fluffy omelet

*Mont St. Michel—"huge fluffy omelets fried in a copper pan over an open fire right before your eyes. . . ."*

*Mont St. Michel—"the best buy, most typical souvenir and sagest advice come in the ashtrays."*

which is fried in a long-handled copper pan over an open fire, right before your eyes. The menu hardly ever changes at Mont St. Michel, the favorite dish being lamb, which is supposed to have a distinctive taste because at low tide sheep graze on the salt-flavored grass flats at the fringes of the rock. The biggest season is June to September, but there is also a big rush at Easter; most of the shops and hotels are open all year around, and off-season there is never any trouble finding a room. The shops carry little kegs trimmed in metal, copperware made at Ville-Dieu-les-Poëles, and china from Quimper which will be cheaper if you buy it in its home town. The kegs run about 1,300 francs for the smallest. Small dolls in magnificent costumes cost about

*In Mont St. Michel's abbey, the friars got wet.* (French National Tourist Office)

4,000 francs and góod antique pieces run proportionately skyward. The best buy, most typical souvenir, and sagest advice come in ashtrays which cost 100 francs. They are inscribed, "Ne faites pas l'amour le samedi, vous ne sauriez quoi faire le dimanche." ("Don't make love on Saturday; you won't know what to do on Sunday.")

*"Like an island cut away . . . and set adrift in time. . . ."*

*Sunday in Finistère—for these ladies a special ration of starch.*

# 5. BRITTANY

SHROUDED in the cobwebby veils of centuries long since passed, clinging to ancient custom with a religious fervor approaching superstition, much of Brittany lives today like an island which ages ago was cut away from civilization, and set adrift in time. Actually, it is a peninsula on the northwest French coast which juts out boldly towards America. It produces fish, ceramics, and hardy seamen whose costumes have been copied by couturiers all over the world. Before the war, its northern coast was a popular watering place for British families. Later, the southern side became equally popular with German submarines which preyed on Allied shipping from the Brittany ports of Lorient and St. Nazaire.

Lower Brittany is the most colorful part of the peninsula, especially the province known as Finistère—"land's end," or as they sometimes say down there, "the end of the earth." Women still wear traditional coifs, white, starched headgear often a foot high. In some outlying villages, farmers continue to sleep in *lits-clos,* beds enclosed in carved wooden cabinets. It used to be the custom for all members of the family to sleep in one room. The *lits-clos* were built into the walls, and each had a sliding panel for privacy.

Bretons are descended from the Celts, and hundreds of their parishes are dedicated to the first immigrants who came over from Ireland. The true natives speak a Celtic tongue called Breton, and many of them are unable to speak French. They suffer from melancholia, congenital

*Bretons are descended from the Celts . . . and many are unable to speak French.*

hip-joint disease, and acutely primitive farming methods which nonetheless produce bountiful crops. Brittany was a bloody battleground in the War of the Succession in the fourteenth century. It was also the homeland of Anne of Brittany (1477-1514), known as *La Petite Brette,* who accomplished the double coup of marrying two French kings in a row, Charles VIII and Louis XII. Coming from one of her trips abroad, Anne landed on what is now the estate of an Englishwoman, a lady who busied herself in the early days of the late war ferrying Frenchmen to England from the very same point.

Of Brittany an old Celtic proverb says, "Kant Bro, Kant giz, Kant parrez, Kant iliz"—"a hundred regions, a hundred manners, a hundred

*". . . melancholia, congenital hip-joint disease, and acutely primitive farm-ing methods. . . ."*

*"Anne landed on what is now the estate of an Englishwoman, a lady who
. . . during the war . . . ferried Frenchmen to England from the very same
point."*

parishes, a hundred churches." There are over two thousand parishes,
each of which has its own type of coif or headgear, and forty-eight
different traditional costumes. The most outlandish are high, white
stovepipe affairs worn by the Bigoudens, and the prettiest are those
of Fouesnant, which are worn with a wide, starched lace collar. Coifs
are said to be disappearing, principally because of the price, now about
ten thousand francs, and the difficulty of obtaining starch. One enter-
prising chamber of commerce in Brittany, with an eye cocked to tourist
appeal, has already requested the government to allot special starch
rations to the local coif wearers.

*Old Breton salts—"as full of superstitions as a Harlem dream book."*

Bretons are as full of superstitions as a Harlem dream book. They still talk of death in hushed allegorical terms, and in the churchyards one can still see ossuaries where the bones of the dead were stored after their graves were exhumed to make room for later arrivals. Breton spinsters who are getting a little anxious have a habit of tossing hairpins on water. If the pin floats it's a good sign their spinsterhood is nearly over. It's an old Breton custom for guests at a bridal party to whip up a dishful of onion soup, and take it to the bride and groom after they have retired. In a ceremony similar to the charivari of early America, the guests, carrying the soup, knock at the door of the bridal couple, and sing a sixteenth-century verse, the opening line of which Tin Pan Alley may find a shade familiar. It goes:

> Open the door, open it
> You newlyweds!

The bride then answers through the door:

> How can I open it?
> I'm in bed.
> My husband is with me
> He holds me in his arms
> And will hold me all the night.
> Wait until tomorrow morning
> He will be at work
> My bed will be made
> My room will be cleaned
> And my little pigeon will have flown.

After going through all that, the bride is obliged to open the door, and drink the damned onion soup anyway.

The best insight into local peasant custom and tradition are the *Pardons,* local feast days conducted by a parish. Although coifs can be seen in Brittany any time, and many costumes are in evidence at the churches on Sundays, every bit of frippery comes out for a *Pardon.* The season for the fêtes runs from May through October, and a list of the dates is published annually by the government's tourist offices in Paris and the United States.

Sitting astride two rivers, the ancient city of Quimper has become the tourist center for Breton lore. It has a number of hotels none of which can be considered continental, but several are pleasantly comfortable. About the best is the Hôtel de L'Epée which is broad and spacious, and run with a certain efficiency by a one-time mail clerk of the Hotel Pennsylvania in New York.

Wednesday and Saturday are market days in Quimper, and tourists should try to be in the city on either of those days. The narrow alleys are clogged from the dark, early hours of the morning. By sunrise, a village of orange, yellow, white, and blue canvas tents has been erected in the square, smack in front of the magnificent cathedral. From carts and cars, and old United States Army duffel bags pours a stream of goods—wool coats, candy bars, plumbing devices, brooches, mirrors, Wrigley's chewing gum, hair nets, combs, rulers, rubber shoe treads, cookies, knives, and thimbles. Bretons sell slippers of molded straw lined with rabbit fur and soled with cork, fine, hand-worked embroidered Juliet caps for girls.

Goods are bought, sold, exchanged in a continuous babble that mixes with the rattle of wooden shoes on the cobblestone pavement—the bargaining in Breton, the haggling in French. Everywhere are the coif-crowned ladies, bobbing around in the crowd like whitecaps in a surging sea. Their men come in black velvet hats with black satin streamers that flow from a huge silver buckle pinned in the back. At sundown, huge buses roll into the market square, and you can always tell the destination of each vehicle by the type of coif worn by the women passengers.

There are tourist shops in Quimper which feature dolls in authentic Breton costume, and pieces of Quimper pottery made in the city. One of the biggest pottery manufacturers is Henriot and Co. on the Allées de Loc Maria which has been doing business at the same stand for some 170 years. They sell to such United States establishments as Macy's and Marshall Field's, and have a museum of old and new pottery, and several authentic pieces of Breton furniture. The pottery collection includes the mate to a huge bowl that was presented to President Wilson when he arrived in France to negotiate the peace after World War I. But one of Henriot's best numbers is a little ashtray with a picture of a schooner. The inscription in French reads, "When this boat sails, England will fall." The ashtray was turned out during the occupation, and was greatly appreciated by the nearsighted

Germans—who never realized that the little painted boat on the little clay sea would never actually set sail.

A number of good trips can be arranged from Quimper: To see the house at Roscoff from which Mary Queen of Scots left France for Scotland; to the unfortunate village of Telgruc, destroyed by American airmen through error after the German retreat in 1944; and to the excellent restaurant Le Moulin de Rosmadec at Pont Aven. But the most interesting point of all is the great sardine and tuna port of Douarnenez. The town is twenty-two kilometers from Quimper, and if you arrive in late afternoon you will not only see red sails in the sunset, but blue nets as well. The fishermen wear red and blue two-piece suits, and broad, flat berets that are not found elsewhere in the province. Old, wrinkled fishermen, who long ago gave up the trade, still affect the traditional costume, sit along the sunny quays, and swap tall tales in Breton.

Although they understand the Welsh traders who come sometimes in their potato and onion boats, the Breton fishermen know very little French, and seem to live like a race apart. Their devotion is to themselves, and many accumulated fortunes during the war ferrying men to England. One French family was blackmailed for 65,000 francs after sending its son by Breton fishing boat to join the de Gaullist forces across the Channel.

Northern Brittany got its first British settlers in 460, and the coast has been popular with Englishmen ever since. Brest has been completely ruined, and must now be discounted as a resort. Morlaix, however, is back in business with a dozen hotels of which L'Hôtel d'Europe is about the best.

Dinard, which likes to call itself "Queen of the Emerald Coast," emerged in fairly good shape, a bit of news that pleased the English and American colony that roosted there for years. The resort was founded by an American named Coppinger, and its success was assured by a summer-long visit of Empress Eugénie. Later came the Comte

*Douarnenez—the Welsh traders who come in their onion boats are under-stood.*

de Paris, the Prince and Princess d'Orléans, Lord Kitchener, and an assortment of Rockefellers and Morgans. One Englishman went into such raptures about Dinard a few years ago, that his tribute was printed and bound into a booklet for public distribution. In part it read: "While Dinard is pleasantly French, it is so delightfully English, too. English people made Dinard, you must know, and if I say it is by us English that Dinard exists, I scarcely exaggerate. So at Dinard you will find just the English things one wants; a pretty ivy-covered, typical English church, an English library, those English comforts to which we so sensibly cling, and above all, an English welcome."

They're getting ready with that English welcome all right. Matter of fact, one hotel has posted signs in all its rooms which read as follows:

NOTICE:

The management well only be responsible for jewellry, money, valuable papers, etc which have been deposited at the Hotel-office against receipt. Cheques are only taken for collection.

Electric light—The electricity is for illumination only. Special permission will be granted for other purposes by the management, extra will be charged on the bill.

Laundry—The hotel takes care of the visitor's laundry and no foreign person is allowed to take same out of the hotel or to bring in customers are kindly requested not to stretch anything at the windows.

Meals—Meals served in the bedroom will be charged extra no wines, beers, liquors ocher than those provided in the Hotel may be taken in the bedroom without extra.

Library—Boofis free of charge are at the deposited of the customers which must bring them back after reading.

Dogs—Dogs pay 2 fr. for their board. It is not allowed to give their good in the restaurant dishes.

Across the harbor from Dinard lies the old corsair city of St. Malo. The bridge has been knocked out, and to get to St. Malo you take the ferry or spend an hour driving around the harbor. St. Malo is renowned for the massive walls that surround the city, for its native sons, Chateaubriand and Jacques Cartier, who explored Canada, and, more recently, as the center of a seventeen-day battle between German and American troops. This latest debacle in the ancient city of St. Malo ruined a good deal of the center of the town. Important streets have vanished altogether, and are now just rows of empty foundations covered with post-war weeds. But the massive walls and the quaint entrances remain as testimonials to the days when the city was a center for pirate operations. At Cancale, 17 kilometers away, you can still find dark, olive-skinned girls who talk with a peculiar accent. The little fishing village is Portuguese, the good burghers being descendants of sailors whose ships were wrecked by the local pirates who set false direction fires along the rocky coast. The people of Cancale refuse to intermarry with others, speaking halting French, sound their "E's" as if they are saying, "eye," and remain as living proof of the high jinks of the old corsairs.

In spite of their historical reputation, however, the men of St. Malo dislike being called pirates, and are otherwise touchy on the subject of Englishmen, with whom they have maintained a long record of differences concerning fishing privileges off the coast. Many of the descendants of the corsairs are engaged today in growing—of all things —mistletoe. Despite the feuds, most of the plants are exported to England, where instead of hard feeling they promote joy and romance.

In summer the French railroads operate regular six-day motor coach tours of Brittany, leaving from Dinard. The trip follows the coastline, past the beach resorts of St. Lunaire, St. Briac, and St. Cast, stopping at fashionable Sables d'Or for lunch. In the afternoon the tour winds through the pine-tree country of Val Indre to St. Brieuc, the first overnight stop. On the second day the group visits Paimpol, where the fishermen go out for months at a time seeking cod in the North Sea, while the women sit at home in pretty coifs and wait. Paimpol was popularized by the writer Pierre Loti as the setting for his book *Pêcheur d'Islande,* which was used widely in the United States as a French primer. Treguier, an afternoon stop, was the home of Renan, a nineteenth-century freethinker who is credited with influencing the ultimate divorce of church and state in France. The second overnight stop is made at Lannion, and the drive the next morning continues through typical Breton countrysides lined with roadside religious shrines all the way to Brest. In the afternoon the motor coaches wind through the strawberry country of Plougastel-Daoulas to Quimper. There is a stop later in the day at the Baie des Trepasses, "the Bay of the Dead," one of the most treacherous bodies of water in the world.

The coaches stop briefly at the colorful ports of Concarneau and Douarnenez, then continue through Quimperle to Carnac to see some 2,000 monoliths, an imposing collection of relics of the Stone Age. Before putting up at Vannes, where the tour ends, the caravan visits Auray, home of the *Pardon* of St. Anne d'Auray, the biggest in all Brittany, which is held every July 25 and 26.

If you would really like to get away from it all, pay a visit to the Ile d'Ouessant, twenty kilometers out in the sea, off Brest. Here the fog rumbles in like a drum roll, the foghorns moan drearily, and the houses themselves are settled into the earth as a protection from the Atlantic winds. The women of the island wear black coifs, let their hair grow down to their shoulders, and while their men are out to sea in ships they till the soil. Yet, because of the nearness of the Gulf Stream, roses, fig trees, and blackberries blossom in abundance on the Ile d'Ouessant, perhaps as a reminder that all the world is not as melancholy as it seems here on the end of the *finistère*.

Chaumont—"here you can walk with kings and courtesans, paramours and queens. . . ."

*Working on the cathedral of Tours—"necessitated by the Germans. . . ."*

# 6. THE CHATEAUS
## of the Loire

In the valley of the Loire, the great chateaus of France still stand today like tombstones of a glory that has vanished, but is often rather enviously remembered. Here you can walk with kings and courtesans, with queens and paramours. Right on location you can trace history's most enervating ennuis, most titillating infatuations, most searing amours.

The chateaus of the Loire were once powerful fortresses, and later became country estates for the kings, the nobility, and the rich. Some are in ruins, but most are well preserved, and many still contain priceless relics of their original days.

The hub of the chateau country is the city of Tours, 235 kilometers from Paris, about three hours by car or rail. It has three excellent, first-class hotels, good moderate accommodations, and daily limousine service to the chateaus from April through September.

Tours is the capital of Touraine, famous as a center of French art, and known variously as "The Smile" or sometimes "The Garden" of France. Tours is a city of some 80,000, and was developed by the Romans who built an amphitheater there which held 12,000. In 903, bands of marauding Norsemen came down from Normandy to St. Nazaire, and then sailed up the Loire to Tours, where they sacked the monastery of Marmoutiers. During the same century Tours was taken over by the royal House of Blois, which lost it in the next century to the House of Anjou. Scarcely a lifetime after the Norse raid, the original cathedral of Tours was begun. It was twice burned, and finally the present structure was started in 1170. It was finished in 1575, after some four centuries of construction.

Now when a resident of Tours would express an unusual length of time he uses the simile, "It took as long as the cathedral." Nonetheless, the edifice remains as one of the most beautiful and famous in France. Construction and remodelling are still going on, a process necessitated by the retreating Germans who fired on the 320-foot twin towers in 1944 in an effort to hit snipers of the local resistance.

Just behind the cathedral is the house where Honoré de Balzac, a hometown boy, wrote his famous novel, *Le Curé de Tours*. A brass plate adorns the building and, with utter disregard for history, announces that one Maurice Damon fixes watches on the premises, between 10 and 12, and 2 and 6.

Anyone reasonably fresh from the movie *Joan of Arc* will find Tours and the chateau country teeming with familiar place names. When, as an unknown country girl, Joan visited Charles VII to plead for an army, she found him at Chinon, which is one of the chateaus of the Loire, forty-six kilometers from Tours. Joan's army was actually formed in Tours, and now, in a tiny street in the city, you can see the house where in April, 1429, 63 years before the discovery of America, the local quartermaster outfitted the Maid of Orleans with a suit of armor, a banner, and a horse. For many years afterwards the building was called "A La Pucelle Armée." Today it is just 32 Rue Colbert, and if it weren't for a brash green sign denoting the presence of a coiffeur, it would almost be possible to see Joan standing there in the doorway, head held high, chin tilted and proud—as pretty, maybe, as Ingrid Bergman.

The Touraine originally became castle country because it was rich, interior land, relatively safe from invasion. Modern armies, however, have had no trouble reaching Tours.

In 1917 American Services of Supply established a bridgehead in

*Tours—"hub of the chateau country . . . capital of the 'The Smile' . . ."*

the city, with headquarters at the Metropole Hotel. In 1932, by which time they must have suspected nobody else was going to do it, the American Army built a monument to their own efforts in Tours. It is a gilded statue, surrounded by a stone fountain inscribed "Erected by the United States of America in grateful recognition of the achievements of the Services of Supply AEF 1917-1918." The American Battle Monuments Commission, in acknowledging engraved responsibility for having built the testimonial, might like to know there are a few chipped places along the base of the fountain, resulting from stray German rifle fire in the late war.

One of the finest structures in Tours is the massive stone bridge, built by Louis XV, which stretches 1,400 feet across the shallow Loire. Because it has fourteen arches, the span has sometimes been called the Wilson Bridge, our war-time president having been similarly associated with those digits. The bridge has twice been partly destroyed, in 1940 by the French, as a holding action to permit its government to flee to the south, and again in 1944 to permit the Germans to flee east.

The bridge of Tours is also forever embedded in the memory of one Harry Alexander, Indiana, U.S.A. In 1944 Harry was a member of the Army's Counter Intelligence Corps, a spy-hunting assemblage of American cops, lawyers, journalists, skip-tracers, ex-FBI agents, and language experts. One sunny summer day that year, when the military situation was rather fluid in France, Harry's outfit somehow got the assignment of scouting the approaches to Tours for signs of the withdrawing Germans. In four jeeps the C.I.C. cautiously mounted a hill that just obscures the bridge at the approach to the city. No Germans. Harry, helmetless, alone in his jeep, decided to go further. He poked his car over the brow of the hill, saw two Germans guarding the bridge, decided to give 'er the gun, and in a twinkling was past the sentries and speeding over the span.

By this time the Nazis realized that the jeep and Harry were both American, and opened fire. There were two guards at the far end of the bridge, but they remained conveniently bewildered until Harry was zigzagging through the streets of Tours and avoiding the enemy at every corner. Somehow the lad from Indiana got his vehicle out of the city and into the suburbs. He joined the maquis, went on raids with them, and earned a reputation for being a dead shot with a .38.

Officially, Alexander is credited with setting fire to German vehicles and playing like a brand of hob with the remaining Nazis, until Tours was finally liberated in September, 1944. It was nearly two months after he had set out in his jeep to scout the enemy forces. After the liberation, Harry hustled about getting affidavits to prove he hadn't been AWOL, and, as a matter of fact, he was later decorated for his exploits. It wouldn't have made a bit of difference to Tours how the American Army took the exploit, however. In the city Harry Alexander was and is a special hero, and his name is as well-known there today as that of Charles VII, Honoré de Balzac, or even Joan of Arc.

There are hundreds of hamlets and counties, and many provinces, in the republic, each of which has its own patois, but the language of the Touraine is renowned as the purest French in France. Students from all over the world come to Tours to study at the Institut de Touraine, a simple little college which offers courses in history, literature, language, and art. Most of this learning is dispensed in the local brand of pure French, and among those in residence are American veterans matriculating by courtesy of the GI Bill of Rights. There are a number of moderately priced pensions, near the school, which students will find pretty nearly within the budget enforced by the United States Government's allowance.

Besides the chateaus, Tours offers a golf course, and swimming, rowing, and sailing on the Cher during the summer. There are a number of antique shops in the city, mostly centered along the Rue de la Scellerye and the Rue de Commerce.

The three big hotels of Tours are the Metropole, the Universe and the Grand, all of which are in good condition, clean, well-run, and surprisingly cosmopolitan. Each has a modestly priced restaurant. The Hôtel de Bordeaux is a well-run, modest establishment, and is very proud of its newly redecorated dining room brilliant with fluorescent tubing and gaudy, red furnishings. The new *décor* hasn't affected the food at the Bordeaux. The cuisine remains excellent.

Specialties of the Touraine are rilettes and rillons, a chopped pork meat traditionally served in a little jug; jelline de Touraine; Saint Maure cheese, made of goat's milk and molded into long round forms and packed with wet straw to keep it moist.

A number of travel agencies operate inexpensive motor coach tours of the chateaus. You can check schedules and make reservations through the concierge of the hotel either in Paris or Tours. Meals and chateau entry fees are nominal but extra. Three typical trips, in this case offered by La Maison du Tourisme, maintain the following schedules:

1. Full day. Leave Tours 8:30 A.M. via Marmoutier, Rochecorbon, Vouvray-les-Vins. Visit the chateaus of Amboise and Chenonceaux. Lunch at Montrichard. Afternoon: visit chateau of Montresor, the Forêt de Loches, the Chartreuse du Liget, the chateau of Loches, and return to Tours by the Vallée de l'Indre, arriving about 7 P.M.
2. Full day. Leave Tours 8:45 A.M. Visit chateau of Villandry and its gardens, visit chateau of Azay-le-Rideau and its park, visit ruins of Chinon. Lunch and visit old city of Chinon. Visit chateau Rigny-Usse, chateau Langeais, return via Cinq Mars and Luynes, arriving in Tours about 6:30 P.M.
3. Half day. Leave Tours 1:30 P.M., visit Villandry, Azay-le-Rideau, Langeais, and return to Tours by 6:15 P.M.

Some chateaus are fully furnished, some are empty shells, and some are ruins. This is what to expect:

*Langeais.* In the center of a little town, twenty-four kilometers from Tours. Originally built by Louis XI in 1465, forty years after Joan of

*Langeais—from the ramparts, "hot lead, boiling oil, and scalding water...."*

Arc. Anne of Brittany and her first husband, Charles VIII, were married here on December 16, 1491, and their seals are still over the door. All the furniture was lost during the French Revolution, but it was reassembled by a French banker named Jacques Siegfried, who once owned the castle. Anne's boudoir is completely furnished in authentic fifteenth-century style, and Charles's bedroom has embroidery from ancient Malta, and a wall decoration that was once a banner used in one of the battles of Joan of Arc. The castle contains a magnificent Spanish, sixteenth-century ivory and wood traveling desk, and in a room which was planned for a chapel but never completed is a model of the cathedral of Colognes made of minuscule chips of calling cards by Siegfried's father. There is a fine view from the towers, where the castle's defenders stationed themselves with such repellents as hot lead, boiling oil, and scalding water. Cut into the tower's catwalks are traps through which the guards dropped rocks calculated to ricochet off the flanges of the foundation and carom into the ranks of invaders.

Langeais is one of the best preserved and most frequently visited chateaus. Sightseers have been scrawling on the towers from Jean and Roland, who carved their names on the 20th of May, 1648, to Dean Patterson who left his in 1945.

\* \* \* \* \*

*Azay-le-Rideau.* Twenty-five kilometers from Tours. Open 9-12 and 1:30-7 in summer; 9-12 and 1:30-4 in fall and winter.

Great shade trees cover the long approach to the chateau, which sits on a tiny island surrounded by a moat. The name *Rideau* is said to have been evolved from Hugues Ridellus, one of the first owners, or perhaps from the *rideau* (curtain) of trees which frame the renaissance castle. At eventide the pointed towers are reflected in the waters of the moat, and the soft, rolling greens, the cedars, weeping willows, and Japanese tuyas are rather reminiscent of the grounds at Tanglewood, Massachusetts.

*Azay-le-Rideau—inside, "Gabrielle d'Estrées in her bath."*

Of the original structure, built in 1150, only the foundation of the kitchen remains. The new building was started in 1518 by Gilles Berthelot, who was treasurer of France and mayor of Tours. It was completed six years later, and was so lavish that the king had Berthelot's books checked, a precaution which resulted in the dismissal of the treasurer in disgrace. It is one of the few chateaus which still contain a kitchen. Azay's middle-age galley has a chimney five yards wide, utensils for baking sixteenth-century *gaufrettes,* and pastry molds manufactured in Nuremburg in the seventeenth century. A Fontainebleau tapestry which Charles I ordered for the city of Rome but which was never delivered hangs today on Azay's walls.

Among the other furnishings is a sixteenth-century trousseau chest with inlaid pornographia, seventeenth-century chinaware from the

Isle of Rhodes with designs, says the guide, a little reminiscent of the new Picasso. There is a royal chamber slept in for one night by Louis XIV, for which occasion a new floor was built. It is still in use. Other attractions are pictures of Gabrielle d'Estrées, mistress of Henri IV, in her bath; several statues by Cellini; an inlaid ivory secretary made in 1633 depicting the miseries and discomfitures of war which (says the guide) were no different from the methods of torture, pillaging and rape visited upon the world by the late Nazi culture; Gobelins and Flanders tapestries, including one designed by Rubens which pictures Constantine I, one of the first Roman emperors to become Christian, carrying the sign of Christ on his banner.

Azay also harbors a collection of stained-glass fragments collected from cathedrals which were sacked during the French Revolution. Some of the glass was broken again in 1944 when the Germans blew a nearby bridge on their way back to the Reich.

*    *    *    *    *

*Villandry.* Seventeen kilometers from Tours. Open daily from 9-12 and 2-6 (winter 2-4).

A privately owned chateau, Villandry is famed for its beautiful gardens, its Spanish museum, and the romantic tale that surrounds its restoration. It was originally converted from an old dungeon by one Jean Lebreton, Secretary of State for François I. Two centuries later, the Marquis of Castellane took over and made some drastic changes. Parts of the chateau were altered, and Lebreton's formal *jardins fran-çais* were changed into a rolling English garden.

Some years ago two medical students, a boy named Cavallo and a wealthy Philadelphia girl named Coleman, were studying together in Paris. After graduation they were married, and together they bought the chateau of Villandry, with the idea of reconstructing it as it was in 1537. Some of the members of the Cavallo family live in the chateau today, and much of the sixteenth-century garden, rebuilt by the original Cavallos, can still be seen.

Nearly ten miles of hedges are used to portray the main pattern, a love motif. Four kinds of love are depicted in the close-cropped box hedge: tender love (a heart design), tragic love (knives), fickle love (butterflies), adulterous love (horns). In these practical times the rest of the Cavallo acres have been given over to vegetables which grow in plain, unsymbolic, geometric designs.

* * * * *

*Chenonceaux.* Thirty-five kilometers from Tours. Open daily 9-12 and from 2 until sundown.

Because of its bold architectural construction and its rich history, Chenonceaux has become a classic. It was begun in 1513 by Thomas Bohier and finished by his wife, Catherine Briconnet, when Bohier went to war in Italy. He died without seeing the castle again, and in the liquidation of his estate the chateau passed to Francois I.

When his son, Henri II, came into power in 1547 he gave Chenonceaux to his indestructible mistress, Diane de Poitiers, a woman twenty years his senior. The chateau lies on a bank of the Cher, and Diane added a bridge to the opposite bank, and a flower garden. Diane's signature and her bedroom can still be seen, but after Henry died, in 1559, Catherine de' Medici insisted on exchanging chateaus with Diane, and the mistress was forced to move to Chaumont. Catherine improved the gardens, imported art from Italy, and built a gallery, for banquets, over Diane's old bridge. The same gallery was converted again during the first World War, this time into a hospital. Over 2,000 Allied wounded were treated there.

In the chapel of the chateau are the usual scrawlings of sightseers, but two inscriptions on the wall are old enough to be preserved under a glass tablet. Says one, "The ire of man reaches not the justice of God." It is dated 1543, and was written by soldiers of the Scotch guard of Mary Stuart. The castle also contains an inlaid ivory chest of the sixteenth century which was a wedding gift from Italy to Mary Stuart and François II. There are some originals by Rubens, furniture pieces

· 147 ·

covered in Aubusson tapestries, and Catherine's own workroom still exists with its original green beamed ceiling bearing her initials.

The floods of May, 1940, and the German bombing in June in the same year completely wrecked the gardens. Stained-glass windows in the chapel were shattered by Allied bombings in 1944, but there was no other damage. The chateau remains in a pure state, unmarred by restorations. One tower on the grounds, now used as a billet for workers, dates from the thirteenth century. The entire estate is owned by M. Menier, who is the "chocolate king" of France.

* * * * *

*Chaumont.* Forty-one kilometers from Tours. Open daily April through September from 9-12 and 2-7; October through March, 10-12 and 2-5.

The very prototype of a feudal castle, Chaumont is perched high on a hill, its imposing towers set amid soft, rolling grounds and great old trees. The castle can still separate itself from the world by pulling up its drawbridge, which the caretaker does each day during the lunch hour and after closing time.

The original fortress constructed on the site in the ninth century was burned by Louis XI at the end of the fifteenth century. Charles II of Amboise undertook the reconstruction, from 1498 until 1510. The nine-foot thick walls of the present castle have enclosed both Diane de Poitiers and Catherine de' Medici, though probably never at the same time. Also, the family Amboise; the Counts of Blois; the Count of Chaumont until the French Revolution; Mme. de Staël, exiled there by Napoléon; and, as recently as 1938, the Princess of Broglie.

Among the sights left over from five centuries of past owners (thirty have owned the chateau since the Revolution), is an ivory embellished musket used at the Battle of Cressy in 1346. The battle is believed to have been the first in which musketry was employed. The floor of the council room is covered with a 2,400-piece mosaic imported from Italy about the sixteenth century. The bed of Catherine de' Medici, who bought the place in 1560 and then traded it for Chenonceaux, is still in existence. The walls of the chateau are covered today by an estimated three hundred yards of tapestries, a priceless collection. Opening directly off one bedroom is a small chapel. The stained-glass windows were changed in 1875, and there is a four-century differential between the chapel and its windows.

* * * * *

*Blois.* Fifty-seven kilometers from Tours. Open 9-12 and 1:30-6 in summer, 1:30 to sundown in winter.

The parapets of the castle overlook the gray slate roofs and red chimney pipes of the old city of Blois. It is a huge, cold, sparsely furnished building, which has become a heterogeneous mixture of many epochs of architecture, after innumerable efforts at restoration. It all started with the Count of Blois, who built it originally as a fortress, and bears the influence of the fifteenth-century Gothic style of Louis XII. The good king is remembered with an equestrian statue over the portal leading to the wing Louis XII. Twenty years later came François I with all the decorations, sculpturings, and architectural fol-de-rol of the renaissance. Perhaps the biggest attraction at Blois is the ornate staircase of François in the inner court. In the seventeenth century Gaston d'Orléans went to work with a classic style resembling that of Versailles, and a wing and a bust have likewise been named for him. It was Gaston's desire to destroy some of the old parts of the chateau and its chapel, but this was not accomplished until 1944, when the Germans tried to retard the American forces advancing into Blois.

Catherine de' Medici slept at Chaumont and lived at Chenonceaux, but she died at Blois on January 5, 1589. Still to be seen are her private chapel, which opens off her bedroom, and her own workroom, decorated with 237 carved panels. Catherine has been handed down to us in history as a rather mystic party who dealt in astrology and cabalistic rites. Her workroom at Blois has a number of secret panels, still in operating order, where she is rumored to have stored her potions and poisons.

They still make a pretty big thing at Blois of the death of the Duke of Guise, who was assassinated by local heavies employed by Henri III. Where the Duke was killed, the route of the assassins and of the dying victim are quite faithfully mapped out by the guides. We are also told why. (Henri III got his comeuppance at St. Cloud, near Paris, just six months later, at the vengeful hands of some of the duke's loyal friends.)

Other Blois attractions include a huge banquet room with a concave wooden ceiling, some fine stained-glass windows, and a collection of thirteenth-century tapestries as full of bright reds and blues as if they had come off the loom last week.

\* \* \* \* \*

*Amboise.* Twenty-four kilometers from Tours. Open 9-12 and 2-6:30 from March through October. From November through February, 9-12 and 2 until sundown.

Amboise was a great center of French art from the time of Louis XI through the era of François I. Artists from all over the world were invited to the chateau, which itself grew into an architectural marvel known all over the world.

Amboise has decayed throughout the centuries, and comparatively little is left of the great citadel that once rose powerfully over the Loire. A chapel built in 1491 by Charles VIII, who was born in the castle in 1470, was partly destroyed by German artillery in 1940 and has since been reinforced. It is believed that Leonardo da Vinci, who died May 2, 1519, was buried in the chapel. At any rate, da Vinci spent considerable time at Amboise, and from its towers he flew what was probably the first model airplane in history.

The guardroom of the chateau has an interesting collection of armor from the fifteenth and sixteenth centuries, and a knight on horseback could still enter the ground floor of the castle and ride right up the tower without dismounting.

When France conquered Algeria in 1831, Abd El Kader, an Arab chieftain, was exiled to Amboise, where he lived for several years. In the soft valley of the Loire, he became a friend of France, and many of his descendants have been officers in the French army.

After a number of confiscations dating from the French Revolution, Amboise is once more owned by the family of Orléans, headed by the present Comte de Paris. Although his wife and two children visit Amboise often, the Count is presently in exile in Spanish Morocco because he is the pretender to the throne of France. Some Frenchmen with nostalgic royalist sentiments have never forgiven American officials who refused to permit the Count to return to France at the time of the liberation.

Amboise is fairly well furnished with period pieces, including some Aubusson tapestries, an 1830 mirror in the bedroom of Louis Philippe, a collection of fifteenth-century furniture, and a new wall destroyed in the war, which has been restored with glass brick. All this is pointed out by a merry little guide who must be nearly as old as Amboise itself. He believes journalists and guides have a lot in common. Both have to be such good liars, he says.

\*     \*     \*     \*     \*

*Loches.* Forty-one kilometers from Tours. Visit includes Porte Royale and museums, Eglise St. Ours, Logis Royaux, and the prison. Museums open 9-12 and 2-7, other attractions open 9-12 and 2-6:30.

High on a hill commanding a valley, Loches is a feudal citadel that has withstood many a siege and many a scandal. The estate comprises a royal residence and a dungeon. The core of the dungeon is a great, square tower built in the eleventh century by Foulque Nerra. Other rulers, until the time of Louis XI, contributed additions, until today there is a group of buildings containing a variety of styles of incarceration. From one adjoining tower there are secret staircases leading to every floor of the chateau. Another encloses the notorious iron cage that once held Cardinal Balue. Prisoners, royal and renegade, have left souvenirs of their stay at Loches. The most famous souvenir is the cell-wall murals of the Duke of Milan.

In the royal residences is the tomb of Agnes Sorel, one of the most beautiful women of France, and favorite of Charles VII. As a fifteenth-century pun had it, Agnes was *La Dame de Beauté,* because she was pretty and owned a manor house called *Beauté.*

According to the accepted story, before her death Agnes contributed two thousand gold pieces to the Collegiate Church of Nôtre Dame du Chateau de Loches, so that she would be buried there. Her wish was carried out, but after her internment some of the elders of the church had some misgivings about the propriety of the likes of Agnes resting in such holy ground. They asked Louis XI to have her removed. The king complied, had her reburied in the chateau, but demanded the return of Agnes's gold. Today, in a black marble tomb surmounted by a white marble statue, Agnes Sorel rests in a chamber high in the castle tower. Two lambs are at her feet, two angels at her head. It's a kind of a nice way to meet history.

\* \* \* \* \*

*Chambord.* Sixty-eight kilometers from Tours. Open 8-12 and 1:30-sundown from March 1 until October 31; otherwise 9-12 and 1:30-4.

Chambord is a huge renaissance chateau of some three hundred sixty-five rooms, a dozen stairways, uncountable corridors, halls, turrets and spires. It is one of the farthest from Tours, and, for all its grand exterior, is rather sparsely furnished. The castle was built in the early sixteenth century and its construction reputedly engaged nearly two thousand workmen for fifteen years. Started by François I, it was continued by Henri II, and redecorated by Louis XIV. In 1748 the Marshal of Saxe moved in with two regiments of Tartar cavalry, some Martinique colonials, and a French actress. The marshal died at 54, his end climaxing one of Chambord's gayest eras. For sixteen days after his death, six cannons boomed every quarter-hour in memory. It had been the marshal's own idea.

Ultimately, the chateau passed into the hands of a prince of Bourbon. When the prince joined the Austrian army in 1914, the chateau was confiscated by the French government. During the recent war, many works of art from all over France were sent to Chambord for safekeeping. Just before the liberation, in August, 1944, the Germans claimed they were being fired upon by snipers hidden in the castle. They threatened to set fire to the whole building, and were restrained only by the efforts of an old Alsatian priest, the curé of Chambord.

The grounds surrounding Chambord comprise several thousand acres, and a wall around the estate measures thirty-two kilometers. It is the longest in France. In the old days, Chambord was a great place for royal hunters, and Francois I once killed a wild boar, that was loose in the castle, with one blow of his sword. He also once engraved a proverb on glass with his diamond ring, thus creating a museum piece which is still preserved in his old study. Other sights are the apartments of Louis XIV and a grand spiral staircase, constructed so that persons who are going up never see those who are coming down.

*   *   *   *   *

There are many other chateaus in the Loire country, and many other sights. Those that have been described are the most popular. Some of the tours take in Vouvray, where acres of grapes are fermented into some of the world's best white wine in caves directly beneath the arbors. Others include the Pile de Cinq Mars, a Roman tower one hundred feet high made entirely of brick. It dates from the first century and nobody has ever been able to explain its meaning.

Sometimes, even in our prosaic times, the chateau country still manages to pick up a little more history that will tumble, glibly, from the bland lips of a guide centuries from now. Things went like that a few years ago when the Duke of Windsor and Wally were married at the chateau of Cange at Monts, about twenty kilometers from Tours.

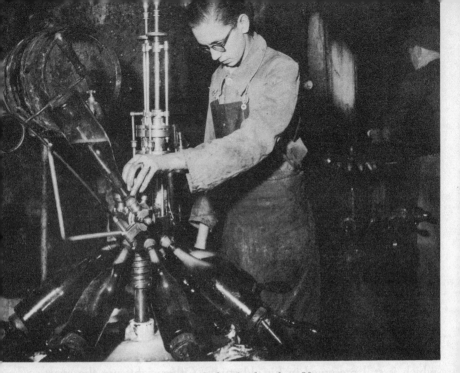

*Between Amboise and Tours, light, fresh, white Vouvray.*

The chateau was owned by M. Bedaux, famous as a factory efficiency expert. M. Bedeaux also devised a rather efficient system of keeping the press out of the wedding.

With the whole world clamoring for news, and editors cabling from a hundred newspapers, the press boys finally got an idea. They descended on the village of Monts, rented a ladder with wheels from the fire department, hooked it on the back of a delivery truck, and went sailing through the castle gates. Once inside, they drove as near as they dared, then set up the ladder. The boys drew lots, and the winner, an AP man, climbed up, and with field glasses got a first-hand view of the proceedings. Then he descended in a hurry, pooled his information with the other reporters, and the word crackled out across the world that Wallis Simpson and Edward, Duke of Windsor, had indeed been duly married in one of the old chateaus in the valley of the Loire.

\*　　\*　　\*　　\*　　\*

Between the two tourist centers of Tours, in the center of France, and Biarritz, in the southwestern corner, runs a pleasant route which can be covered by rail or car. Southward out of Tours it winds through the small spa of La Roche-Posay to Poitiers, city of churches, where you can choose between two good restaurants, the Chapon Fin and Maxim's, and can find also one fair hotel, the France. Another sixty-eight miles take one to Angoulême, the next big city which, although of little tourist interest itself, is flanked by Limoges, the china center sixty-five miles to the east, and Cognac, the liquor center, twenty-five miles to the west.

The fame of Cognac, the brandy, has, of course, far overshadowed that of Cognac, the city where it is made. During World War II, after Cognac was liberated, American Army trucks rolled into the town in unending streams, and rolled out again, loaded with cases of brandy. The GIs' aptitude for cognac was alarming to French doctors who implored Americans to be wary; this was not whisky.

François I was born in Cognac, but that prosaic historical fact has been all but lost in the welter of alcoholic renown in which the city is steeped. The chateau in which he was born now houses the firm of Otard Dupuy. Two other famous brands, Martell and Hennessy, among the best known of France's export products, were started by Britons. Jean Martell, an Englishman, migrated from the Channel Islands to Cognac in 1715, and Richard Hennessy, an Irishman, came from Cobh some years afterward.

Until that time Cognac had produced a poor grade of wine that could not compare with that which flowed from the vineyards of Bordeaux, just to the south. A process of distilling the wines of Cognac into a liquor was begun, and the result was popular from the start. Fresh cognac is seventy per cent alcohol by volume, and gradually weakens as it is aged in wooden casks. According to the gourmets, the best cognac is aged for sixty years, until it reaches an alcohol content of forty per cent. In our hurry-up world, however, the ordinary brands of cognac are about five years old, and are diluted with distilled water, and colored. If cognac manufacturers were forced to rely upon aging for its dilution, the loss in volume by evaporation would make the cost in the United States prohibitive.

The city of Cognac today is a well established, prosperous community, living on the reputation spread by its bottled ambassadors. Once, when a number of church dignitaries had been invited to Rome and introductions were in order, one French prelate introduced himself as the Bishop of Angoulême. Everyone looked blank. Finally, he added, "I am also the Bishop of Cognac." Knowing smiles of understanding broke out among the holy men. "Ah, yes," they said, "the superb See of Cognac!"

From Angoulême it is seventy-two miles to Bordeaux, another city whose name has been sent all over the world on the labels of bottles. Bordeaux is an important port at the end of a long estuary that leads to the Atlantic. It is, in essence, a drab city, of no tourist interest, except that it is a byway for travelers on their way to Biarritz, Pau, Lourdes, Luchon, and the rest of the Pyrenees. There is an American consulate in Bordeaux, also branches of the Paris department stores and a big, sprawling hotel which is a little worn but still modern.

The Bordeaux section, which probably produces more wine than almost any other region on the continent, stretches southward for nearly forty miles, and north along the Gironde estuary virtually to the ocean. The soft, pleasant, grape-covered hills produce both red and white wines, and have been cultivated since the days of the Romans.

The wines of Bordeaux are classified according to region and label.

Among the best: Médoc—Château Lafite, Château Margaux; Graves —Château Haut-Brion (Pessac), Château Haut-Brilly (Leognan), Château la Mission Haut-Brion (Talence); Saint Emilion—Château Ausonne; Pomerol—Château Certain, Château La Conseillante, Château Petit Village; Sauternes—Le Château d'Yquem, la Tour Blanche (Bommes).

Most of the oysters of France come from Arcachon, a seaside resort thirty-five miles from Bordeaux. Fashionable as well as commercial, Arcachon has some excellent hotels, among them Le Grand and the Regina et Angleterre. A sea-bordering road twists along the shore from Arcachon to Bayonne and Biarritz, there is a direct route from Bordeaux bypassing the oyster resort, and via railroad you can take the place or leave it.

*A French Basque—berets, Borotra, pelote, and Uzcudun.*

# 7. THE PYRENEES

◇◇◇◇◇◇◇◇◇◇◇◇◇◇◇◇◇◇◇◇◇◇◇◇◇◇◇◇◇◇◇◇◇◇◇◇◇◇◇◇◇◇◇◇◇◇◇◇◇◇

THE Pyrenees are long and high, and provide a natural border between France and Spain, from the Atlantic to the Mediterranean. There is no national character to the Pyrenees, but strung across the heights and the foothills, from sea to sea, are all manner of sights and all kinds of people—the Basques, Biarritz, also the miracle city of Lourdes, hot springs that send therapeutic waters bubbling naturally from the earth, cable cars that swing between snowy peaks, ski runs that cut through mountain forests, and medieval fortresses that still stand guard over the empty past.

Nobody knows where the Basques came from. They are the "forgotten men" of Europe. The world has a half million Basques, most of whom live in seven Basque provinces, four Spanish and three French, which are crowded into the corner of the Pyrenees where France and Spain and the Atlantic Ocean come together. Basque is a language by itself, and many of its words are reputedly derivatives of Indian and Japanese. Basque villages have names like Itxassou, Jutxu, and Esterençuby. *Eskualduna* in Basque means "Basque."

There have been many separatist movements among the Basques, and, as a matter of fact, they had their own laws in Spain until the nineteenth century. In the recent Spanish civil war, many Basques supported the Communist cause, because the Loyalists had promised to give them back their private laws. Basque men always wear suits, never wear ties, bury their dead under keyhole-shaped tombstones, burn rope candles in church, hang cheese from the ceilings to dry, and use solid wheels on their carts.

In spite of their comparatively small numbers, the Basques have given the world the beret Basque (which we call the beret), the Basque game of pelote (which we call jai alai), the Bouncing Basque (Jean Borotra), and the Battling Basque, a heavyweight boxer named Paulino Uzcudun (whom the sportswriters called Paulino Upside-down, for a number of obvious reasons).

The Basques were always good sailors, and the French city of Bayonne became a chocolate center because the Basques brought back cocoa from America. In fact, they claimed to have made a landing in the western hemisphere before Columbus. Actually, the first man around the world was not Magellan, who died on the trip, but a Basque named Juan Sebastian del Cano, the ultimate commander of the crew that finished the circuit in 1522.

Every Basque town has a church, a pelote court, and many white houses with red tile roofs and green shutters. Come Sundays, everyone goes to church, the women sitting downstairs, the men in the gallery. After the services the Basques lounge under the shade of the old platane trees, and watch the youngsters bat a hard goatskin ball around the village pelote court, which is often just one wall of the village church.

The Basque beast of burden is the ox, which farmers decorate with a red fringe headdress, and cover with a white blanket to keep off the flies. For personal transportation the peasants use two-seater donkeys, rigging a chair on either side of the animal, one balancing the other. In summer each province has a feast day, and the more spry Basques dress up in brilliant white and red costumes, and perform traditional tambourine dances. In a progression similar to the Irish emigration to the United States, Basques have gotten into the habit of moving on to the richer fields of Argentina, Uruguay, and Chile as soon as they have transportation money. Sometimes, when

*...asque village—"many of the words are derivatives of Indian and Japanese."*

...ey have grown rich in the foreign pampas, they return to live out ...eir days as influential citizens in their homeland.

The famed seaside resort of Biarritz is the center of the Basque ...oast. Once a scrubby fishing village, it was put in vogue by the ...mpress Eugénie, who built a villa there. In September, its most ...shionable month, Biarritz swarms with a high-toned international ...t of Portuguese, South Americans, Americans, and Belgians. There ...e a number of villas in the surrounding pines, one owned by the ...rince and Princess Murat, another, called "the Black Panther," ...wned by the Doderos, whose claim to prominence is a friendship with ...vita Péron.

At the height of the season, Biarritz can accommodate some 10,000 in sixty hotels, all of which are on the American plan. The Palais, which is on the beach, and the Miramar and the Carlton are the top hotels of the resort; they get upwards of $25 a day per person, food included. There are three beaches, the Grand Plage, Port Vieux, and Plages des Basques, all broad, sandy and shallow, framed in rocky formations reminiscent of Bermuda. There are two casinos right on the beach, offering music, dancing, theater, and gambling, the main attraction. Smart nightclubs like Les Ambassadeurs, the Savoy, and the Mayfair hew to the Paris-Riviera line of insisting that you take at least one bottle of champagne during the evening.

The Germans occupied a good bit of the Basque coast during the war, and heavily fortified it against invasion, the Lord knows from where. The Organization Todt requisitioned and wrecked the old Regina Hotel by the normally passive process of just living there. The world-famous Chiberta golf course, in the tall pines outside town, will take 15 million francs and a lot of doing to get back in shape. German block houses stud the beautiful holes that ran along the sea, and some of the finest, rolling greens were ground to hash by the tread of the invaders' tanks.

No wonder Biarritz was a bit apprehensive when word came down, after the liberation, that American forces were requisitioning most of the hotels. As it turned out, we opened a post-war college called Biarritz American University, referred to popularly as B.A.U., and everybody got along fine. As well as facts can be reconstructed today, the time while B.A.U. was in session in the Pyrenees was just one long Roman holiday for all parties concerned. One of the most popular figures was the American commander, General McCoskey. Shortly after he arrived, when the Army's post-war retrenchment policy was put into effect, the general was slipped back a notch to his regular rank of colonel. The gallant French never recognized the Army's order, never referred to him as anything less than general, and flaunted their indignation by naming a street that remains today the Rue Général McCoskey. Another rue, smaller than the general's, is called Rue de L'Université Américaine. Everybody admits the new names add some distinction to the city, the roads having been formerly known as Rock and Seagull Streets.

If anyone gets bored with the Biarritz beaches, there are a number of de luxe motor coach excursions into the neighboring country; one half-day trip covers St. Jean de Luz, Hendaye, Ascain, and Cambo; another, St. Jean Pied de Port and St. Etienne de Baigorry. There is also service across the border to San Sebastian, in Spain. A one-day trip runs to Lourdes and return, a distance of 160 kilometers; a two-day trip goes all the way across the Pyrenees to Perpignan, on the Mediterranean, by way of Pau, Lourdes, Luchon, and Font Romeu—names which will be reckoned with later.

For those who like things plain and quiet, Guethary is a comfortable family resort just outside Biarritz. Wrecked during the war, it is being rebuilt with its own casino, hotel, restaurant, and bathing beach.

St. Jean de Luz, towards the Spanish frontier, is a combination resort and fishing port. The Maison de L'Infante, where Marie Thérèse stayed before her marriage to Louis XIV, still sits on the edge of the bay. Across the water, nearly covered with the bright blue and green sardine fishing boats, is Ciboure, birthplace of Maurice Ravel. The cathedral at St. Jean de Luz, where Louis XIV was married, is typically Basque, and boats still hang from the ceiling as a token of good fortune to the fishermen of the community. St. Jean de Luz also has its own golf course, called Chantaco, which boasts the greenest greens in the province. The groundkeeper's secret is to let sheep graze on the links during the winter. The sheep clip the grass closer than a mower, fertilize the earth themselves, and stamp the manure into the ground where it does the most good. At Chantaco they say it's an unbeatable combination.

One hundred and fourteen kilometers from Biarritz, over the mountain roads of the Pyrenees, is the city of Pau, a winter resort without winter sports. Pau was discovered by the English after the Napoleonic wars, who found the city had warm winter breezes, mild weather, and virtually no wind. Wilbur and Orville Wright flew at Pau some forty years ago, and a plaque erected in a barren, weedy corner of the airfield commemorates their experiments in France. The field was occupied by the Luftwaffe during the war, and most of the facilities were wrecked in bombings. A French military parachute school operates from the field now.

A rich American named F. H. Prince was the social wheel in Pau for many years. Under his patronage, fox-hunts were held three times a week, and the social season flourished elegantly and quietly during the winter months. Many Americans and Britons still own villas in Pau, and some of them are located on Avenue Norman Prince, named for the son of F. H., who was killed with the Lafayette Escadrille in 1916.

Pau's biggest attraction today is its Boulevard of the Pyrenees, a fine avenue of hotels and glass-fronted tea shops, that seems to be suspended from the very edge of the snow-covered mountains. The city operates a Municipal Casino in Beaumont Park, offering dining and dancing on outdoor terraces, theater, and the usual gambling tables. The castle of Henri IV is open to visitors, and displays a turtle shell which was Henri's cradle in 1543. Pau has a golf course, a race track, and during the rugby season develops the same partisan passion that is kindled in the fall at Ann Arbor.

Some redecorating efforts have gone into the cavernous Hôtel France, which came out of the war old and seedy. The most interesting visitor in the city is the Bey of Tunis, who is living in exile with an entourage of some forty attendants, in a modest villa overlooking the mountains. Most any day his three-foot midget Jester can be seen scuffling along the streets, a scarlet four-foot muffler flowing behind him in Pau's windless weather. Some international intellectuals study

*A fair at Pau—in the city, windless weather and the Bey of Tunis.*

during the summer at the Lycée de Pau, a crumbling old school whose honor roll dates from 1808. In addition to the few Americans who come each year, the lycée maintains a cultural link with the United States by decorating its ancient walls with such Americana as pictures of the Yankee Stadium, the Great Smoky Mountains National Park, and Walla Walla County, Washington, general view.

Deep in the fastnesses of the Pyrenees, midway between Biarritz and Toulouse, is Lourdes, city of 20,000 inhabitants. The story of Lourdes is the story of the faith of a people, so modern that it cannot be called a legend, so powerful that it must be called a miracle. To the shrine of Lourdes each year come the stricken of the world, not only Catholics but people of all religions, and some of none. They are people who have only two things in common—affliction and hope. And they come by the hundred thousand. Each year some "incurables" return home from Lourdes, cured.

Lourdes' religious history is no embroidered tale of the Middle Ages. It dates from 1858, and centers about a miller named Soubirous who was miserably poor. One day the miller sent his two daughters, Antonia and Bernadette, to gather wood in the forest. Antonia and a friend crossed a river, but Bernadette, who was a sickly child, stayed on the near side. While she was alone, Bernadette heard a rustling sound, and felt a strong gust of wind. She looked around— and there in a grotto, on the side of a hill, she saw an apparition of the Virgin. The vision asked Bernadette to recite the rosary, and afterwards disappeared in a golden blur.

Almost daily thereafter, Bernadette returned to the grotto, and each time the vision appeared before her. By the fifth apparition, on February 20, a hundred persons had gathered at the grotto. By the sixth apparition, on the 21st, Bernadette was enjoined by the civil authorities not to return to the grotto. On the 23rd she went again, despite the order, and the Virgin imparted to her a personal secret which she never divulged. On the 24th, as a gesture of humility, the

*The Basilica at Lourdes—"a story so modern it cannot be called a legend."*

Virgin asked Bernadette to kiss the ground, a symbol which has been repeated by thousands of pilgrims in the years that have followed. The following day, before four hundred, the Virgin told the young girl to drink from a spring. Bernadette saw no spring, but, searching at the bottom of the grotto, she discovered the source of the water which has since evoked so many miracles.

By the tenth apparition, the next day, the spring gushed water in a steady stream. At the time it was correctly analyzed as plain drinking water, possessing no curative properties. During the eleventh apparition on February 28, Bernadette drank from the spring and as an act of penitence ate of the herbs that grew at the grotto's edge, and she received an order from the Virgin. She was directed to tell the priests to build a church at the site. On the 28th of February the first miraculous cures took place, and by the time of the thirteenth apparition, on the 1st of March, there were thirteen hundred at the grotto. At the fourteenth apparition, on March 2, the vision told Bernadette that she wished the faithful to visit the grotto in processions.

On March 26, at the sixteenth apparition, Bernadette asked the vision her name and who she was. The answer came in the local patois of Lourdes, "I am the Immaculate Conception." By the time of the seventeenth apparition, which did not take place until the 7th of April, nearly ten thousand had gathered at Lourdes. Bernadette, on her knees, held a lighted candle in her hands, and fell so deeply into a trance that she did not notice the flame burning about her fingers. She was unhurt and unscarred by the experience, in spite of the fact that a doctor who stood near her in attendance figured she held the burning taper for fifteen minutes. After the apparition was over, the doctor tested Bernadette with another candle, and the girl jumped back, burned.

The last apparition took place on the 16th of July. Following a succession of interviews and interrogations by representatives of the

"... by the tenth apparition ... a steady stream ..."

government, the clergy, and the press, Bernadette decided, in September, to enter the convent of the Sisters of Nevers.

Today the grotto at Lourdes has become a great shrine, with three churches—the Basilica, the Crypt, and the Rosary. Stained-glass windows in the Basilica depict the story of Bernadette and the miraculous cures of Lourdes. The flags of sixty nations hang in the church as offerings from pilgrimages. Many veterans have left their medals as a thanksgiving for their safe return from the war. Some of the groups that come to Lourdes donate funds for memorial chapels. There are now a hundred such chapels in the three churches. A typical one was offered by the village of Niort, which was traveling en masse to Lourdes on July 2, 1876, when the train was badly wrecked. Not a soul was injured, and the pilgrims believe they saw the vision of the Virgin in the smoke of the engine. The scene is depicted in the chapel. In the crypt below the Basilica, the walls are lined with forty confessionals, all hewn out of solid rock. Everywhere are engraved tablets offering the thanks of pilgrims who have found solace, serenity, or new hope at Lourdes.

All three churches are just in front of the original grotto. An altar has been built within the rocks, and a statue of the Virgin has been mounted at the exact spot where the apparitions appeared to Bernadette. There are benches in the tree-shaded plaza in front of the grotto, and alongside are twelve water taps fed by the spring discovered by Bernadette. Visitors habitually light a taper and kneel at the grotto, then visit the fountains to drink of the water of Lourdes. Many fill canteens, thermos bottles and gourds, and some unbelievers stay for hours seeking absolution or remedy by a continual process of washing and drinking.

Nearby are nine compartments where the afflicted may bathe in the water of Lourdes. Pilgrims unable to walk are wheeled to the bath on stretchers. They remove their clothes, and cover themselves with a plain white cloth. They are then transferred to a canvas stretcher,

*Bernadette's bed and her closest living relation, Mme. Jean Soubirous.*

and as a priest chants a prayer they are lowered into the chilly waters. Some two thousand persons a day are bathed in this manner. There is never a charge, and if the rooms are unoccupied, individuals may just walk in. Pilgrims arriving in groups can make their arrangements for the baths with the priest assigned to their party.

Rising up the mountainside behind the grotto are the fourteen stations of the cross depicted in life-size bronze figures. At the first station, pilgrims mount a holy stairway on their knees, reciting a prayer at each step. For the crippled and the paralytic, wheel chairs are available for rent at the grotto hospital.

Bernadette's home in Lourdes has been rather faithfully preserved, and some of the girl's family still live there, despite the hundreds of thousands of visitors who file through the building each year. The bed in which Bernadette slept has been placed behind a chicken-wire screen, and it is covered with medals, photographs, bits of ribbon, fourragères, and military shoulder patches from Poland, Belgium, Malta, the Philippines, and points unknown. Little marble plaques of remembrance left by visitors are all over the walls. The bed in which Bernadette's father died is framed in family portraits, and pictures of Bernadette as a nun. The old Soubirous mill is still in existence in the basement, and the kitchen has its original utensils from the time of the apparitions. Rosary beads, money, and photographs left by pilgrims are everywhere, the stairway railings have been whittled thin by souvenir hunters, and the ancient plaster walls are covered from roof to ceiling with carved and pencilled initials. In a little dusty room upstairs, as a reminder of the brevity of the history of Lourdes, there lives Bernadette's closest living relative, a cousin, Mme. Jean Marie Soubirous, whose late husband was present at the grotto at the miracle of the candle.

The hotels of Lourdes can now collectively take care of about one hundred thousand a day. There are ten first-class hotels, of which the Moderne, the Bethanie, and the Londres-Gallia are among the best.

Best of the second-class hotels are the Bellevue, Heins, Metropole, and Europe. In any case, prices are considerably lower than those of comparable establishments in Paris and the fashionable French resorts. Most of the hotels are on the American plan, and the two or three first-rate restaurants in town will probably charge as much for a meal as a full-day pension at a hotel.

Excursions into the beautiful mountain country surrounding Lourdes are arranged by local travel agencies in the city. One of the best organized bureaus is the Office Catholique de Voyages, which schedules classic tours to Gavarnie and the Spanish frontier, a full-day trip to the mountain resort of Cauterets and Pont d'Espagne, and another to the thermal station of Luchon via the mountain passes. Cars also run to Bayonne and Biarritz, and to the Caves of Betherran to see the underground river.

More than a million persons visit Lourdes each year, and the town has become, next to Rome, the most important center of Catholicism in the world. Although the church only recognizes five miracles, the forest of crutches and discarded braces that hang in the grotto are evidence of the hundreds who have been cured at Lourdes. Some say it is extreme will, others call it supernatural, and the practical insist it is nothing but the shock of cold water on a warm body.

Doctors assigned by the church supervise each case that comes to Lourdes, and record its history. One of the most important miracles happened to a Belgian who had broken both tibia, the bones refusing to join. He was cured by a lady who bathed his leg in the water of Lourdes while he was on a pilgrimage to the shrine. After his death, some time later, a plaster cast was taken of the healed bones; it is now on exhibition at the Bureau of Consultations. The case is still unexplained by medical science.

An Englishman named Jack Traynor was severely wounded in the first World War and was paralyzed for four years. The British Medical Corps declared him incurable. In 1923 he joined a pilgrimage

*Lourdes' grotto—"the forest of crutches . . . is evidence. . . ."*

from his home town of Liverpool. After bathing in the waters he was suddenly cured, and actually walked to the railroad station on his way home. The British Army re-examined him, found him fit, and took away his pension. Every year thereafter Traynor came to Lourdes. He was the last British pilgrim to make the trip in 1940, and in 1943 he died.

Pagans, Moslems, Negroes and whites, every species of man, has been to Lourdes. In the summer the vast esplanade in front of the Basilica is massed solid with kneeling visitors, the blind, the diseased, beggars, paralytics, cripples, and sometimes, incognito, kings. Often the summer rains pour down all day, but the crowd never thins. Battle-scarred veterans have come to Lourdes in blocs of a hundred thousand. Sometimes mass is said in all three churches continuously from four in the morning until midnight.

And there have been times, too, when the power of Lourdes has been a handrail of faith to people far from the miracle of its grotto. Once, during the recent war, a lad who had been brought up near Lourdes was captured by the Japanese in Indo-China and sentenced to death. As he languished in his rotten cell in the cold hours before execution, he prayed and vowed that if he somehow got out alive he would walk barefoot from his home in Tarbes to the grotto in Lourdes, twenty kilometers away. The hour of execution came, he was herded into the courtyard, and the grisly scene began. One by one, his friends were beheaded. And then suddenly, before the executioner got to him, the Japs changed their minds, and the rest of the prisoners were sent back to their cells. Eventually he was freed and returned home, happy to walk the twenty kilometers from Tarbes to Lourdes in his bare feet.

When the Germans overran France, in June, 1940, the writer Franz Werfel and his wife fled to the Pyrenees. Hardly a step in front of the enemy, they found refuge in Lourdes, where they listened to the London radio announce that they had been captured and murdered by the Nazis. While he hid in Lourdes, never knowing when he and his wife would be discovered, Werfel came to know the story of Bernadette. He vowed that if he ever escaped and reached America safely, he would put aside all other tasks and sing the song of Bernadette. And so it happened that not a Catholic but a Jew sang the song of Bernadette, and the miracle of Lourdes came to be known even better wherever books are read and movies are shown.

Of the little miller's daughter, there is very little to record. She died in 1878, and her body was conveyed to Nevers, where she still lies in state. Outside of a small black mark on one cheek, she just looks white, saintly, and asleep.

*     *     *     *     *

In the travel folders, Luchon is called "the Queen of the Pyrenees." All hyperbole aside, the resort is probably more heavily endowed than any other in France. It has a summer and a winter season, a thermal station, and some of the best ski runs in the country. (At Luchon, as somebody once said about Saratoga, you can clean up at the baths during the day, and get cleaned in the casino at night.)

Luchon looks into Spain, and can be reached through Toulouse, which is what the French like to call the *plaque-tournante* for all the resorts of the Pyrenees. On the Toulouse-Pau railroad line, passengers must change at the switching station of Montrejeau for the run south towards the Spanish border to the resort.

Nearly all of Luchon's hotels are right and left down one main street. There are a hundred of them, and collectively they can hold about two thousand. The summer season runs from the middle of June through September, the winter season from December until March. The best hotels are the Pyrenees Palace, the Sacaron, and the Angle-terre, all of which have somewhat higher rates in winter than in summer.

Built on the site of the old Roman baths, Luchon now uses forty of its sixty natural warm sulphur springs. The water comes bubbling to the surface anywhere from 71.6 degrees to 150.8 degrees fahrenheit, at the rate of 600,000 liters a day ( a liter equals 1.05 quarts).

Speaking in terms of chemistry, the water is charged with sodium sulphide, carbonates, silicates, and an assortment of metals. In 1908 a professor, whose name now seems unimportant, found the waters of Luchon to be radioactive. As a matter of fact they contain — or they did in 1927 — fifty millimicrocuries to the liter of water (in case anyone is counting).

In view of all the current hoopla about radioactivity, the discovery was all in Luchon's favor, and the 1927 count put the resort a considerable number of millimicrocuries ahead of any other French spa, especially La Bourboule, which was its rival.

Among doctors, Luchon is best known for its cures in cases of ear, nose, throat, and respiratory afflictions. Specially designed apparatus converts the hot sulphur waters into vapor for treating chronic sore throats, catarrh, adenoids in children, pharyngitis, laryngitis, and also deafness. There are treatments for certain skin diseases, a special dry vapor has been developed for asthmatics, and a hot, pressurized shower is available for those who are just plain tired. Fatigue cases, nerve disorders, and lymphatic children are treated in the hundred-foot-long, naturally heated sulphur caves of the radioactive vaporarium.

While all this is going on, a band plays in front of the baths each morning, and everyone taking the cure stops at the Buvette du Pré, a thatched-roof Pyrenees-style cottage that dispenses more sulphur water than an Atlanta drug store sells Cokes in July.

On a pleasant plain at the foot of the mountains are Luchon's tennis courts, open-air swimming pool, and golf course. Nearby, the casino nestles innocently in a tree-shaded park. It is open in summer, and again for a short season in winter.

Most of Luchon's winter sports take place at Superbagnères, a six-thousand-foot peak reached by a mountain railway that leaves from the center of town. There is usually snow from November to May, and sometimes it gets to be ten feet deep. There are five sports shops in town, and two at the top of the mountain. The summit is crowned with a magnificent stone and marble inn known as the Grand Hotel of Superbagnères. It is open from June 15 to September 30 and for the winter season from December 20 until the 15th of March. The hotel has 180 rooms, holds 225 people, charges about 1,400 francs a day for full pension in winter and just over half that in summer.

It is very pleasant in winter to sit in the steam-heated, glass-enclosed terrace, and look over the tops of the Pyrenees into Spain. The Grand's isolated position was resistance enough to the occupying armies during the war years, and, therefore, the appointments are like new. Movies, dancing, and a gay bar are defense against the long winter evenings.

There is radio service to Luchon in case any one wants to maintain contact with the outside world; a resident doctor tapes twisted ankles, and the rooms have cabinets for heating towels.

For those who venture outside, there are excellent ski runs that start at the door of the hotel, and pause conveniently at each stop of the mountain railway. Three ski tows help to make life in the great outdoors a little easier, and a cable car swings between slopes. Ascent or descent, it takes forty-five minutes on the railway between Luchon and the top of Superbagnères. Skiers, however, can slip through the pine-bordered trails all the way to town in fourteen minutes flat.

Southeast of Luchon is another thermal station called Ax les Thermes which is less pretentious, and therefore less expensive. Like Luchon, it was originally discovered and used by the Romans who called it "acqs" for "water." The little town lies in a valley completely surrounded by mountains, and because of its natural position it was, circa 800 A.D., a fortified village on the road to Spain. It has been a modest little watering place for the past two hundred years, with four stations for baths and some twenty hotels. It is reached via the regular railroad south from Toulouse by way of Foix.

In the center of the village is a natural, open-air hot-water sulphur pool which was once a public bath. It is still used for public washing on laundry days.

Ax's biggest and only first-class hotel is the Grand, which has eighty rooms. Le Teich, a large and ancient establishment, sits right over a roaring mountain stream and is a hotel and thermal station in one. The Thermes du Couloubret is the newest and most modern of Ax's baths.

Right in town are a modest casino, a fair clay tennis court, a fresh-water swimming pool, and some excellent trout streams. There is a long summer and a short winter season, mainly because Ax has no handy mountains or nearby cable cars. Even when it snows there is

*The Grand at Font Romeu—"in January sunbaths on the terrace. . . ."*

never any snow in the center of town, because the natural hot-water sulphur springs flow directly under the pavement.

Font Romeu, eighty kilometers from the Mediterranean, at the same latitude as Florence, Italy, is the most southerly resort in France. It is also probably the gayest, clearest, warmest and most healthful in the Pyrenees. In January and February the guests take sun-baths on the terrace of the Grand Hotel, and in summer there are sun and rest, tennis, horseback riding, and golf on a nine-hole course, the highest in France. Several of the hotels organize picnics in the tall pine woods that remind one of Canada, and there is excellent trout fishing in some twenty-five lakes in the vicinity.

Font Romeu has twelve ski slopes, two tows, and a winter sports plant complete with instructors, equipment, ice hockey rink, and skating rink. The snow is fine and dry in December and January, but the skiing goes on well into the spring, when the ladies take to the slopes in the contraption of knots and ribbons that passes for a bathing suit on the Riviera.

A number of ski shops carry skis from 2,000 to 4,500 francs, excellent boots at 4,000 francs, and all manner of other winter sports apparel.

Font Romeu has fifteen hotels which can put up about fourteen hundred. Fanciest is the Grand, which is under the same management as the Grand at Superbagnères, and bears it a strong family resemblance. Font Romeu's Grand suffered some twenty million francs' worth of damage during the German occupation, but has been completely refurnished, and will accommodate 300 at a time, all in fine style. The Bellevue and the Hôtel des Pyrénées are comfortable establishments, and the revived Ermitage, which is fun and inexpensive, gets them young and gay.

The resort is so near to Spain you can spit into it, and, in the days before Franco, the hotels used to organize trips to the bull-fights in Barcelona, which is only an hour and a half away. It may come to that again, now that the border is open. Sometimes in summer the guests can still get a nostalgic earful of castanets when the colorful Catalan dancers who live along the border make the rounds of the resorts.

To reach Font Romeu by rail, take the Toulouse-Foix line as far as La Tour de Carol, which is the end of the run. A bright little yellow mountain railway takes it from there, rattling around the slopes until it reaches the foot of Font Romeu. Buses and taxis meet the train and transport passengers up the last mountainside to the hotels, which sit high in the clean air at 5,400 feet. It's easier than you'd think.

Carcassonne anchors the eastern end of the tourist's Pyrenees with a

*Carcassonne—"rising on the fringe of town like a medieval dream . . . crossbow-men flinging arrows . . . flaming oil over the side . . . a symbol of tribal insecurity. . . ."*

huge fortification that dates from the third century before Christ, and is one of the great sights of France. The city of Carcassonne is north and east of Font Romeu, sits directly on the railroad line from Toulouse, and is thirty-five miles from the Mediterranean.

The massive citadel of Carcassonne is ten minutes from the city, and is built in a circle about one mile in circumference. It has some fifty towers, and two sets of encircling walls. This unsubtle architecture represents the insecurity of a number of tribes and nations who have inhabited the castle for twenty-three centuries of time.

An ancient tribe of Gauls known as the Volcae Tectosages first established a fortress they called Carcaso, to command the route from Toulouse to the Alps. About 118 B.C., the Romans took over, turning the place into a bulwark of defense against the Spanish frontier. The Franks won the fort from the Romans in 350 A.D., but later the Romans turned the trick. Theodoric, King of the Visigoths, settled the indecision by taking the castle himself in 436. Three hundred years later the Saracens successfully invaded the ramparts. The Franks promptly attacked again, and during a siege that ensued the following legend was born:

After a long battle, the besieged Saracens were said to be down to one pig and one sack of corn. A lady by the name of Dame Carcas fed the corn to the pig, and then threw the animal over the side of the castle to impress the Franks that the defense was well stocked with food. The not-so-wily Franks said, Well, if there were pigs enough and corn enough to throw away, then the siege was useless. So they retired, and Carcassonne was saved.

Nearly every force which held Carcassonne at some point of its history has left a souvenir of its architecture. Julius Caesar made Carcaso a federal city, and there are, to this day, some Roman ruins in the citadel. The Visigoth influence is clearly evident in the Visigothic towers, which were constructed with alternating layers of brick and stone, and remain formidable even today.

Rising on a mound on the fringe of town, the citadel looks like a medieval dream. Its double walls enclose a separate little village of over a thousand persons, who operate tea rooms and souvenir shops within the enclosure. In the open-air Antique Theater, which dates from the twelfth century, road companies from Paris give operas and Shakespearean plays all during July. Every Bastille Day, July 14, it is customary to place red flares all around the walls of the citadel. For miles around, people gather on the surrounding hills to watch the spectacle.

The Hôtel de la Cité, inside the walls of the citadel, is the only good hotel in Carcassonne. Open from April to October, it has achieved so world-wide a reputation that its guest book is a global list of statesmen, royalty, and millionaires who came to Carcassonne to visit the fortress. Among the great names which date back through the years are those of Queen Victoria of Spain, the King and Queen of Portugal, the Sultan of Morocco, Grand Duke Boris of Russia, and Gaston Doumergue, once President of France. Back in the old days, Pétain was a visitor and so was Raymond Poincaré, Myron T. Herrick, the garrulous Lady Astor, and the gallant General Pershing. Otto H. Kahn, John D. Rockefeller, Jr., and Mistinguett were guests, and the Hôtel de la Cité has entertained such Hollywood celebrities as Mary Pickford and Douglas Fairbanks, Norma Talmadge, Buster Keaton, and William Powell.

The book says that Cecil B. de Mille, the greatest spectacle duplicator of them all, slept there, too. A couple of days inside the gaunt castle walls must have stirred his imagination with visions of crossbowmen flinging hundreds of arrows against the attackers, of flaming oil going over the side, of great, wooden stone-hurtling devices sending projectiles across the ramparts, armored warriors scrambling up portable scaling walls, the air filled with burning fagots and agonized screams. He must have passed some restless nights in Carcassonne.

# PROVENCE

*In the Arizona climate, Roman ruins.*

# 8. PROVENCE
## and Roman Ruins

◇◇◇◇◇◇◇◇◇◇◇◇◇◇◇◇◇◇◇◇◇◇◇◇◇◇◇◇◇◇◇◇◇◇◇◇◇◇◇◇◇◇◇◇◇◇◇◇

It is a complaint of the French that North and South Americans come to France, spend a week in Paris, a week at the Riviera, and believe they know the country. It is rather like giving a visitor to America a peek at New York, a whirl in Miami, and saying, "There you have us, old man; we are gay, gaudy, bright-lacquered, expensive and neon-lighted all over these United States."

One of the most individual and little known corners of France is Provence, which sometimes resembles Italy, sometimes Palestine, and sometimes looks like no other place on earth. Provence is mostly dry, scrubby, rocky, arid land, flowered with endless miles of olive trees, and bordered with rows of towering, deep-green cypress. But bleached in the sun of the Arizona-like climate for the past two thousand years is probably the greatest collection of Roman ruins this side of Rome itself.

Provence is a triangle of land bordering on the Mediterranean — roughly speaking, between the Riviera and the Spanish peninsula. It has a language quite its own, which is sometimes spoken, sometimes sung in folk songs, and sometimes used on restaurant menus for old times' sake. The tongue is a type of patois, only more so. It differs widely from French, as witness this stanza:

> Le Petit Chose vient d'acheter un moulin;
> Il a laissé Paris, ses quais, la Seine brune
> Pour l'air natal, vibrant, enivrant et salin.

which in Provençal becomes:

> Chose, lou pichounet, ven de croumpa'n moulin;
> Vous a leissa Paris, si quei, la Seino bruno
> Per l'er enebriant de soun pais salin. . . .

The biggest city of Provence, and the most untypical, is Marseilles, which is also France's largest port and second largest city. Big and brawling Marseilles is the *plaque-tournante* for southeastern France. East is the Riviera, south across the sea lie the island of Corsica and the cities of North Africa, and up the north road are Nîmes, Arles, Avignon, and the ruins of the empire that was Rome.

Marseilles is, for the tourist, a place to eat and sleep in, when one is en route between Provence and the Riviera. The city teems with Arabs, Senegalese, Spahis, turbans, fezzes, and also with sailors from every fleet afloat. It has comfortable hotels, and, along the waterfront, some of the world's most famous restaurants.

The Noailles and the Grand, both on the Canebière (called "Can of Beer" by the GIs), the main avenue of Marseilles, are big, first-rate, international hotels. The huge Terminus, at the depot, is one of the better run of the commercial, station-side hotels in France. A walk along the broad Canebière, lined with hotels, cafés and movie houses, leads one directly to the Vieux Port, where the Phoenicians landed in 600 B.C. In the twisting alleys of this old quarter are restaurants like the hundred-year-old Pascal, at 27 Place Thiars, Mont Ventoux, at 1 Quai Belges, and the colorful Brun, which has a prix fixé dinner which includes wine.

Bouillabaisse, a mélange of seafood, is the best known of the dishes Marseillaise. But if you have a pioneering spirit and a strong stomach, try pieds et paquets, an equal mixture of cow and sheep intestines which takes thirty-six hours to cook — and as far as I'm concerned, they could have saved the time. Bourride is a white fish with a mayonnaise sauce, and Aioli is codfish soaked in garlic gravy. The national drink in these parts is pastis, an anise extract similar to Pernod. It is clear, yellow, and potent, turns milky when mixed with water, and goes down over there quite as often, but not as easily, as soda pop over here.

Either Nîmes or Avignon makes a suitable base of operations for visiting the Roman ruins. From Marseilles, by car, Avignon can be reached by following N538, a short, direct route. The train service between Avignon and Marseilles — a distance of 104 kilometers — is via Arles, and from the north there is a direct run to the city from Lyon. Nîmes is on a direct railroad route from Paris via Clermont-Ferrand.

Of the two cities, Nîmes has more classic beauty. Its Jardin de la Fontaine must be one of the loveliest public parks in the world. Its pools, arches, and colonnades, built in the eighteenth century, bespeak an ancient glory. The city calls itself La Rome Française, and is, in fact, a preserve of Roman ruins. Remnants of the Temple of Diana still stand in Fontaine Park. The temple was partly wrecked during the religious wars at the end of the sixteenth century, and some of the stones bear the inscription of the *tailleurs de pierre*, who came later to visit, study, and repair. On a hill overlooking the park is La Tour Magne, the oldest monument in Nîmes, which commemorates a victory of the Roman general Domitius. During the recent war, the French air-raid service placed a siren on the tower, and later the Germans used it as an observation post.

Incongruously encircled by trolley cars and civic buildings in downtown Nîmes is the Maison Carrée, a temple of religion built toward the end of the Roman period in the year 2. It is a remarkably preserved one-room, square edifice, boxed in by tall Corinthian columns. Inside is a priceless collection of Roman coins, one bearing the inscription of Octavius Augustus. There are some Roman kitchen utensils which are about the same as those we are using today, and a Roman helmet worn two thousand years ago is hardly different from the headgear that was fashionable in 1944. The Maison Carrée also displays a

*The Arena at Nîmes—"the seal of Augustus looks out on a solid bank of cafés...."*

stone tomb, three feet square, which contained, when found, an urn of ashes believed to be the remains of a young girl. Buried with the urn were some first-century toys, a gold ring, an embroidery needle, and an embroidery frame made of ivory, a basin, a tiny lamp, and a pan for burning incense.

The biggest attraction in Nîmes is its Roman amphitheater, probably the best preserved of all the world's seventy such structures. It sits in the midst of the bustling city, and is bordered by the Rue Victor Hugo and the Rue de la Republique. Its bull-headed seal of Augustus, over the main portal, looks out on a solid bank of cafés across the street.

The amphitheater is built entirely of stone and entirely without cement. There are holes along the top where the Romans must have planted flags, on the days devoted to what passed for alumni home-coming games in those times. There is not a railing in the house, in spite of the gaping holes through which the builders hoisted stones, making it altogether easy for a spectator to come a cropper the Roman way.

Many ages did many curious things to the arena. In the fifth cen-tury A.D. the Visigoths turned it into a fortress. Later, its portals were sealed, houses were built into its walls, and it became a village with 2,000 inhabitants. Finally, in the nineteenth century, it was restored as an historical monument. At the beginning of the recent war, how-ever, it came into new use, this time as an air-raid shelter. The people thought it would be spared from bombing. Soon after their arrival in France the Nazis caught on, and started to fortify it, adding some monumental stone walls of their own; the Germanic "improvements" have since been obliterated. The Nîmes arena is now strung with floodlights, and used in the summer for movies, opera, and bullfights.

For all their architectural heritage, the citizens of Nîmes are none-theless fiercely prideful of the Fountain Pradier, which stands in a big square across from the arena. It was designed by the sculptor Pradier, a native of Nîmes, who became a local hero when he was com-missioned to execute part of the square marble base of the tomb of Napoléon at the Invalides in Paris. For his own home town, M. Pradier designed the fountain named for him, using a woman as the central figure. Atop the lady's head sits a model of the Maison Carrée, proving that, if nothing more, M. Pradier was a millinery genius of his day.

In passing, it may be remarked that Nîmes is also the home of Perrier water, which bubbles on bars all over the world. It has an excellent hotel in the Imperator, and several lesser establishments, the best of which is the Cheval Blanc. The Lisita restaurant, in the shadow of the arena, has a chef imported from the Savoy in London who talks in English but cooks in French—and that's as it should be.

*　　*　　*　　*　　*

Avignon, twenty-six miles from Nîmes, still lives behind high, protective stone walls built in the fourteenth century. But there is nothing archaic about the atmosphere inside the city. Its main street is like that of a typical small town, ablaze with neon lights and alive with people. The shops, bars, restaurants, and movies are crowded, and the cafés are crammed with soldiers of an engineer battalion billeted in the city.

When there were French Popes, Avignon was for a time the seat of the Papacy, and the old Palais des Papes is one of the showplaces today. The city has no Roman ruins. The village square was once the site of a Roman forum, but the structure was razed, and the stones were built into surrounding buildings. Avignon is, however, a center for excursions to Roman ruins nearby.

As for its own attractions, Avignon's Palais des Papes is right in town, a short walk from the hotels. A mass of halls and walls, the palace is about as complicated as a floor plan of the Pentagon. Suffice it to say that the first French Pope was Clement V, who began his reign in 1305. By the time Benedict XII became Pope in 1334, it was clear that French Popes were not going back to Rome, and work was begun on a combination fortress and palace in Avignon.

Benedict's building is cold and austere and reflective of his personality, and is referred to now as the "old palace." By comparison, Clement VI, who was seated in 1342, was a modern. The wing he built, likewise reflective, is called the "new palace."

Regular tours through both buildings are conducted several times daily by a nattily uniformed, handsomely mustachioed, singing guide, probably the only one of his kind in France. Visitors see "the Window of Indulgence," where the Popes appeared publicly, the bridge built by Innocent VI, who was a cripple, the grand dining room used for

*Avignon—"there's nothing archaic inside . . . the 14th-century walls. . . ."*

*Avignon's Palais des Papes—the Wehrmacht played a game. . . .*

*. . . and the singing guide took an encore. . . .*

Papal banquets which still has five Gobelin tapestries. Much of the palace shows evidence of destruction and vandalism which occurred during the Revolution. The great pontifical chapel became a barracks after the Revolution, and remained under military control until 1906. A slab of the old altar is still emplaced in the huge hall. Before it the singing guide breaks into an aria. It is a demonstration, he explains, of the remarkable resonance of the room. A full twenty seconds after he has stopped singing the sound of his voice still echoes in the chapel. As an encore, the guide may pull from his repertoire a song in pure Provençal, most beautiful language in the world, he says.

In a smaller chapel in the palace, holes remain in the once beautiful walls, where soldiers chopped out the heads of frescoes and sold them to art dealers. During the recent war, the visiting Wehrmacht got into the habit of playing a game in one vestiary that contained a statue of Charles IV. They decorated him with a swastika, put a bottle in his outstretched hand, and then tried to knock it off with stones. An objection by the curator was met with a rebuff by the Nazi sergeant. But the curator finally reported to the lieutenant that Charles IV, King of Bohemia, was a German, not a Frenchman, and the statue was saved.

The palace became a huge air-raid shelter, and was capable, within all its myriad passages, of giving protection, of a sort, to over six thousand. Once, during a bombing, six hundred persons scurried into one cave under the building, and after the "all clear," six hundred and two came out. Two babies had been born during the raid.

Above the palace is the Promenade du Rocher des Doms, a lovely park overlooking the Rhone. At the left is a bridge which officialdom insists on calling Pont St. Benezet, even though anyone who was ever a child remembers it as the Pont d'Avignon. A flood destroyed most of Avignon's bridge in 1670, and only four spans remain of the original twenty-two.

Across the Rhone is Villeneuve-les-Avignons, topped by an old

*"Anyone who was ever a child remembers . . . the Pont d'Avignon."*

castle which once held the tomb of Innocent VI. Villeneuve was once the site of cardinals' palaces, and functioned as a Versailles of Avignon. There, amid the quiet cloisters, at eight A.M. on the 8th of August, 1944, an American flyer parachuted down from a crippled Flying Fortress, and was hidden in the catacombs until the Americans liberated the village. Buses run on regular schedule from Avignon across the river to Villeneuve. There is an excellent restaurant in the village called Le Prieuré, furnished entirely in early Provençal, and decorated on the outside with some seven testimonials from touring and gastronomical clubs of Europe.

Avignon has no hotels of palace category. The best is the Hôtel Europe which, in one form or another, dates all the way back to 1580. It has been redecorated a number of times, but is still proud of its old heritage. Napoléon stayed at the hotel on a number of occasions, always signing the register simply "Bonaparte." During the Russian campaign, Napoléon, after listening to the grumblings of some of his officers, worn out by privation and cold, is said to have said something like, "Confound it, boys, we are not back at the Hôtel Europe!"

The Terminus is a trifle less sedate, but more equitably priced, than the Crillon Hotel across the street. Up the avenue, the Regina is a comfortable, moderate price hotel, and near the Palais des Papes is the Hiely, an excellent restaurant.

Wherever you eat in Avignon, you should try a bottle of Châteauneuf du Pape, one of the wines of the Rhone produced on lands near Avignon once owned by the Popes. The castle itself, at one time the summer home of the Popes, is in ruins, but it has given its name to one of the great wines of France.

Midway between Avignon and Nîmes is a perfect Roman aqueduct one hundred feet high, built before the time of Jesus Christ. Rising in three decks over the River Gard, the structure is twice the height of the Nîmes arena, and was used by the Romans as part of the pipe line carrying water to the city. Every time there was a war, the water, running in a trough across the top of the aqueduct, was cut off, and three separate layers of sediment are now clearly discernible. The lower tier of the aqueduct has long since been paved for use as a roadway, and is actually along the right of way of Route N581 between Arles and Nîmes. On the north bank of the river, a path cut through the olive trees leads up the hill to the top of the aqueduct. Daring travelers traverse the length of the bridge along the top, which is three feet wide and unprotected by railings. Those who think twice walk along the covered water trough, which really is just a long, stone corridor. The sediment is so thick in some places it is necessary to turn sideways to get through. In the tunnel, the original red caulking placed in the seams by the Romans is still apparent.

Hundreds of visitors have left their initials on the inside of the aqueduct's stone walls. A certain Jeanne swabbed hers in black paint in 1906; one M. Lafont wrote in brown paint on August 29, 1926, and A. Bechard left his notice in blue ink on the underside of a step on June 13, 1886. I would like to report to Fanny, Jeanne, and Alex that their notice, painted in 1936, is showing signs of weather

*The aqueduct near Nîmes—"Fanny, Jeanne and Alex . . . show signs of weather. . . ."*

and M. Blanc's inscription nicked right into the stone back in 1860 looks a little moth-eaten too.

Near the base of the bridge is a prehistoric grotto which the Germans used during the war for storing ammunition. An inn nearby calls itself, grandly, the Hôtel du Pont du Gard. And sometimes, not so grandly, it sends off scratchy American dance music which echoes against the two-thousand-year-old stones and goes screeching down the peaceful olive-bordered valley like a runaway brewery horse upsetting a funeral.

From Nîmes there is a once-a-day commercial bus service to the Pont du Gard, leaving at 8:30 in the morning and returning to pick up passengers going back to Nîmes at 5:30 in the afternoon. The hotel serves lunch. From Avignon the bus companies run a regular excursion which visits Villeneuve and Uzès in the morning, stops at Nîmes for lunch, visits the Pont du Gard, and returns to Avignon in the late afternoon. Another itinerary from Avignon takes in Tarascon, Arles, Les Baux, and St. Remy, also a full day's trip.

Tarascon is equidistant from Nîmes and Avignon, was famous for its fairs, and is mildly interesting now for its chateau of King René, a great specimen of military architecture of the fifteenth century. The chateau later became a country home for the Counts of Provence, and still later was a prison. On May 27, 1944, American airmen making simultaneous passes over Tarascon, Nîmes, and Marseilles, knocked out the suspension bridge over the Rhone at Tarascon; it took with it most of the Church of St. Marthe, once celebrated for its tall belfry.

There is much to see in Arles, and you can buy one combination ticket for all the sights. Crowded now by seedy buildings of the present village are ruins of a Roman theater, an obelisk, an arena, and a Roman cemetery called Les Alyscamps. It is plain that Arles was once a greater city than the archeological graveyard it has become. Situated as it is near the Mediterranean at the mouth of the Rhone, Arles became important after Caesar wrecked Marseilles in 49 B.C. Its markets filled with exotic treasure from Africa and the East. As its wealth mounted, so did its political importance. It became a religious center, the seat of an archbishop.

Then, as with all inflations, the crash came to Arles. The city was laid waste during the invasions of the barbarians. Marseilles stepped in quickly to regain its lost position in the economic order, Aix rose as a political center, and Arles was reduced to a tourists' museum clutching to its bourgeois bosom its last worldly possessions, the crumbling ruins of its once proud empire.

Just before the Christian era began, the Roman theater of Arles was playing Greek tragedies to a house that could hold twelve thousand. The theater is not as well preserved as the one at Orange, north of Avignon, but in June and July it still stages plays in the open air, and

*Arles' Roman arena—"will the guidebooks of 3949 mention the World Series?"*

it still packs them in. Destroyed in the fifth century A.D., and buried, the playhouse was excavated in the nineteenth century. Statues found at the time went to the Musée Lapidaire, in town, or to the Louvre, in Paris. But the semi-circular seating section is intact, the stage is discernible if not existent, and two whole pillars and a number of broken ones rise on location.

The arena of Arles rises in the shadow of the antique theater. It dates from 46 B.C., the date of origin of the city itself, and is in excellent condition, except for the third tier of portals, which somehow became misplaced through the ages. Like the amphitheater at Nîmes, the Arles arena was fortified in the tenth century, and the interior was filled with houses and churches. In the fourteenth century the arena was excavated, and in the nineteenth century it was restored.

In the old Roman days, the sports promoters used to pit gladiators against animals, and animals against each other. Just as now, the big cities got the primary attractions involving lions, tigers, and elephants. Secondary circuits, on which Arles must have been a stop, were booked with wolves, bears, and bulls. Gladiators were often matched against each other, and if the defeated fighter didn't please the crowd, there was no refund—the loser was obliged to have his throat slit by the victor. As a precaution against such blood-letting showing, the turf was always covered with a red powder beforehand.

Restoration work still goes on at the Arles arena, and if just as good care is taken of the Yankee Stadium, the Rose Bowl, and Madison Square Garden, what will our ancestors have to say of our civilization in another two thousand years? Will the guidebooks of 3949 mention the World Series, outdoor rodeos, wrestling matches in the mud? Will the legend of football games before crowds of 100,000 survive the centuries? Certainly, historians with a straight face won't be able to tell the story of the variety of the shows in Madison Square Garden, where they have boxing one night and ice hockey the next. They used to pull that at Nîmes before the opening of our present era, when

Les Alyscamps—"original Roman coffins lie in a quietude that has lasted for over nineteen centuries. . . ."

they flooded the arena and had the gladiators do battle with crocodiles and seals. By the time another two hundred decades roll around, the stunt will be 4,000 years old.

Les Alyscamps, one of the most celebrated cemeteries of the Roman epoch, still exists in Arles. It was the Roman custom to bury the dead in sculptured stone coffins. Les Alyscamps has been re-established as it once was. Original Roman coffins lie in neat lines along a poplar-bordered road, in a quietude that seems to have lasted for over nineteen centuries.

Once there were seventeen chapels in the cemetery; now only a few buildings remain at the end of the central roadway. The most interesting is the Temple of Jupiter. Two urns that once held Roman ashes flank the entrance of the temple,. and inside is a room where the Romans allegedly indulged in child sacrifice. Some graves lie exposed in front of the temple, but the most handsome of the tombs disinterred so far are kept inside the chapels.

A guide who is nearly blind has been conducting visitors around Les Alyscamps for some thirty years, and in his spare time fashions plaster cigarette boxes in the form of sculptured tombs. If the thought of such a souvenir reposing in your living room three thousand miles away is not too macabre, perhaps you will also be interested in taking along a femur or a tibia from the piles of bones that lie around. The bones are advertised as bona fide Roman, but there is no guarantee that they are not remains of some old dead cows.

Arles was also the home, during the last years of his short life, of Vincent Van Gogh, the Dutch painter who died in 1890. After a boyhood in Holland, and some early years in London and Paris, Van Gogh came finally to Provence, where he lived in a simple room and painted the towering cypress trees, the fields in the strong, southern sun, and "L'Arlesienne," the wife of an inn keeper. Gauguin, an old Paris friend, joined Van Gogh in Arles, and they worked together until

Van Gogh's health failed completely. He went insane, and finally shot himself at the age of thirty-seven.

The road from Arles to Les Baux runs through the country of Alphonse Daudet, a great French story-teller. Daudet's *Letters from My Mill* centered about the mill at Fontvieille, and the village has become a literary shrine. One of his most famous stories in the collection explains how the idiom "le coup de pied de la mule" ("the kick of the mule") came to mean "the taking of revenge." A page boy who was in charge of the Pope's mule made the animal walk up the narrow stairs in the tower of the Pope's palace. When they got to the top the mule couldn't turn around and walk back down. The page boy tried every which way to get him down, and finally the mule had to be placed in a cradle and lowered over the side with ropes. It was a very embarrassing position for the mule, and he never forget the indignities to which he had been subjected. As for the page, he was a bright lad, and ultimately was sent to Naples for ecclesiastical training. Seven years later he returned as a church dignitary, and while he was walking in a Papal procession the same mule, who never forgot, broke away from his handler and dealt the ex-page a forceful kick of revenge.

Les Baux sits atop a wild, craggy rock formation, just east of Arles. From its name came the name of bauxite, which was mined in the nearby country. The ancient village of Les Baux is an eerie ruin of classic buildings said to have been inhabited by descendants of the Celts. Later, Les Baux had its own royal families, and great wealth, two factors that caused considerable unrest in the southern provinces. In 1372, one Raymond de Turenne, related to two Popes, touched off a minor civil war which was finally quelled by royal troops. When the last of the princesses of Les Baux died, the house became a barony and was merged into Provence. In a fit of royal temper, in 1632, Louis XIII announced that he was distraught with the riotous history of Les Baux, ordered the castle torn down, and exacted a huge fine from the local citizenry.

*In the rocks of Les Baux, a chic restaurant and a smart crowd.*

All that's left of the early pomp are a few tumbledown shops that sell antiques and the little painted clay figures for which Provence is noted. Each Christmas the shepherds and the village folk hold at Les Baux a renowned church service which is arranged to resemble the first Christmas.

One of the best restaurants in France sits at the bottom of the flat plateau formed by the Les Baux rock formations. It is known formally as "L'Oustau de Baumaniere," is chic and expensive, and gets a smart crowd who motor up from Marseilles for a swim in the pool and lunch in the cactus-bordered patio. Specialty of the house: canapés of fish eggs and an oily butter mixed to a mash, and spread on bread.

By no means do these notes on Provence mention all the relics of the Roman empire that existed in Southern France. On the side of

the road from Les Baux to Avignon a whole Roman village lies un-
covered. A dozen columns still stand, foundations of houses remain,
street outlines are clearly discernible, and in some floors there are fine
mosaics, perfectly preserved, which felt the tread of Roman sandals.

What's more, archeologists believe that under the roots of olive trees,
beneath the sandy soil of Provence, untold other Roman ruins still lie
buried. Whole cities? A clew to Roman culture? A key to a life older
than the time of Christ?

Who knows?

*Monte Carlo—on the tired face of Europe, a lacquered eyelash still fluttered.* (Monaco Information Bureau)

# 9. THE RIVIERA

◇◇◇◇◇◇◇◇◇◇◇◇◇◇◇◇◇◇◇◇◇◇◇◇◇◇◇◇◇◇◇◇◇◇◇◇◇◇◇◇◇◇◇◇◇◇◇◇◇◇◇◇

LIKE a long, lacquered eyelash, the Riviera is still fluttering gaily on the tired face of Europe. It would seem as if all the lush, well-heeled, white-tie, champagne life had been pushed off the continent, except this one strip of insulated fringe where the sporty crowd still clings to an existence—albeit with one foot in the sea.

Exactly three years after the Riviera was liberated by some American gentlemen of the 36th Division, the whole Azure Coast from St. Tropez to Menton was alive again with a jiggling mass of narcissists, sun-worshippers, tipplers of whisky and dealers in the *marché noir, de facto* socialites, barons with defunct titles, party-throwers, and dethroned royalties.

There were a lot of new faces around that had never before been toasted by the southern French sun, when the Riviera opened for business again after the war. But the new, and what was left of the old, had one thing in common: money. As usual, that was the common denominator. The new faces and the old faces soon came to recognize each other. Every day they met on the Riviera run—from breakfast to beach to bar to swim to lunch to beach to bar to swim to bar to dinner to Casino. If times were uncertain, at least one thing was sure: the Riviera was back in the big swing. All was very gay.

The whole Côte d'Azur—by which appellation the Riviera is also known—is making its re-entry as both a summer and a winter resort, a double-pronged idea that never had a chance to catch on in the years

· 213 ·

before the war. More Americans than ever before have come to know the coast. As each resort town was successively liberated, Special Services representatives from the American Army buzzed about requisitioning hotels. It seems clear now, in the calm, post-war light, that the area was ticketed as a rest center before our invasion ships ever left Africa.

True enough, nearly the entire stretch was made one gigantic resort for troops in the European theater. The city of Nice went, in toto, to the enlisted men. To the Red Cross girls, nurses, OSS, OWI, and other female accouterments was handed the resort of Juan-les-Pins. The male officers got Cannes. The army's own rail and air services were set up. Men were flown directly out of battle areas, and were landed on the palm-fringed Nice airport a few hours later. It was probably the first time in history that any army had erected signs which read: "No Saluting." Ties and caps were out, too, and for awhile, it wasn't necessary to wear insignia, but some of the brass got a little skittish about that, and the bars, leaves, eagles—yes, and stars— went back on.

Soldiers were allowed to stay on the Riviera for seven days, not counting transportation time, and the whole cost, including room and board for the seven days, ran to something like $37. The top hotels of the Riviera were retained by the United States Army on a reverse lend-lease basis. Life in some of the same rooms now runs $37 for a couple of days.

Along the seventy-five-mile stretch of the Côte d'Azur there are perhaps half a hundred resorts, of which Nice is the largest, and Cannes the best known. Reading from left to right as a yachtsman views the coast, the westernmost point is anchored by St. Tropez.

On the fifteenth of August, 1944, American invasion forces put ashore at St. Tropez, landing at a beach called Pampelune. They hit the sand about five years after a faithful colony of artists had left, and about ten centuries after a group of invading Saracens had arrived.

The Americans' attempt was eminently more successful than that of a large Spanish fleet which was repulsed at the same spot in 1637. In the years before the war, St. Tropez developed a rather flamboyant reputation which only artists, beach-browned beauties, free-spending tourists, two dozen saloons, and a waterfront can produce.

Eastward along the golden Corniche, the seaside road, are the modern resort of St. Raphael and its neighbor Fréjus, an ancient Roman city. Napoléon got to St. Raphael on two occasions—once on his way from Egypt to Paris to effect his *coup,* and again on his way to Elba fifteen years later. That was hardly the end of the military life for St. Raphael. Consider the history of the Golf Hotel in the recent war: First it was a French hospital, then it was taken over by the Italians. The Germans imprisoned the Italians inside the place, and finally the Americans took over, established the 78th Station Hospital, and put up tents all over the golf course. Now the Golf Hotel is back in business as a moderate-price Riviera resort, with golf course and tennis courts functioning as heretofore.

Three kilometers away, the town of Fréjus is like an old derelict with aristocratic antecedents. From its decadent present it can hark back to its origin in 49 B.C., to its originator, Julius Caesar, and to its standing, which once rivaled that of Marseilles.

Of all the resorts, Cannes is probably the most representative of the Riviera's reputation. It has a long sand beach, and magnificent casinos. Great hotels share the seafront along the Croisette with fine shops; among the latter are Cartier, Worth, Van Cleef and Arpels, Jeanne Lanvin. Elsa Maxwell has a villa in Cannes, and so have Antoine and Chevalier and a score of other personalities. Lily Pons was born in Cannes, and it was there that Jimmy Walker married Betty Compton. After abdicating as King Edward VIII, the (later) Duke of Windsor hurried to Cannes to meet Wally, and they went into seclusion at Villa Lou Viel owned by Mr. and Mrs. Herman Rogers.

Cannes is elegant and smart and flossy. Sleek new American cars

*Along the Croisette—under the skies, stars . . . Orson Welles . . . Chevalier . . . Boyer. (Essi)*

with New York and California license plates, and loaded with more celebrities than the Super Chief, whiz under the palms.

Merle Oberon, Michele Morgan, Greta Garbo (in funny looking shorts), Sonja Henie, Jack Warner, Doris Duke, Orson Welles, Chico Marx, and Johnny Meyer, seeking to escape the heat of Washington, have all dropped in at Cannes since the war. Nobody has counted the rajahs, maharajahs, amahs, pashas, and shahs, but in Cannes you can meet anybody and see anything.

On the broad Riviera beaches, children run untamed and naked. The bathing suits for ladies, as you must know by now, even bare the essentials, and what is affected by the men would shock a model for a Bauer and Black advertisement.

It all started with an Englishman and an epidemic of cholera. The Englishman was Lord Brougham, who, in addition to founding

*The beach at Cannes—"under the palms . . . sleek new American cars. . . ."*

Cannes, also gave his name to a type of one-horse carriage. In 1830 the lord was on his way from England to Italy when he learned of an outbreak of cholera, and decided to put in at Cannes, at the time a small fishing village. In the middle of winter Brougham returned to England, a rather unpleasant place at that time of year, and explained to his countrymen what they were missing. Soon afterwards, English people began to flock to Cannes, and, aside from the war years, they kept coming until the British government slapped down its ban on pleasure travel in 1947.

Today Cannes has some thirty-five hotels, of which a dozen are on the beach. Five of these are what the French call palace-type hotels. One of the best is the famous Carlton, run by jolly little Jean Mero. Both M. Mero and Cap de Ville, his front man and assistant, insist that the luxurious Carlton is no more expensive than its luxurious counter-

*The ladies "even bare the essentials. . . ."*

parts in the United States. (They've got menus from the Colony in New York to prove it.)

The huge Martinez, largest hotel on the Riviera, is still doing business behind its yellow and blue Air Corps *décor*. When the Riviera was a military rest center, the Martinez was, in fact, an Air Corps hotel, and its bright yellow walls and bright blue shutters shuddered to many a "Wild Blue Yonder" ere the peace was signed. One Air Corps colonel became pretty well entranced with the Martinez when he was there. He expressed an interest in coming back some day and buying the place—presumably with the money he saved from his flight pay. They still talk of the chap wistfully, along the Croisette. They wish he'd come back, and make good his word. Some of the big

"It all started with an Englishman and an epidemic of cholera. . . ."
(A. Traverso)

*The Carlton Hotel—next door ". . . many a 'Wild Blue Yonder' . . ."*

hotels are being bought up by real-estate operators and remodelled into co-operative apartments.

That fate has already befallen part of the Miramar Hotel, whose Red Cross Club got to be about as famous during the war as the Stage Door Canteen. Like every red-blooded American on vacation, officers at Cannes would sleep late during their leaves, even though it meant missing breakfast. Everyone lay abed, content in the thought that he could stumble over to the Red Cross at eleven A.M. and revitalize with coffee and doughnuts on the sun-scorched terrace of the Miramar. It was a place where soldiers fresh from the front could talk with American girls, sip Cokes, and read new magazines—all in deep, leather chairs.

A couple of times a week there were dances, and that's when the corps of French hostesses really rang the bell. The mademoiselles were paid assistants, hired by the Red Cross. If the army never had it so good, neither had they. They were danced, dated, wined, dined, and adored. One of the girls, captain of the assistants, and daughter of the then mayor of Cannes, was especially beautiful; her name was Simone Picaud. During the time the Americans were in her father's city she played ping-pong with, darned the socks of, was waltzed by, brewed coffee for, listened to proposals from, and said "no" to no less than one thousand goggle-eyed Yankee officers.

Now it came to be that not every officer was at Cannes for seven days; some were stationed there *permanently*. One of these was Captain Donald Elliott, of Burlingame, California. Don had come up through the ranks in pretty normal fashion. He graduated from Officers' Candidate School at Fort Benning, and went overseas with the 102nd Division. He saw action in Germany, and in due course was made captain. Towards the end of 1944 his regimental commander was replaced by a big, bruff colonel who had a violent tongue and a violent temper. One day the colonel and Captain Elliott, normally a rather mild individual, crossed paths. Shortly thereafter Don found himself yanked out of his outfit and redeployed to the Pacific. He was actually climbing the gangplank at Marseilles on his way to the other side of the world when he received new orders to proceed to Cannes. He was assigned to permanent duty with the Riviera Rest Command, and finished the war under the swaying palms. It was Don Elliott who finally married Simone Picaud.

Cannes has two casinos, one for each season. The Palm Beach Casino is open in summer, when the coast gets a mixed crowd. In addition to its gaming tables, the Palm Beach has a swimming pool, cabaret, floor shows, restaurant, and bar. In the winter, the arch-socialite set flocks to the Municipal Casino, at the opposite end of town, which is under the same management as the casino at Deauville. Most of the hotels have open-air terrace bars along the Croisette, and there are a number of cafés tucked away in odd corners all over town and usually frequented by the same faithful patrons year after year.

A barkeep named Felix, who runs the Blue Bar on the Croisette, became so friendly with Philip Mountbatten that he found himself with a ticket to the royal wedding when Philip married Princess Elizabeth. It's been one windfall after another for the Blue Bar. The building which contains the saloon is being remodelled to become the permanent base for the Cannes Film Festival, held each September.

In the interests of good reporting, it should be noted that the old Arizona, opposite the Miramar, where you could get a fine black-market steak at four A.M. in the first post-war years, now does business under the name of Chez Antoinette. Outside of that, the town is pretty much the same. The shops in the commercial quarter along the Rue d'Antibes still offer glazed fruits, pottery, as well as perfumes from Grasse. There are a lot of oranges around, a product in short supply elsewhere in France, and every now and then Arab rug sellers make the rounds carrying their stock on their shoulders, Casbah fashion.

A low range of mountains, called l'Esterel, curves out into the sea from the west end of Cannes, forming a small harbor at the edge of the city's busy section. Most any time of the year you can sit under the shade trees of the Alliées de la Liberté Park, along the waterfront, and watch the sailboats, the fishing smacks, and the yachts bob in the blue-green Mediterranean. Music blares from the municipal bandstand from time to time, and in winter and spring the flower market sets up shop in the open, filling the air with ambrosia.

Cannes has two golf courses and a number of championship tennis courts. The weather is balmy all year around, but it's only warm enough for swimming in summer. An hour's ride, as the Duesenberg flies, will put you in Beuil-Valberg, one of three fine ski resorts just that near to the warm Mediterranean sands.

Twelve miles up the mountain road from Cannes is the perfume center of Grasse, which produces about ten million pounds of roses, orange blossoms, jasmine, and carnations every year. Nearly every perfume a woman dabs on her ear lobes as a come-on in the old bees-and-flowers routine, contains a drop of Grasse's jasmine. During the jasmine season the flower pickers at Grasse must rise at dawn, pick the flower before the sun's heat sends the perfume into the air to attract the birds and the bees. Grasse is a favorite stop on excursions out of Cannes and Nice. Among the visitors who drop into several of the eighteen firms who do business in the city is Mme. Molotov, one of the big-wigs in the Russian perfume industry. The city is further commemorated as the home town of a famous admiral, the Comte de Grasse, whose name now rides the waves on the bows of a French transatlantic liner.

When the Riviera Rest Command was functioning, the traffic got to be pretty heavy between the officers' base in Cannes and the nurses, WACs, and Red Cross girls lolling in the luxury of Juan-les-Pins on the edge of the Antibes peninsula. In the warm, tropical nights, the war seemed a couple of continents away. Today there isn't much traffic between the two resorts. Cannes is still elegant, while Juan-les-Pins has slipped a bit in class and price. Out along the peninsula, however, towards Cap d'Antibes, things get pretty chic again. The Duke and Duchess of Windsor have their own villa out there, called Chateau de la Croe, and so had the Princess of Montenegro. Eisenhower himself relaxed in the rarefied atmosphere of the cape, during the war. At the end of the promontory is the famed Hôtel du Cap d'Antibes whose ninety rooms are usually filled with the plushiest characters of the international set. Hardly a precious stone's throw away is world-famous Eden Roc, an expensive watering place with attached swimming pool, restaurant, and bar.

Another favorite place for excursions is the town of Cagnes, an artist colony between Antibes and Nice. The Greeks founded the city along with Antibes, and later lost them both to the Romans. Renoir really put the place on the map in a single-handed sweep, by painting some of his great works there. He died in Cagnes in 1919.

Cannes is smart, Cap d'Antibes is elegant, but Nice is all of that and a great city, besides. Nice, betimes, is graceful and sedate, swaggering and lusty, old and sentimental. It has a broad, palm-fringed avenue by the sea. It has ultra-modern apartment houses with glass balconies hanging over the azure sea, luxurious hotels, casinos as big as the Music Hall in New York, a carnival to rival the New Orleans Mardi Gras, a dusty old quarter, and a language all its own. The people who operate all these variations in the life of Nice add up to a quarter of a million, or about 25,000 more than live in Miami and Miami Beach combined.

Nice's avenue by the sea is called the Promenade des Anglais. Along it runs a string of fine hotels like the Ruhl and the huge white Negresco. It is a magnificent boulevard, with a broad walk, and with more new American cars than the Merritt Parkway sees on the first warm Sunday in May. The sidewalks along the Promenade des Anglais are strewn as with confetti with multi-colored chairs where strollers stop and sit in the hot Mediterranean sunshine.

The Negresco is as nice a hotel as you will find in Nice, or most anywhere else, for that matter. It lies smack in front of a hairpin turn along the course of an annual automobile race, was the home of the Commission de Controle during the German occupation, and later became headquarters of the Riviera Rest Command under the Americans. There are any number of lesser establishments, like the Hôtel Albert I which overlooks a beautiful flowered park by the same name, and all manner of pensions, boarding houses, furnished rooms, and families who take in guests.

Virtually only one category of night life exists in Nice—brassy and expensive. Most of the after-dark entertainment centers about the casinos. Le Casino Municipal in Place Masséna will be remembered by a lot of American soldiers who found a companionable friend in one of the managers of the place, a gentleman promptly dubbed Joe Casino. Gambling rooms in those days were off limits for soldiers, but Joe used to keep a stock of tuxedo jackets which the military could don, and therein sneak into the Salons de Jeux incognito. Joe's friends never forgot him, and all kinds of offers have poured in, inviting him to pack up and come to the States. Joe thinks he's too old to take such a drastic step. He prefers to stay in Nice, where he supervises such sprightly Municipal Casino attractions as the nightclub with a dance band and an American singer, a music hall offering continuous entertainment, a complete theater, and a scattering of gaming rooms.

But inside, Joe Casino is not content. "Hell, when the Americans were here," the nightclub manager says, wistfully, "there was a party every night."

Most ornate of Nice's casinos is the Palais de la Méditerranée, a great marble barn by the sea. A bit more *intime* is the Nouveau Casino, which is new, fancifully furnished, and features the usual French vaudeville—extravagant costuming, ornate staging and weak talent. Every French city has a nightclub named Maxim's. The Maxim's in Nice, totally unrelated to any other, is next to the Hôtel Albert I, and, in the Parisian tradition, is low, velvety, and smoky. Some of the clubs in Nice proudly advertise that they do not require patrons to accept a bottle of champagne at about $5 to $8 the quart, as is an old Parisian custom. And with the new devaluation of the franc, whiskey, if you order it, will come to about the equivalent of 65 cents a drink.

Wherever you go and whatever you spend—which is likely to be plenty, you end up at a dive called Le Chat Noir, a rather disreputable emporium in the middle of the market that opens at midnight and closes when the last of the customers goes home. Since the nightclub is reached via a long, descending stairway bordered by many colored bulbs, it is quite impossible to determine the arrival of daylight. The place attracts the current crop of artists and actors, who sit amid the risqué scrawlings and sober up on onion soup, oysters, snails, tripe, and mussels. Americans will be glad to know that this rather Gallic bill of fare also includes ham sandwiches, and that, hard by the pornographia, is a sketch of the Statue of Liberty. One Jean Tomas functions as the local *compère,* which means he greets customers, sings, dances, and counts the take. Most any night you can see in the Black Cat a Mistinguett or a Chevalier, and if you leave too late you are likely to run into a cab driver or a vegetable huckster having breakfast in the resturant upstairs which does business in normal hours, willy-nilly.

In Nice you have the choice of eating Provençal, Niçois or plain native French. All the casinos have one or more elegant restaurants serving the usual fare. Eastward along the extension of the Promenade des Anglais, which becomes the Quai des Etats-Unis, is a battery of high-priced establishments overlooking the sea. In the order of their

appearance they are La Maison Rouge, Le Cabaret, and Raynaud. Dinner: expensive.

But the crumbling walls of the old city hold many a wonderful restaurant known only to the initiated and the informed. The most colorful of these is Da Bouttau which has been doing business in the same ramshackle building since 1860. The *décor* is strictly old-quarter. Salamis and cheeses hang from the ceiling, red-checkered tablecloths set off the ancient plaster walls. There are no partitions to contain the kitchen, no menus, and no checks. Waiters wear lumber shirts and white aprons, and get arbitrary about serving what *they want* instead of what *you like,* in the manner perfected in Lindy's loxhouse in New York. Among these pseudo-woodsmen is Jean Bouttau, one of the owners. His brother Maurice, a quiet and gentle type, runs the kitchen. On this combination, Jean's raucous, gravel voice explains: "They call us the cowboys—he's the cow and I'm the boy."

While all this by-play is going on, street singers perch on a stairway behind the kitchen, and sadly serenade the roomful of celebrities who munch octopus, quaff red wine, and inscribe immortal verses in Da Bouttau's famous guest book. Daladier himself signed the book, and so have actresses from Lucienne Boyer to Norma and Constance Talmadge, who set the Riviera agog in 1929, through to Rita Hayworth in 1948. One whole page carries a sketch penned in a frivolous moment on September 25, 1928, entitled "Just four bad boys from the U.S.A." The four boys in question identified themselves as (1) Baron Orin Gould; (2) Bad Bill Byrne; and (3) J. C. Finitney, Keokuk, Iowa. Number 4, with certain lack of self-effacement, concealed himself under the *nom de vin* of "The Tri-Nightly Express." If this needed further clarification he wrote "The Great Lover," and as if anyone wanted an additional testimonial, he added *"au lit extraordinaire."*

But neither a Talmadge nor a scrap of pre-war gaiety provokes more nostalgia than a copy of Da Bouttau's menu in 1927:

| | |
|---|---|
| Homard à la Americaine.................... | 16 and 13 francs |
| Sandwich au foie gras...................... | 3 francs |
| Escargots de Bourgogne.................... | 3 francs |
| Bouillon de poule......................... | 2 francs |
| Gigot agneau Roti......................... | 3 francs |
| Rosbeef saignant.......................... | 3 francs |
| Marron glacés............................. | 3 francs |
| Corbeille de fruit........................ | 1½ francs la pièce |

In forty years the prices are about the only thing in Da Bouttau that have changed. Today you remind Jean what you had, and he sketches each item on a piece of cardboard. Then he slaps down some round figure, probably about 500 francs per person, and that's your bill. You get the drawings as a souvenir.

Once a year, usually early in February, the good burghers of Nice throw a huge party called the Carnival of Nice. It's been going on as long as anyone cares to remember; a magazine called *Les Guepes* reported in 1859 that "people threw candy, beans, flowers, wisecrackers, and eggs filled with plaster and soot at each other." Things have calmed down a lot since those gay days, and the hardest thing thrown on the Riviera nowadays is a bag of confetti. Besides being an annual ten-day binge, the Carnival also provides a year-round industry to painters and decorators. It takes six months to build the floats, and another six months to knock them down and store them for the following year. The big sight is entirely free, and, as a matter of fact, the carnival procession is prohibited by tradition from passing before grandstands occupied by people who have been forced to pay admission.

While something of such recent vintage as the arrival of the *Mayflower* has become the yardstick of ancient heritage in America, the people of Nice can go all the way back to the Ligurians who were conquered by the Greeks from the settlement at Marseilles in 4 B.C. The Greeks had a word for Nice. It was "Niké," meaning "victory." As it turned out, the name was a bit optimistic, because in short order the Romans took over, and, in fact, established what is now the suburb of Cimiez as the seat of the province. Cimiez declined, along with Rome, and is now just a stop on excursions out of Nice.

Everyone was so busy fighting over Nice during the Middle Ages, nobody stopped there long enough to enjoy the place. The first British visitors began to come in the middle of the eighteenth century, and the French revolutionaries, in 1793, issued an edict rejoining the city to the French nation. Napoléon used Nice as a base of operations against Italy, as a result of which the city went to the King of Sardinia with the decline of Napoléon. Princess Helena of Russia finally made a fashionable resort of Nice, by establishing her winter residence in the city in 1858. Two years later, the townspeople held a plebiscite, and Nice went back to France. Mussolini made a few passes at the city in 1939, but failed, thus not spoiling his perfect record. The old Chateau de Nice is still camouflaged, but there are few other marks of the war, in spite of the fact that the place was crawling with Gestapo.

Nice was buffeted around so much that it grew up like a child of divorce, and developed a certain independence. It has its own language, which derives from the low Latin, with overtones of Italian, Celtic, and whatever was spoken by the Ligurians. The first poem in Niçois was written in 1823; there is a Niçois dictionary, and there are a half dozen academies where the language is taught.

The old parts of the city are a curious spectacle, and in some places the streets are so narrow the citizens can toss a piece of string to their neighbors across the alley and hang their wash thereon. All the exotic foods which are strictly Niçois—or, at any rate, southern French —are on display during the winter at the Marché Courssaleya. In summer the market moves over behind the Casino Municipal, and sets up shop on top of the River Paillon, which runs underground. Flowers are a staple of life in Nice, and you buy them in the marketplace as you might a sack of beans or a pound of potatoes. Nice's goods are spread over an area equal to that of about a dozen California super markets, and no bazaar ever reeked of more entrancing smells, resounded to more strange tongues, or displayed so weird an assortment of vegetation. Here you will find *sanguins,* a queer sort of mushroom that grows on pine trees in southern France and is eaten fried with garlic, and *kakis,* a tart kind of orange from which you cut out the middle and then treat the rest with rum and sugar, before you ice and eat it. The fish section specializes in octopus, which ordinarily makes French mouths water and American stomachs churn. The larger ones are called *poulpes,* the smaller, *seiches.* Big, round, pale yellow *panis* are cakes molded from a chestnut flour, and if eaten hot they are slightly more digestible than paving blocks. Also in the baked-goods department is what is described as a tart that is made with onions and goes under the startling appellation of *pissaladiera.*

But the Riviera doesn't end with Nice. Three roads lead on towards the Italian frontier. They are called, with a certain nursery-book flavor, the Corniche, the Middle Corniche, and the Grand Corniche. All the Corniches run on different levels, the sea route leading to Villefranche, Cap Ferrat, and Beaulieu. Anything that is afloat in the neighborhood puts in at Villefranche. It's almost a custom. The sardine and lobster boats from Sardinia stop by, transatlantic liners running between Naples and New York put in, and the town has always been a favorite with the ships of the United States Navy. It is said to be the ambition of every local maid to ensnare an American sailor when the fleet is in, and many maidens have turned the trick.

A press agent who could read a thermometer once figured out that Beaulieu is the hottest place on the Riviera. It has since been called "Little Africa." The mountains rise abruptly from the sea at Beaulieu, and the place is teeming with bananas and Englishmen. Tepid temperature has also served to promote a lush retreat called La Reserve de Beaulieu. La Reserve is a pink fairy palace decorated with beautiful greens and elements of the choicest clientele on the Riviera. In summer a bejeweled set dines expensively on a long terrace that overhangs

*Nice's Flower Market—Princess Helena finally did it.*

*An octopus at Nice—strange tongues, entrancing smells, and a dozen Cali-fornia markets.*

the Bay of Beaulieu and the Reserve's own private yacht harbor. Come winter, the guests are preserved inside a glass dining room next to the terrace. The Reserve has some forty rooms, all designed in different motifs, and all spanking new. Work on the establishment ceased at the time of the German occupation, and was resumed after the war. Since it opened, in July, 1946, La Reserve's fancy threshold has been crossed by many a celebrity. Rita Hayworth, who must have been the most ubiquitous tourist France has ever known, stayed here.

La Reserve's magnificent moon-swept terrace was the scene of a famous meeting between Lord Beaverbrook and the Duke of Windsor.

After a lavish meal, lubricated by many old vintage wines, somebody acting under orders steered the Duchess out under the palms, and the other guests wandered off to leave Beaverbrook and Windsor by themselves. Nobody knows what the conference was about, but the eavesdroppers did manage to catch the opening sally. Said the Duke to the Lord: "How in the world do you manage to eat in a place like this on the allowance the British government permits today?"

The last French outpost before Monaco is the resort of Cap d'Ail, surmounted by the famed Hôtel Eden. Cap d'Ail means "Garlic Cape," a linguistic technicality that hasn't deterred the Eden from attracting more movie stars than Warner's commissary.

Monaco is an independent principality crammed into a tiny strip of land along the Côte d'Azur. It has two cities, Monaco and Monte Carlo, whose square, red houses are stuck all over the surrounding hillsides like those of a Hollywood set for a low-budget picture. Monaco has no income tax and no customs barriers, and its entire life revolves around one industry—gambling. It is a toy, make-believe, candy-box land, of which William Gaxton must be king and Victor Moore chief of police, with music by Rodgers and Hammerstein.

Actually, the country is governed by a prince who has a palace by the sea. Red and white sentry boxes that look as though they were copied from Otto Soglow's cartoons stand on either side of the palace gate. The entrance is protected by a footman decorated in yellow and green, and two musical-comedy guardsmen done up in costumes by Brooks with blue bobbies' helmets splattered with encrusted seals, scarlet epaulets, red and white fourragères, and a red and blue tunic and trouser combination that makes Roxy's doorman look like a pallbearer. They carry huge rifles with fixed bayonets, and when the Princess, fresh from a cocktail party at Cannes, comes swooping onto the palace grounds in her new convertible Cadillac, the whole shebang snaps to attention so you can hear it rattle in Corsica, 107 miles across the open sea. Said a Frenchman who viewed the spectacle

*The Palace at Monaco—"William Gaxton must be king . . . Victor Moore, chief of police. . . ."*

recently: "Next war don't bother sending help; we'll use the Monaco guard."

Some of the local take has been sunk into an extensive Oceano-graphic Museum built by the reigning family as an absolution of guilt and the indulgence of a hobby. It's a little out of character with the tempo of the place, but if you are so inclined it's worth a look.

Around the bay, where the Prince's fine yacht often rides at anchor, lies Monte Carlo, a city built to patronize pleasure. It has two sporting clubs, seven hotels, a beach, a pool, two dozen superb tennis courts, and a two-season program packed with auto races, flower battles, swimming meets, fashion shows, concerts, open-air ballets, water carnivals, and a social schedule that would flap the wings off the hardiest social butterfly.

The city is also the seat of the Monte Carlo Casino—biggest, fanciest, most fabulous, most refined den of iniquity in the world. To get inside its great hallowed, high-ceilinged halls, guests must show a passport, and slap down a fee of twenty francs for admittance to the public rooms, fifty francs to play in semi-privacy. The passport check was instituted by the Prince as a way of refusing entrance to residents of Monaco and surrounding areas. Of course, explains the gatekeeper, people owning villas are admitted. The rule is designed to keep "salaried people" from gambling away their wages. Another Casino rule prohibits women from entering if dressed in shorts, but the management confides that if you're a big spender you can get in that way, too. Barbara Hutton Mdivani Haugwitz-Reventlow Grant Troubetzkoy did.

The great ornate building, muralled, mirrored, and hung with sparkling chandeliers, was built by no less a personage than the architect Garnier, who also planned the Opéra in Paris. It costs 1,000,000 francs a day to run the place, nobody ever committed suicide there, and nobody ever broke the bank, either. We had all this on the word of Monte Carlo's manager who wades through all the marble, the marquetry, and the money while smoking cigarettes which he rolls himself.

Lines of old ladies form in front of the Casino each morning as if a hat sale or a garden club convention were going on inside. When the doors open at ten, they make a bargain-basement dash for their favorite seats—and a sharp fingernail and a finely honed tongue for anyone who gets in the way. Later come the fine old biddies, trimmed in lace collars, combs perched on their gray, grandmotherly heads, glasses extended out on their noses as if they were about to focus on a good old hymn. In they toddle on the arms of uniformed attendants. They sit down in seats they've held as long as the family plots. Then they pull out colored pencils, pads, and rulers, and mark each play and record their every bet. Around them swirl the gay sporting women, the cultured accents, the expensive scents, the clack of chips being raked in, and the smoke which streams from the long cigarette holders clamped in the teeth of sleek, patent-leather Balkan men.

The big Monte Carlo Casino is neither too blasé nor too business-like to make a fuss over the celebrities who come to try their luck. Faithfully preserved among the management's souvenirs are autographs that read:

> The Happy Loser
> Ha! Ha! Ha!
> Bob "13" Hope

"I've been robbed." Jerry Colonna.

Monte Carlo was officially off limits for military personnel during the war, but officers who were influential enough could be admitted with a pass. M.P.'s were stationed at the door, and at least one American colonel was slapped with a stiff fine for arriving without a pass. There is evidence, however, of the visits of an amazing number of generals, among them General Ben Lear, Lieutenant General W. H. Simpson, Commander of the Ninth Army, and Brigadier General Charles M. Busbee.

A number of Congressmen, presumably overseas to investigate war conditions or the post-war food problem, carried on at least some of their research in the Monte Carlo Casino. In case their constituents may be interested, the calling cards of these lawmakers are on file over there now: William E. Hess, Donald C. Cook, Lyndon B. Johnson, and W. Sterling Cole. Jean Brunner, Commander-in-Chief of the Veterans of Foreign Wars, did a little investigating, too, and so did one Colonel Michael Grimaldi, once of the 305th Quartermaster Battalion, now removed to 526 East Monroe, Springfield, Mo. The colonel discovered that he possessed the same family name as that of the royal house of Monaco. When the Prince found it out, he received the colonel like a long-lost cousin.

During the war days, youngsters in the neighborhood used to peddle the Casino's chips to the soldiers as souvenirs. They were getting three cigarettes a chip until someone discovered the merchandise was counterfeit. The Casino, meanwhile, was having its own difficulties with souvenir hunters. Officers with duly accredited passes were buying chips at the gaming tables, and purposely neglecting to cash them in upon leaving. Each month the house was losing that way 30,000 chips, every one of which contained a sizable chunk of silver.

Monte Carlo has six hotels of its own. The Old Beach and the New Beach are open for the summer season, the Nouvel, Hermitage, and Grand for the winter season. The great old Hôtel de Paris, across the street from the Casino, which has been in business since 1875, is open all year round. It has closed only once in its history, in June, 1940, when Italy declared war on France.

Although nearly every crowned head of Europe has rested on its fluffy pillows, the Paris is proudest of the fact that it is the only hotel in the world connected with two casinos by an underground tunnel.

Besides the royalty, the Hôtel de Paris has been host to Churchill, Beaverbrook, Anthony Eden, and others whom the management calls "nearly all the members of the Third Republic." Sir Basil Zaharoff, Lord Rothermere, and the omnipresent Aga Khan have put up there. So have Gracie Fields and her husband, Monte Banks, Barbara Hutton, Charlie Chaplin, Mary Pickford, and both Douglas Fairbankses. One patron, the Count de Keralhallet, has been coming every summer since 1892.

The old Paris is that kind of hotel. It is downright sentimental about its fine and faithful guests who pay top Riviera prices for good rooms facing the sea and three very square meals. In the archives of the house are some priceless photo albums depicting the great personalities of the world, who, decade after decade, for some seventy years, have signed the register of the Hôtel de Paris. Here is the Aga Khan, again, almost arrogantly debonair in straw hat, spats, cane, and cultivated mustache. Paderewski in white Panama, J. Pierpont Morgan, Lloyd George, and W. K. Vanderbilt. Tod Sloan in a somber derby posing in a paddock, and Gaby Deslys in a great picture hat, pearls down to her waist, and a satin dress down to her ankles, proof that the new look is old. In a snap-brim hat and carrying a walking stick is the French playwright Francis de Croisset, strolling with Albert Wolf, and on the next page Mme. de Croisset and Marthe Brandes, both done up in styles of the early twentieth century. The de Croissets' son, Philippe, is now head of the French tourist offices in the United States.

It was a gay old Riviera, even in those days. Times change, skirts plunge, people and money come and go, but nobody ever gets tired of pleasure. In 1946, the first full post-war year, visitors from some thirty nations came to the Côte d'Azur by car alone. They included, besides the usual European representations, tourists from China, Turkey, Iran, and even Russia. Cannes, during its first full post-war summer, already showed an increase in visitors over 1938. As somebody named Pierre Frondaie has written in a travel folder put out by the Principality of Monaco: "In the spring the young earth blossoms in the gardens. In the summer, sea breezes float over the terrace and lend to the very heat the quality of iced cocktails."

Yessir, that's the Riviera, right down to the last ice cube.

# CORSICA

*An hour from the Riviera, a new Cuba.*

# 10. CORSICA

◇◇◇◇◇◇◇◇◇◇◇◇◇◇◇◇◇◇◇◇◇◇◇◇◇◇◇◇◇◇◇◇◇◇◇◇◇◇◇◇◇◇◇◇◇◇◇

STANDING on the heights over Monte Carlo, on a clear day you can look south across a hundred miles of Mediterranean, and see the mountains of Corsica silhouetted against the sky.

Tourists used to come to Corsica in small steamers which took nine hours to negotiate the journey from Nice, twelve hours from Marseilles. Corsica today could well become the Cuba of the Riviera. Service by Air France takes little over an hour from the mainland. After the lacquered luxury of the Riviera, Corsica is rough, refreshing, and unexploited. The island is 110 miles long, 50 miles wide, and 650 miles around. About one-seventh of that territory is forest. A good deal of the rest is covered with wildbrush called "maquis," a name tacked on to the underground bush fighters of the French resistance during the late war.

Corsica is most beautiful in Spring when the maquis blooms in white and pink and blue and violet, growing so high sometimes that the blossoms can conceal a man on horseback. In September the maquis gets dry, turns brown, and burns easily. Often the shepherds who roam the hills with flocks of sheep and goats deliberately set the brush on fire; the ashes and rain water make a fertilizer that grows a verdant pasture land in two years.

Nestling in semi-tropical lushness in the middle of the Mediterranean, Corsica produces cork, chestnut wood, and chestnut dye extract, asbestos, yellow and green marble, olives, limes, tangerines, and melons. There is also a pretty active industry in briar pipes which are made from maquis roots and carved into heads of Napoléon, who was born on the island. Cap Corse, the aperitif, comes from Corsica. It is made from Corsican wine mixed with quinquina bark and sugar. That mess is allowed to settle for three years, and the clear liquid that is filtered off is called Cap Corse. It is served with cracked ice, soda, and lemon peel.

But the favorite drink of the island is still Pastis, which has been described elsewhere on these pages as a licorice concoction to be mixed with water and sipped. The Corsicans have not forgotten how American soldiers tossed off the stuff straight, no water added.

The Corsican peasant is a versatile fellow with a chestnut. The nuts are ground into a flour from which is made a pudding called *polenta.* If you take the word of the local gourmets, it is best when eaten with ripe goat and sheep cheese. When the chestnut-flour paste is dropped into hot óil, as we fry a doughnut, you have *beignets,* a pastry eaten with sugar, but when the same batter is baked into round, flat cakes, sprinkled with ground almonds, and eaten hot from the oven, it becomes *tortas.*

Although the chamber of commerce of Roquefort, France, will never admit it, most of the cheese that is sold all over the world under the name of that city is originally prepared in Corsica. The natives make it from sheep's milk, mixing in a fair amount of bread crumbs. The preparation is sent to Roquefort, where it is aged for five or six months in the caves of the Cevennes Mountains, until the bread takes on the green and black mould characteristic of the cheese.

Corsican men like to wear their coats over their shoulders, and sometimes even affect black capes, which makes them all look like old-style Corsican bandits. Up in the hills Corsicans wear dark corduroy coats, black felt hats, striped shirts, and red flannel cummerbunds three yards long. They smoke Corsican briar pipes which are usually half-hidden in the brush of huge beards, ride donkeys all over the place,

*Corsican peasants are also "pretty versatile . . . with a chestnut."*

*"Up in the hills . . . dark corduroy coats, black felt hats, striped shirts, and red flannel cummerbunds three yards long. . . ."*

"... *on the kitchen table* ... eau de vie...."

and make a big megillah about inviting you over for a drink of *eau de vie*, which is always handy on the kitchen table. A mild, sticky liquid, *eau de vie* is nothing but home-made brandy, the condensation of boiled wine with prunes or cherries added for flavor.

Although they are slow, inherently indolent, shy of new production methods, Corsican farmers grew rich during the war on crops of artichokes, cauliflower, and beans. Many own huge flocks of sheep, goats, and pigs, and lately have gotten into the habit of flying over to the mainland on business deals, and returning to the hills with their pockets bulging with wads of francs.

Herds of sheep graze on the fringes of the airport, and goats are all over the place. Pigs are allowed to root wild, too, and they have developed black hides and long snoots quite like wild boars. Some twenty kilometers from Ajaccio you can actually hunt boars in their native habitat. It's not on the official schedule but the Ajaccio Syndicat d'Initatives will arrange safaris.

In all of Corsica there is probably one hotel only that can honestly be termed first-class. Inevitably called the Napoléon Bonaparte, it is located at Ile Rousse, contains 150 rooms, each with a private bath, and is perched three hundred yards from a sand beach two miles long. Unfortunately, to reach Ile Rousse it is necessary to take a plane to Bastia (45 minutes from Nice), then go by train and bus.

The accepted tourist center of the island is the city of Ajaccio, main stop in Corsica on the Air France route. Ajaccio (they say Ajaxeeo) is colorful and interesting, all right, and from a tourist standpoint it would be fine if only there were some good hotels and restaurants. As the local hotelkeepers tell it, Ajaccio's hotels were ruined by the war. And so they were. The war wrecked tourist facilities all over the world, but everybody has gotten around to rebuilding except the Corsicans. In Ajaccio travelers must rely on the ancient Continental, which is a shambles. All around the outskirts of the city are magnificent beaches, secluded, unoccupied, unused, never enjoyed. The Corsican lacks the ambition to develop the country, and he strongly resents the intrusion of outside labor or capital. There it stands.

Napoléon was born in Ajaccio, and the house has long since been bought by the government and turned into a national museum. Just a simple town lawyer when Napoléon was born, old man Bonaparte later became an *avocat general* when his son came into power. As everybody knows, Napoléon worked his way along during the French Revolution. As a lieutenant of artillery he was forced to flee Ajaccio because of political differences. He returned to his birthplace only once after that. It was after the Battle of the Pyramids in Egypt that he visited Corsica with his entire staff.

Quite a few Americans who were stationed in Corsica during the war married native girls. The American methods of courtship were rather revolutionary—especially in Ajaccio, where it has long been the custom for young people to show their wares by parading back and forth on the Avenue Napoléon every night between six and eight. In summer it lasts a little longer, and sometimes the crowd gets so thick it is virtually impossible to drive through in a car.

One of Ajaccio's new night spots is called the American Bar, and is a rather attractively furnished post-war café where everybody stops for coffee and a liqueur after dinner. Corsicans are great troubadours, and you can hear the real stuff at a place called Au Son des Guitares. Young Corsicans use the place as a club, and like to gather in the evenings, play their guitars, sing folk songs, and sip cognac sweetened with cube sugar from a shot glass. Most any night you can count on anywhere from two to fifteen guitars playing at once, and anyone who feels inclined just starts singing. Corsicans have fine, high-tenor voices, and all of them sound quite like Tino Rossi, a local boy who made good. A lot of the music is sung in Corsican dialect, and every third number is a militant thing called "L'Ajaccienne." It was origi-

*Les Roches Rouges—"in the lacy rock formation . . . a bleeding heart. . . .*

nally played to honor Napoléon's mother, but the Bonapartists adopted the song in 1947 and sang it as a paean to political victory over the Communists, who had held sway since the liberation.

The French railroads have a rather elaborate system of motor-car excursions in Corsica. Trips begin at Ajaccio or Bastia, and you can arrange your itinerary before arriving on the island, by applying to the Service d'Autocars S.N.C.F., 2 Rue Maréchal Joffre, in Nice.

Some of the classic tours take in the Greek village of Cargese, established at the time of the Turkish persecutions in 1676. Descendants of the original Greek settlers now speak a Corsican dialect, but a Greek Orthodox church still flourishes in a land otherwise strictly Roman

*Porto has "a lovely view . . . and a restaurant so informal as to be name-*
*less. . . ."*

Catholic.  Farther along on the twisting mountain roads are the red
rocks of Calanches.  Here, in the lacy rock formation, guides claim to
see a praying bishop, the head of Poincaré, and even a bleeding heart,
all fashioned by nature.  Between Cargese and Calanches is the Hôtêl
Les Roches Rouges, one of the better of the Hôtels Corse, an island
chain.  Porto has a lovely view and three restaurants, which has made
it a noon-time excursion stop.  One of the restaurants facing the sea—
so informal as to be nameless—has a soft spot in its heart for Americans.
The only daughter of the owner ran off with a lieutenant colonel, and
lives now in Hasbrouck Heights, N. J.—which is, no matter how you
measure it, a long pull from Porto.

*"What with daughters running off with Americans . . . it was a helluva war. . . ."*

Farther up the coast, Calvi is a pleasant seaside town founded by the Genoese in 1268. Across the island, on the eastern coast, lies Bastia, a commercial city that was badly battered in the war, and is hardly of tourist interest. Bonifacio, on the southern tip of the island, facing Sardinia, is a queer town built on sheer cliffs that overhang the sea.

There are, all told, some five natural mineral springs in Corsica, three of which run hot and contain iron and sulphur deposits. The largest, at Orezza, catered to sufferers from stomach maladies, but it was blown up by the Germans in retaliation for a little *malaise* engendered by the local maquis.

What with daughters running off with Americans, cities being bombed, hotels being requisitioned, Corsica had a helluva war. Between 1939 and 1945 everybody invaded the island but the Japanese. First it was the Italians, 70,000 of them. They were all shined up, and concentrated on making the girls. Then came the remnants of the German Afrika Korps, who arrived in a nasty mood and concentrated on throwing out the Italians. In September, 1943, when Italy collapsed, French troops, supported by the French fleet and the American Air Force, took over. Bastia was liberated on October 4, 1943. A couple of days later the Americans moved in with their baggage, and set up Air Command Corsica.

Although Allied-held Corsica sat in the sea only forty-five minutes from German-held Nice and an hour from Marseilles, the island was only bombed twice from October, 1943, until August, 1944. One German run, in May, 1944, was a dilly. It caught us unprepared, for a change, and Germans managed to shoot up a lot of aircraft and kill forty Americans, among them four nurses.

The palm-grown island will, nonetheless, always provide a nostalgic memory to a lot of members of the 63rd Fighter Wing, and the 312th and 323rd Bombardment Group, who used it as a pleasant place to bunk in, between runs over northern and central Italy, Austria, and Hungary.

Don't bring up the subject of war at the Hôtel Continental in Ajaccio, however. It was requisitioned by five different armies for six solid years, and the proprietors are rather unhappy about the whole thing.

THE ALPS

Annecy—"in spring great willows bend to brush the hair of lovers. . . ."

# 11. THE ALPS

THE mountain fastnesses of the French Alps hold great centers of winter sports, soft little summer resorts, and some places that double as both. This is snow country, lake country, mountain-climbing country. Geographically, it extends from Grenoble north to Geneva and the shores of Lake Leman, and bulges east to the Italian border.

From Paris the route into the Alps usually runs through Dijon, the mustard center, and Lyon, home of French silks. The southern approach from Nice across the mountains to Grenoble has been rendered historic by two military units, one headed by Napoléon and the other by Brigadier General Frederic B. Butler, United States Army.

Escaping from Elba in 1814, Napoléon made his way over the twisting, tortuous mountain roads to Grenoble in three days. So began his famous Hundred Days. In August, 1944, General Butler, heading a task force from the American 36th Division, made straight for Grenoble from the landing beaches, over the same Route Napoléon. Today it still takes one full day by S.N.C.F. bus from Nice or Cannes.

Like an oriental Buddha, Grenoble sits on a plateau 300 kilometers from the Riviera; it is completely surrounded by mountains. However, Latin tempers burn furiously in the cool mountain air of Grenoble. In 1789 the French Revolution was touched off by riots in Grenoble, and the city was also the seat of the most active French resistance groups during the late war. Maquis hidden in the nearby mountains raised merry hell with the Germans, who retaliated with

*The University of Grenoble—" 'Learn French while visiting in the Alps.' "*

some of the most outrageous atrocities of the war, including the murder of five professors from the University of Grenoble who were taken from their homes and shot.

Grenoble's famous seat of learning is a progressive institution that specializes in courses for foreign students. Soon after the city was liberated, on August 22, 1944, a GI educational program was set up at the University. It has proved quite successful. Particularly the program seems to endear Americans to the faculty, and the school authorities are looking forward to increased enrollment from the United States. In a land where higher learning is serious business, the sophomoric high jinks of Grenoble's students sometimes seem self-consciously collegiate. Classes are co-educational.

*Grenoble—Seventh Heaven had naked angels.*

The University sponsors excursions all over the neighboring resorts and as far afield as Cannes, Monte Carlo, and the Roman ruins in Provence. "Learn French while visiting in the Alps," says the University of Grenoble. It's a rather pleasant way, at that.

Comparatively modern apartments line some of the streets of ancient Grenoble, and there is a wide selection of hotels, of which the Moderne is perhaps the best. A cable car known as the "Telepherique de la Bastille" whips you across the River Isère to a lofty peak that looks down on Grenoble and the lands beyond. A restaurant called the *Septième Ciel*—Seventh Heaven—serves food and drink on the mountaintop. The ceiling is decorated with a lot of boys and girls I take to be angels, gamboling naked and unafraid among the stars. Perhaps that's supposed to be Seventh Heaven. Anyway, it's enough to give John Sumner, who suppresses vice in New York, a thumping case of apoplexy right on the spot.

Since Grenoble sends a lot of skiers into the resorts of the Alps, there are any number of sports shops in town carrying a complete line of equipment. Some of the best ski boots in the world are made near Grenoble, and they are available but expensive if you buy them without shoe-ration coupons. French after-ski boots for women are the smartest being shown on either side of the Atlantic, but likewise costly without tickets. Skis designed by Emile Allais, sold under the label of Allais-Rossignol, are among the best you can buy. Shoe harnesses, metal poles, heavy gabardine ski pants, gale cloth parkas, are all on hand.

Perrin gloves, a famous French brand, are made in Grenoble, and the company operates a retail outlet in town.

Virtually all the 150 resorts of the Alps are grouped in the Province of Savoy. Like Nice, Savoy has been a royal football for hundreds of years. When Charlemagne's empire was cut up, Savoy was part of Burgundy. In 1008, one Rudolph, King of Burgundy, gave Savoy to one of his generals, and that was the beginning of the House of Savoy. In appreciation of the active part played by Prince Eugène of Savoy in the Battle of Blenheim in 1704, and other skirmishes in Bavaria, the Duke of Savoy, at the Peace of Utrecht in 1713, got the island of Sicily. The Duke proclaimed himself King of Sicily, but five years later swapped the island for Sardinia, making the Dukes of Savoy also Kings of Sardinia.

During the French Revolution, Savoy went to France without a blow, but after Napoléon's downfall the Congress of Vienna returned the territory to the Kingdom of Sardinia, which was by then a part of Italy. Napoléon III and a French Army came to the aid of Italy when Austria made war in 1859. For the assistance rendered Italy, France wanted Savoy and Nice. In a plebiscite held in 1860, the people

*Savoy—"from the mountains come fresh trout, mountain smoked ham, and Alps honey. . . ."*

voted 130,533 to 255 in favor of returning to France. Italy ceded the provinces, and they have been French ever since.

A few nationalistic customs still remain in Savoy, but they seem to be disappearing. Men wear blue wool peaked hats rather than berets, a custom which seems to have been dictated by practicality instead of tradition. Savoy women, particularly the Tarentaise, affect a demure, heart-shaped coif embroidered with gold ribbons and bright colors, fringed silk shawls, and silk aprons. The young girls like to wear gold crosses. Because the days are short and the winter nights long, sport in winter in the Alps has narrowed down to sitting around a big log fire swapping stories. Often, in the remote regions, the tales are told in the local *patois,* which differs a good deal from the pure French of Touraine, for instance.

What in French would be: *Les grand peupliers tremblant et les haies ont des frissons,* in Savoyard becomes: *Lo grands poblo ont la gravoula et lo cize le frezon.*

It's an old Savoy proverb that says:

> Quand ma borsa fat tin-tin
> Tot le monde est mon cosin
> Mais quand le fat ta, ta
> Tot le mond s'en va.

These pessimistic words say that all the world is your friend when you're rich, but when you're broke everyone disappears.

Savoy produces certain wines, among them a bubbling white wine known as Crepy, something called Savoy roussette, and ayse, which is similar to Crepy.

Good restaurants in the Alps specialize in lake fish, particularly lavaret du Leman; fera, from Lake Annecy; and omble chevalier, from Lake Bourget and Lake Annecy. From the mountains come fresh trout, smoked ham, and Alps honey which has a characteristic flowery smell. The valley of Thones specializes in milk cheeses, particularly roblochon and tomme.

There are no less than thirty thousand guest rooms tucked away in the Alps, in imposing palace hotels and tiny mountain châlets. One of the best developed of the resorts is Aix-les-Bains, a watering place which sits in a valley at the so-called gateway to Savoy. The first man to take a bath at Aix was, most certainly, a Roman laborer employed by Domitius, who built the first spa on the site in 122 B.C. The King of Sardinia laid the cornerstone for another thermal establishment at Aix in 1776—which must have been a busy year all over the earth. Today there are two thermal stations at Aix, one built in 1857 and a new building put up in 1934. Both are owned and

*The baths at Aix-les-Bains—a bashful Queen of Sheba and the barefoot tread of the Duke of Windsor.* (Essi)

operated by the government, and so are called the Aix-les-Bains National Spas. Like French railway cars, steamships, and sailors, the baths at Aix are graded into classes. The old building, which is open all year round, is second and third class. The new building, open only in the summer, is reserved for first-class bathers.

Over a million gallons of water pour from Aix's spring every day, hitting the surface at nearly 115 degrees F. The spa has been famous for years because of its "Aix shower" and a treatment called the "Berthollet." In the "Aix shower" treatment a pair of muscular masseurs dressed in weird cotton jumpers give you a good working over for six minutes, spraying you meanwhile with a hoseful of hot sulphur water. Then the patient is wrapped in a *maillot*, a woolen bathrobe, and placed on a hot bed to induce what they like to call "sudation." Modern as tomorrow, the resort has masseurs who can massage under water, and there are also facilities for treating one limb at a time without requiring the patient to undress fully.

Berthollet was a Savoy chemist who developed a steam box powered by natural vapors. Patients sit in the "Berthollet cabins" completely boxed in except for the head, and are subjected to hot, damp air currents condensed from the natural hot springs.

Aix-les-Bains is often irreverently referred to as "aches and pains," principally because it deals in cures for rheumatism and gout. But in the new building there are a variety of trick showers, among them the submarine douche, for sciatica; the circle shower and the spinal shower, for nerves; the perineal shower for prostate trouble and pelvic congestions; and the hydrotherapy shower, a contraption of power hoses capable of giving a five-alarm blaze a thorough soaking.

If your attending physician has prescribed no "sudation," the original shower treatment is followed by a Scotch shower, which is alternating hot and cold sprays, finishing cold. It used to be that patients were wrapped in a wad of towels, placed inside a little covered carriage with long handles on either end, and carted off, like a bashful Queen of Sheba, to the dressing rooms, by a pair of porters. Now, if "sudation" is prescribed, the patient is wrapped like a mummy and put through a series of chambers to avoid catching cold, much as a diver is treated for the bends.

Among its other attractions the thermal station offers colonic irrigations with hot sulphur water, a *bain profond*, specially constructed for invalid patients, and nose and throat treatment with fine sulphur vapors which is followed by external massage. Hot mud bath treatments will soon be available, too.

The new building contains a standard Olympic swimming pool filled with fresh water, which is often the scene of swimming competition and water polo games. Actually, the first-class station was built on the very site of the Roman baths, and the building has been constructed so that the Roman excavations are enclosed in one large room. Two thousand years ago the Romans also had a swimming pool and their own steam bath. Bits of round and square Roman pipe can still be seen, Latin writing on the constructions is as clear as if it had been written the day before yesterday, and there are two fine examples of sculptured Roman and Greek heads still on display.

Some forty-odd doctors, many of whom are specialists, are attached to the thermal establishments. After a consultation with a patient, the doctor prescribes a specific treatment, and the patient reports to a masseur with his prescription. Masseurs, incidentally, are forbidden in three languages from taking tips.

Patients taking the cure at Aix are advised to drink from Aix's springs before lunch and dinner. Every morning and evening an orchestra plays outdoors at the St. Simon Pavillion while the guests flush their kidneys at the spring before going up to their hotels to eat.

Even before the war, Aix was extremely popular with royalty and the right people. Queen Victoria was a frequent visitor at Aix, and a statue in town commemorates her many visits. Victor Emmanuel II bathed here, and so did Napoléon III, Wilhelmina, George of Greece, and Leopold of Belgium. In the new building the government has built a royal bathing salon for distinguished guests. It has five rooms done in blue mosaic, and a bathtub worthy of Cecil B. de Mille. The shining tiles have known the barefooted tread of the Aga Khan, the Duke of Windsor, and Premier Herriot.

As long ago as 1910, Pierpont Morgan financed a public hospital at Aix called, directly enough, L'Hôpital Pierpont Morgan. There is also a boulevard by that name, and another honors Franklin Roosevelt. Americans and English alike have made a success of the resort. To this day the town officially celebrates Empire Day each May 24, and the Fourth of July as well.

*Revolving solarium at Aix-les-Bains, one of the three in the world.*

During the first World War, Aix became a rest center for American troops, much in the same manner as the Riviera was used in 1944. Most of the hotels contained American troops, and the activity centered about the magnificent casino called the Grand Cercle, which was run by the Y.M.C.A. One feature of the contract permitting the Y to use the building required the organization to rehire all the casino's employees. It was probably the only time in history that the Y.M.C.A. carried a supervisor of gambling on its payrolls.

Rebuilt in 1937, the Grand Cercle still maintains a tablet originally erected by the Y.M.C.A. "in appreciation of the hospitality of the citizens of this town during the great War." During the greater war that followed there was no damage to the fine, white building. Guests once more play boule, roulette, and baccarat under cover of a beautiful ceiling, placed in 1884, which would be a credit to a church. There is, of course, a restaurant, a gilded indoor theater, and one under the stars as well.

Aside from the Grand Cercle, Aix has a number of good restaurants, a nightclub called L'Amiral, a tea-room with tan plaster colonnades called La Rotonde, and an elevated solarium that each day rotates with the sun across the Savoy sky. The solarium looks like a windmill and is one of three of its kind in the world. Another is located at Cannes, and the third in India. The huge arms of the turning solarium are fitted with built-in mattresses on which patients relax and get the sun through vari-colored filters, depending on the vitamins they seek.

The town of Aix is very nearly on the edge of Lac du Bourget, which is eleven miles long and therefore the longest lake in France. Municipal bus service plies back and forth from the hotels to a land-scaped sand beach, which has lockers, floats, and diving towers. Sailboats and motorboats can be rented, and old paddle steamers ply up and down the soft waters making excursions to the Abbaye d'Hautecombe where the House of Savoy used to bury its royal dead.

A first-class hotel, called the Splendide, gets Aix's smart summer crowd. Its richly carpeted lobby, lined with heavy, blue marble columns, and showcases from the best Paris shops, is known as the Rue de la Paix. Its double-sized elevators, originally built to accommodate handicapped guests, are a favorite with Americans, who ordinarily find the match-box French elevators claustrophobic. Most of the Splendide's rooms open on white alabaster terraces overlooking the Alps, and an outdoor dance floor. The Splendide is run on an expensive American plan, but Aix can offer some five thousand other accommodations, in sixty hotels, at varying prices.

Thirty-three kilometers north of Aix is a nice old town called Annecy, which sits at one end of a quiet mountain lake. Canals flow

*Annecy—"canals flow under the ancient houses . . . making a kind of Venice in Savoy. . . ."*

under the red-tiled ancient houses, and thread their way through the old streets, making a kind of Venice in Savoy. In spring, great willows bend over to brush the hair of lovers who paddle flat-bottom boats under the Pont des Amours and out onto the lake.

Annecy can be real old-world. You can climb among the steep, narrow, cobblestoned streets, that look like Montmartre, or watch the townfolk clatter along on the sidewalks with arcades, built to protect citizens from the heavy winter snows. There are a broad selection of restaurants, lots of pastry shops, a modest casino, and one small-town nightclub concisely called Le Club. But on the edge of town a great, comfortable hotel rises quietly at the foot of the mountains, and casts a soft reflection on the lake which stretches out from its front door. It is

Up "among the steep cobblestoned streets that look like Montmarte, Annecy can be real Old World...."

called the Imperial, and it's a great place to get away from it all. Right alongside is a bathing club, and there are excursions up to the top of Mont Veyrier where you can see the French, Swiss, and Italian Alps all spread out on a platter. Annecy is only twenty-five miles from Geneva, and there is a Swiss consul in town—but more on this later.

During the pleasant summer evenings the shores of Lake Annecy are aglow with the lights of the picturesque inns. They deal in fine food and quaint settings. One is run by Leon Francis Ball, of Great Falls, Montana, a good-looking, balding young man who has an attractive wife and a blonde baby daughter smothered in curls. When Leon Francis Ball hitched up his parachute and prepared to jump into German-held Savoy in 1944, he knew he might not come out, but he never thought it would be like this. He had been yanked out of a combat division because he spoke fluent French. He had been sent to a school in London, and asked how he would like to be a spy. He would like it fine. He had been interviewed by a full colonel, who looked him straight in the eye and asked him a lot of questions. The colonel turned out to be the late General Patch, commander of the Seventh Army, who had borrowed the eagles so as not to arouse suspicion. Then, one night, Leon Francis Ball of Great Falls, Montana, became Monsieur Nivault, of Annecy, France, and he jumped into Savoy to organize the maquis.

The first day on the ground he met an attractive girl, who refused to believe he was French, but thought he was handsome, all the same. Somebody thought he was a German spy, and they called Dr. Picaud, a well-known Alpine surgeon who was an underground leader—and, incidentally, brother of Simone Picaud, the belle of the Riviera. The doctor observed that Nivault met often with a Frenchman who was known to have been in London the previous month. Nivault was cleared, and his mission assured. Around Annecy, today, nobody has ever heard of Leon Francis Ball, but a chap known merely as Nivault is a local hero.

The Imperial at Annecy "casts a soft reflection on the lake which stretches
out from its front door."

In summer, Nivault and his wife run her parents' hotel called Les Glaieuls, on the lake shore. In winter they go up to Mégève, where he has his own place, known as Les Alpettes. It is high up in the mountains, and to get there you have to take two cable cars and a ski tow. Here, in the deep snow and also in the warm spring sun, Ball and his wife serve lunch, on an outdoor terrace, to a ski crowd that usually numbers over a hundred every day. Ball still wears his army pinks and keeps his feet warm with loud argyles which Mrs. B. knits for him. His father-in-law is a Communist, and since Ball is still an out-and-out American, he says they spend hours making each other see the light of day. Otherwise, he thinks the life is much easier than it is in the States. Mrs. Ball likes things the way they are, too, excepting that the dashing parachutist is beginning to lose his hair. He's not as handsome as he used to be, she says.

Farther down the lake, at Talloires, is a famous old abbey built in the year 1,000 by Hermangarde, an early Queen of France. In the old days, the Benedictine monks established quite a reputation, not alone for their ecclesiastical efforts, but also because they could brew a tasty white wine called Vin de Talloires. Today the wine is still manufactured in the village, but the monks have long since gone. Sixty years ago the place was turned into an inn called Hôtel de L'Abbaye. There are sixty rooms, rather fancifully furnished, all on modest-price full pension. Specialties of the house are the desserts like "Merveille Abbaye," a concoction that would make a monk turn in his robe on the spot. Building on a base of biscuits, the chef adds vanilla, chocolate, and coffee ice cream in layers, then tops that with Creme Chantilly, with flaming brandy over all. Fish from the lake is a specialty, too, especially when stuffed with pâté foie gras and cooked in port, The season at the abbey opens the 15th of May, ends in October. When things get warm enough there is swimming, and most any time you can have dinner in the grape arbor by the edge of the lake.

As if this isn't pleasant enough, one of the best restaurants in France

*"The only thing that moves in a Mégève winter are . . . sleighs . . . baby carriages mounted on skis, and skiers themselves. . . ."*

is just up the road. It is the famous Chez le Père Bise, which is likewise open from Easter to October, takes in a few guests, and is quite expensive. It is right on the lake.

A lot of people try to compare the resorts of Chamonix and Mégève. There really is no comparison. Mégève is gay and cute and full of sun. Chamonix is older, more sedate, settled in a valley like a fine matron. Mégève is a new and sporty Alpine village, full of Tyrolean huts colored red, blue and yellow, and people so irreverent as to call their homes L'Igloo, or Châlet de L'Inconnu. The snow comes early in Mégève, piles up three to five feet high, and stays until April. The only thing that moves in the middle of a Mégève winter are horse-drawn sleighs painted in bright colors, baby carriages mounted on skis, and the skiers themselves.

The Nationale de Ski Français was started in Mégève by Emile Allais, now the foremost exponent in the world of the French method of skiing. Allais was born a son of a baker, became a baker himself, and turned to bicycle racing before trying skiing.

In Austria, and now in the United States and Canada, skiers practice the Arlberg technique, based on the basic snow-plow and stem-turn. As you might suspect, the French do it differently. Allais devised a turn effected with parallel skis, and proved his method by winning the world's championship three times. His system has become accepted as the French ski technique. Allais designed a red ski sold under his name, and spread his gospel in the resorts of Chile, and later in Canada.

The school he developed at Mégève now employs sixty teachers, nice-looking, smartly dressed young men, who spend their winters skiing with the wealthy, and their summers digging on farms. Guests can sign up for ski lessons in town and present their tickets on the slopes. They are started on easy inclines, then advanced to the ski tows, and finally to the cable cars that swing up through the peaks to Mont d'Arbois and the Rochebrune, which is the highest point in Mégève. High on top of the Rochebrune is the winter inn run by Nivault, the former American parachutist.

The oldest hotel in Mégève is the Soleil d'Or, which was originally a way station for stagecoaches going through the mountain pass on their way from Albertville. Second oldest is believed to be the Hôtel de Panorama, which has since been turned into a nightclub called Le Centra. Smugglers running the border at Geneva used to make their deals in laces and alcohol at the Panorama, and the place got to be rather well known as a rendezvous for picaroons.

Mégève came to be a ski resort in a roundabout way. In 1915, soon after the outbreak of the first World War, the Baroness de

Rothschild, a fiercely patriotic lady, was making arrangements for her customary winter sojourn in St. Moritz. This time, however, she demanded that her hotel be cleared of Germans. The management assured her it would bend every effort. The baroness arrived, but when she entered the dining room the first person she encountered was a famous German industrialist. Upon her insistence that the German leave the hotel, the management tactfully suggested to the gentleman that he indulge the caprice of the woman, and find quarters elsewhere. The German obliged, and according to one version, the next day he sent the baroness a box of flowers. Nonetheless, the patriotic lady was nettled, and said that it was a shame that France did not provide its own winter sports stations. Accordingly, the French Alps were forthwith scoured for an attractive village with sunny ski slopes.

If you'll have the word of what passes for the local chamber of commerce, the scourers picked Mégève, and there the baroness built the Hôtel Mont d'Arbois. The Rothschild family still owns the Mont d'Arbois, and it remains the plushiest hotel in town. During the recent war, false ownership papers were made out, and the hotel was assigned to a nonexistent syndicate that included the Carlton in Cannes, the de Paris in Monaco, and the Scribe in Paris. Things are back to normal now, the golf course is in good shape for the summer guests, and the cable car runs up to the slopes from the front door.

A typical winter day at Mégève begins at the ski school at nine. Skiers usually take three or four runs in the morning, then stop for a hot grog while waiting for the tow. Lunch outdoors if the highly advertised Mégève sun is shining, and back to the slopes until four. Everybody goes tea dancing in ski clothes at the Centra or the Isaba, which looks like an old Russian log cabin. Dinner at the hotels is usually late. Afterwards the crowd retires to the Casino, a pine-paneled emporium erected, with certain forethought, at the confluence of five roads. Should anyone wish to deviate from the normal schematic winter programs at Mégève, the Casino remains open twenty-four hours a day. There are also two ice skating rinks, one of which becomes a swimming pool in summer, and in nearby streams there is lots of trout fishing in season.

Besides the fancy Mont d'Arbois there are some twenty or more establishments of varying prices, of which the Hermitage is a rather comfortably moderate-priced institution.

For students on a budget an organization with the formidable title of Fonds Mondial de Secours aux Etudiants runs a vacation spot of its own at Combloux, just outside Mégève. Any foreign student is eligible to apply for a room in the hotel, which is called the Châlet International des Etudiants. The walls are plastered with photos of healthy looking young people who come down to Combloux for a week or two, and live in the châlet where all the rooms open on balconies that hang over the Alps. They ski in winter, go picnicking in summer, and participate in the student programs, all for about four dollars a day.

Chamonix bulges way over into the wedge of France that fits between Switzerland and Italy. It is a good forty miles east of Geneva, and farther east than a couple of unimportant towns in Italy. Deep and dank, it settles on the cellar floor of a valley completely surrounded by mountains. The mountains that provide the scenic surroundings also manage to keep out a lot of sun, a point emphasized by the people over at Mégève, but one which has never handicapped the development of Chamonix. It has more facilities for winter sports than any other resort in France, and a good deal more than most others in Europe. In 1924 it was the seat of the winter Olympics.

Oddly enough, Chamonix started as a summer resort, and a good many years ago at that. It first came to world attention when Jacques Balmat, all by himself, climbed nearby Mont Blanc, the highest peak in Europe. In the 1800's English climbers began to come to Chamonix in summer to try the 15,000-foot ascent to the top of Mont Blanc. In winter, however, they all turned to the Swiss resorts. By the early

*"The snow falls heavily around Chamonix, covering the châlets like a deep white frosting on gingerbread cake."* (G. Tairraz)

twentieth century, Chamonix became popular with the English for winter sports as well, and their presence is still reflected in the cold, rather bland architecture of the place.

In summer the resort offers climbing, walking, cable-car rides to the magnificent peaks, and a funicular railroad. Mountain climbers will find both glaciers and rocks at Chamonix. There are some one hundred and twenty accredited guides, many of whom have scaled the Rockies, the Himalayas, and some peaks between. For those who prefer milder sport there are a swimming pool, a golf course, tennis courts, and daily excursions to the Mer de Glace, a flat glacier between Chamonix and Les Pratz, which is viewed from a terrace 6,000 feet above sea level. There are three cable-car systems—called "telephe-

*Cable car station in Chamonix—from the top, a walk to Italy.*

riques" in France—which carry skiers in winter and outdoor enthusiasts in summer high among the hills. Le Brevent, directly facing Mont Blanc, sails upward to a height of 7,600 feet. The Telepherique des Glaciers swings you some 7,200 feet via two stages. A third stage is now under construction which will make the Telepherique des Glaciers the highest in the world. From the top of the new station it will be an hour's walk to a telepherique on the other side of the mountain that descends to Courmayeur, the Chamonix of Italy. A new ski run sixteen kilometers long will be developed, giving beginners an easy two-hour descent down the Vallée Blanche all the way to Chamonix. Meanwhile, workmen ride little baskets and two-plank platforms to the top of the construction. A watchman is assigned to each of the stations

*Chamonix's slopes—"with all the equipment . . . man-made and heaven-sent, it's possible to ski twenty miles cross-country."* (G. Tairraz)

of the telepherique system. All alone, stranded in the middle of the bitterly cold mountains for a whole week at a time, the lonely guardians spend most of their time reading. One of their favorite books is *Kabloona,* a story of life in the North.

Up in the barren, frozen heights there's more activity than one might expect. At 3,600 meters a bearded French scientist lives alone, studying the effect of cosmic rays. Nearby, they are back at work again on the Mont Blanc Tunnel, a project that has been under discussion for forty years. Engineers plan to bore eight miles through the middle of Mont Blanc from Chamonix to Courmayeur, making a direct link between Paris and Rome. The plan will also permit Italy to provide electricity from its ample resources to France, which is habitually short on current in winter. Work on the Italian side began in 1945, and is progressing at the rate of one kilometer a year.

The third telepherique of Chamonix is called Les Houches Belle-vue, and it was built expressly for winter sports. A small cozy hotel, newly remodelled, it is perched very high, and attracts students and ski clubs. Les Houches has a ski tow, the French Air Force tests airplane parts nearby, and the site was also the location of the Gainsborough film "Rescue," based on the successful recovery of the American plane that was wrecked in the Swiss Alps shortly after the war.

In case anyone keeps track of such addenda—the skating rink at Chamonix is the biggest in Europe. You can have lunch, served by skating waiters, right on the ice. Skiing guests on pension can make some arrangement with their hotels for lunches at the slopes. No eating arrangements for bobsledders or ski jumpers, but there are plenty of facilities for such horseplay all the same.

The snow falls heavily around Chamonix, covering the châlets like a deep, white frosting on a gingerbread cake. On the high slopes the snow often stays as late as May, when the girls go skiing in bras and short shorts. With all the facilities in the area, man-made and heaven-sent, it's possible to ski twenty miles cross-country to Mégève. The trip includes locomotion via telepheriques, downhill ski runs, funicular railway, and tows.

Chamonix has some two dozen hotels, most of which are open on a dual-season basis. The largest is the Majestic, which is off by itself in a quiet little setting. Opened in 1919, the Majestic's first customer was the Y.M.C.A., which took the place over as a rest camp for American troops. When the winter Olympics were held at Chamonix in 1924, the Majestic was official headquarters, and there are some people around the place who remember Sonja Henie making her first public appearance that year. During the second World War the Majestic became a German hospital, and on August 17, 1944, the FFI accepted the German surrender in the lobby. By spring, the Majestic was back to being a rest home for Americans again.

It got to be pretty gay in the war. Every Monday, Wednesday, and Friday night, and every Sunday afternoon, there was a big party in the Majestic's immense ballroom. Major Glenn Miller, leading his sixty-piece band, played the Majestic just before he was lost over the Channel. It was one of his last engagements.

Since the war, the Majestic has modernized its lounge, and has brightened up the foyers that look out over the Alps. They expect a lot of Army people to come back, and many have returned already.

The Savoy is a smaller but equally elegant establishment, that likes to take its guests for not less than a week at a time. Moderately expensive, the Savoy lowers its rates in summer, but always has its own orchestra playing for tea dancing and after dinner, and manages to run three galas a season, with formal dress required.

It was an officers' rest home during the late war, and once seven generals ate together in the dining room, a fact that left a rather lasting impression. Patton once sent a resplendent aide down to look things over, but the old man never showed up himself. A twenty-piece GI orchestra, which was stationed in Chamonix, played often at the Savoy. Naturally, the officers only invited those among the French youth who were girls, a narrow choice that left the French boys frothing at the mouth.

The Savoy has particularly fond remembrances for the American troops, principally because they brought in gasoline for the tractors and lawn mowers, and got the golf course in shape long before it might have been refurbished had the French been left to their own devices. The Savoy also offers an open-air terrace that faces south directly on Mont Blanc, two tennis courts, and a ski lift that rises just about out of the backyard.

Three brothers—Charles, Jules and André Lavaivre—get an awful lot of fun out of life running the four-star Grand Hôtel Alpes, and their own nightclub next door called L'Outa. The hotel holds 150, and about half the rooms have private baths. The service is excellent, and the same customers have been trekking back for years. L'Outa has outdoor tea dancing in summer, and is very gay during the four-till-eight tea time in winter.

Probably nobody on either side of the Atlantic wears more campaign ribbons than the Grand Hôtel Alpes. First came the French troops in 1939. Then, for a short spell in 1940, the English arrived to train for service in Scandinavia. Soon the place was swarming with Italian Alpine troops decorated with feather plumes in their hats, who kept busy serenading the girls. When Germany drove eastward, the Nazis turned the hotel into a hospital for the treatment of eyes frozen on the Russian front. There was a spell with the FFI, inevitably the hard-drinking GIs arrived for a rest, and the occupation finished with the British who liked their mustaches and their brandy, and were always inviting you to join them in an ABL—the "absolutely bloody last."

No less than fifty bottles of cognac a night were being sold, drink by drink, over the bar of the hotel during that fateful summer of 1945 when the Americans were around. In August, when V-J Day arrived, the Lavaivre boys held a hasty consultation. They decided, to hell with the furniture, the devil with the cost, this was a night to celebrate. They ordered drinks on the house—a free bar—for the whole night, and then they retired to await the worst. As it turned out, V-J night was the quietest night in the history of the Americans' stay at the hotel. By 7 P.M. not a soul stirred. Everybody had passed out.

There was nothing very pleasant about the war that went on in and around Chamonix. Before the shooting had even begun in 1939, a band of Italian fascists climbed Mont Blanc, planted the Italian flag, and renamed the peak Mont Mussolini. The next day the flag was gone.

The maquis thereabouts were busy during the whole war ferrying

*Casino in Chamonix—for the Americans, fifty bottles a night.*

English and American pilots across the mountains into Switzerland, and so eventually back to England. After the FFI liberated Chamonix, they encamped on top of the glaciers all during the fall and winter of 1944-45, twice engaging the Germans. The second battle must have been one of the most eerie of the war. The Germans wore their customary white uniforms. The FFI was outfitted the same way, in uniforms stolen from the Nazis. One night the two forces met in the fog on top of a snow-covered glacier.

Sports-conscious Chamonix inaugurated the post-war sports season with a skiing competition of English, American, and French military teams, in the winter of 1946. The Americans, who were looked upon as supple, but unskilled, took the meet.

Like Mégève, Chamonix has some fine shops for ski equipment. Much of the sportswear is quite highly styled, and probably the ski stations have a bigger selection than you will find in Paris. One store is owned by Harold Snell of Douglas, Kansas, a wrinkled doughboy left over from the first World War. He came over in 1918 as a private first class with the 7th Division. While on leave he met one Marthe Devouassoud, whose father manufactured cow-bells, and it was love at first sight. He went home after the war, but got kind of lonesome, as one may do in Kansas, and came back three years later to claim the cow-bell heiress as his own. He hid in a monastery during the German occupation, and was liberated by three American tanks. He returned to open his shop in Chamonix, which became a lively trading post for exchanging cigarettes for merchandise when the American Army moved in. But he speaks perfectly awful French.

Aside from the famous resorts, there are perhaps fifty other vacation spots in the Alps that offer comfortable if not extensive facilities. Evian on Lac Leman has a fine beach, tennis, an 18-hole golf course, water skiing, a climbing school, and thermal baths. Evian bottled mineral water is sold all over France. A mile away is Amphion-les-Bains, yet another spa. Annemasse, five miles from Geneva, offers sightseeing. Morzine has winter sports, and clean, high air. You can ski at Val d'Isère, Peisey-Nancroix, Les Gets, Praz-sur-Arly, Nôtre Dame de Bellecombe, St. Gervais, and also at Les Contamines, which calls itself the little resort with the big snow.

\*    \*    \*    \*    \*

*Geneva.* Sitting as it does, up there on Lac Leman, forty minutes from Annecy and ten minutes from the border, Geneva seems more a part of French Savoy than it does of Switzerland. It was French until 1815.

In the first post-war years, when times were difficult in France, Switzerland had everything. Going from one country to the other would perhaps be like traveling, at the height of the wartime shortages in the United States, from a rationed New York to a ration-free Yonkers. In the desert of Europe's barren shelves Switzerland was an oasis of croissants and brioches. Its shops are usually stocked with piles of baked goods, chocolates, oranges, grapefruit, bananas, and green vegetables. In the restaurants the bread is white and the beer is creamy. There is soap in the washrooms, and there are towels on the rack.

Along Geneva's prim streets, stern-faced, cape-covered policemen direct the bustling traffic (exacting more acquiescence to authority than Toscanini gets from his fourth violinist). At the officers' commands the gangling hordes of bicyclists stop and start with almost military precision.

Yet Switzerland is no police state. The life is free, but the Swiss have visited upon themselves a certain self-discipline which has indeed paid off. Signs in mosaic tiles cemented in the sidewalk remind citizens not to spit in the street. It is against the law to blow your auto horn. New, massive, shining steel trolley cars skim quietly over the rails. American cars are everywhere, and there is no rationing of gas.

The good Swiss burghers are well fed, well dressed, healthy, content. They do not have the trudging step of other post-war Europeans. They walk with assurance, on well heeled shoes, over clean pavements. Their stomachs are well filled. They are as full of solicitude for you as Grover Whalen welcoming a king. They thank you for coming into their shops, thank you for buying, thank you for just browsing. Even the purchase of a three-cent paper is worth a bow and a greeting, and you are struck suddenly with the realization that not only are you a customer in a customer's market, but that here in Europe you have found someone who is content with his lot.

To keep their country prosperous, the Swiss make a big effort to draw tourists to their lakeside summer resorts and winter ski stations. Americans are invited to exchange a limited number of travelers' checks at favorable rates.

No visas are needed for Americans entering Switzerland, but it is necessary, nonetheless, to stop at the border and present your regular passport. Persons crossing from France, Americans included, are not permitted by French authority to take more than a stipulated amount of francs into Switzerland. It is a wise precaution to check French customs before arriving at the border. Persons attempting to cross with too many francs may be required to deposit the excess with the customs, against receipt. (It's a fancy trick, trying to get the wad back at some other customs house.)

Coming back from Switzerland, if you have just crossed for a short visit, you are not permitted more gas in your car than you had when you left France. It almost seems like an import tariff to protect the black market in gasoline, but that's the French law. There are further rules—about chocolate, baked goods, and cigarettes—which vary from time to time.

Swiss tobacco shops carry a bigger selection of foreign labels than the cloakroom at the U.N. All brands of American cigarettes are available at about double the States price, or one-third the cost in France. Unknown brands of blended Turkish and American tobaccos are normal United States price for known brands. Every other store sells watches, and the prices are about half of what you would pay in the States. It is possible, for example, to buy a gold-filled, seventeen-jewel chronometer, with second hand and stop-watch mechanism, for 122 francs, or about $30. For $50 you can get a watch that tells the month, day and year, and, incidentally, the time.

As most everywhere else in the world, the luxury life comes high in Switzerland. But a good, substantial, middle-class restaurant, with potted palms, rathskellar tilings, and racks of newspapers for regular patrons, advertises a fixed-price lunch for just about what you would pay at a similar place in the United States. A ten per cent tip is automatically added to your check, by custom. If you leave the waiter an extra amount, he may protest and say, in good English, "If that's for me, sir, I want to let you know that I have already charged you for service."

(In Toots Shor's tabernacle, nobody ever had it that good.)

# BURGUNDY

*"On its slopes . . . the finest, richest, most famous, and most expensive wines of France. . . ."* (Julius Wile)

# 12. BURGUNDY

◇◇◇◇◇◇◇◇◇◇◇◇◇◇◇◇◇◇◇◇◇◇◇◇◇◇◇◇◇◇◇◇◇◇◇◇◇◇◇◇◇◇◇◇◇◇◇◇◇◇◇

ALTHOUGH Burgundy is often called the Côte d'Or, it posseses neither coastline nor gold—unless you count the harvest of its grapes. Burgundy lies southeast of Paris, towards Switzerland, and on its slopes grow grapes that produce some of the finest, richest, most famous, and most expensive wines of France. Also, from the Cassis, a black currant, it distills a liqueur known as crème de cassis.

The capital of Burgundy is Dijon, an old city en route from Paris to Geneva. There is one fairly good place to stay in Dijon, the Hôtel de la Cloche, a broad-beamed, roomy old establishment with an attractive, modern dining room that serves good, expensive meals. In the center of the country that produces some of the most famous wines in the world, Dijon has established its own reputation as the hot mustard center of the world. It exports white porcelain jars, full of French mustard, to all parts of the world.

While nominally not tourist country, Burgundy has a big attraction in the importance it places on the production of good food and drink. The hills of the Côte d'Or, entirely given over to wine production, extend nearly forty miles south and southeast of Dijon. The Dijon-Corton section produces the wines of the Côte de Nuits; Corton-Santenay, the Côte de Beaune. The origin of fine wines is what every visitor to Burgundy should know. Here is where the rich red Burgundies come from:

| *Côte de Nuits* | *Côte de Beaune* |
|---|---|
| Chambertin | Aloxe Corton |
| Clos de Bèze | Pernand |
| Clos de Tart | Beaune |
| Musigny | Pommard |
| Clos de Vougeot | Volnay |
| Grands Echezeaux | Chassagne |
| Romanée Conti | Santenay |
| Richebourg | |
| Nuits de St. Georges | |

Burgundy also produces excellent white wines, among them such famous labels as Montrachet and Meursault.

As for the application of Burgundy wines, local intelligence suggests this formula:

> With soups and hors d'oeuvres:
> Aligotes de Beaune and de Nuits
> Pinot Rose de Marsannay
> With fish and shellfish:
> Montrachet, Meursault, Corton Charlemagne, Chablis
> With entrees:
> Beaune, Pommard, Volnay
> With roasts and game:
> Chambolle, Musigny, Vosne Romanée
> With cheese:
> Romanée Conti, Chambertin, Musigny, Clos Vougeot, Corton, Richebourg

Although eating and drinking is a serious business to everyone inside the confines of the Côte d'Or, nobody takes it more seriously than a fraternal order known as the Confrérie des Chevaliers du Tastevin, a world organization for the worship of wine. The universal headquarters of the Tastevin is located at Nuits St. Georges, just outside Dijon.

"... *what every visitor to Burgundy should know.* ..." (Julius Wile)

Once every two months the local order meets in the Château du Clos Vougeot, an eleventh-century castle surrounded by vineyards stretching as far as the eye can see. Banquets are held in a grand hall which has a gravel floor and columns decorated with flowers placed in gourds which once held wine. The best wine years of history are commemorated on the columns; among them are 1108, 1371, 1499, 1551, 1660, and 1947. A big sign at one end of the hall says *Jamais en vain, toujours en vin,* the slogan of the Tastevin brotherhood, meaning, "Never in vain, always in wine."

Across the courtyard tourists can see three primitive wine presses dating from 1249, and wine vats from the same period. The original kitchen of the castle, nearly twenty-five feet wide, is now filled with stoves used to prepare the banquets of the Tastevin.

When the Chevaliers of Tastevin meet at the castle, the brothers in good standing deck themselves out in square hats, long red and gold robes trimmed with ermine—all very ecclesiastical. Suspended from their necks by a bright colored ribbon is the *tastevin,* a small silver dish, badge of the society, ostensibly used for tasting wine. Costumed heralds announce with a fanfare of trumpets the arrival of the officers of the Tastevin. During the banquet, the Cadets of Burgundy sing Latin odes to the glory of the grape. At each ceremony the Chevaliers du Tastevin initiate into the order a few chosen diplomats, politicians, writers, and artists. A new American ambassador always rates a reception, a custom which began with the introduction of Ambassador Bullitt in 1936. The society has a chapter in the United States, which meets from time to time at the Waldorf-Astoria, the Ritz, or the St. Regis, in New York. One of its members was the late Selmer Fougner of the New York *Sun,* a grand gourmet whose *tastevin* was later taken up by no less qualified a wine taster than Lucius Beebe of the New York *Herald Tribune.* Once, when the Chevaliers were meeting in New York, photographers and researchers from an American magazine descended upon the banquet hall, explained the great publicity value of their publication, and insisted that the ceremonies of initiation be put on before the banquet was served instead of afterwards, as planned. With a cold eye, Fougner rose and asked them: "Do you suppose for one minute that the Chevaliers du Tastevin would take a chance of spoiling this gastronomical masterpiece which the chef is ready to serve us?" He added, coldly, "If you can't come back for the ceremonies, make it some other time." The astonished journalists retired from the hall, and in an official report to headquarters in France the head of the Tastevin fraternity in New York made note of this brave "act of respect for the principles of gastronomy," in the teeth of prevailing American mentality. "It was a performance worthy of elevating the entire brotherhood to a pedestal," he wrote to the head office in Burgundy.

At Beaune, thirty-five kilometers south of Dijon, visitors are permitted to see the famous hospital, the most artistic edifice in Burgundy, which dates from 1443. The roof is, unexpectedly, decorated with iron spires and red, yellow, black, and green shingles. It is now a charitable institution, but hardly any of the original architecture or appearance of the place has been changed. The nuns still skim, with almost imperceptible motion, across the red-cobblestoned courtyard. They wear huge, white, starched, unusual headgear. Even the pharmacy has retained its ancient mortars, pestles, and porcelain containers. The Beaune hospital supports itself, in the local tradition, by making wine which is the most expensive of all French vintages. An annual auction, held on the hospital grounds on the third Sunday in November, is an event among the wine makers of France. In a recent auction, the last before the revaluation of the franc, 224 barrels of red and white wine brought eighteen million francs.

The Hôtel de la Poste is a small hotel with a long list of testimonials. In the town of Beaune, visitors can buy woodcuts of wine cellar scenes, miniature wine casks, silver wine bottle holders, jugs, cups, and virtually any other appurtenance which aids in the dispensing of beverages. Tours of wine cellars are arranged by the tourist office in Beaune, and travelers who come in October can see the wine pressed and manufactured. Any time of the year, the Beaune office says, visitors can taste it.

However famous Burgundy is around the world as a well-spring of wine, the name originally derives from a tribe of people, the Burgundians. Any red-blooded Burgundian will raise a loud cry of protest at the mere suggestion, but, nonetheless, history indicates that the first Burgundians were Germanic. Like everyone else in those days, they got into a war with the truculent Germanic tribe known as Alamanni, and in 411 they took refuge in Gaul. The Burgundians developed the land in which they lived, and the chief towns emerged as Lyon, Besançon, and Geneva. The last King of Burgundy was Rudolph III,

*"In its history . . . a flow of dukes. . . ."* (Julius Wile)

"... at West Point ... slum and gravy. ..." (Julius Wile)

who was born in 993 and died in 1032. After fighting a war that lasted for some thirteen years, the French King, Robert II, united Burgundy to his kingdom. Later he gave the province to his son Henri, who sometime afterwards became Henri I. In 1032 King Henri I gave Burgundy to his brother Robert, and Burgundy was established as a duchy. Throughout its ensuing history Burgundy was almost as prolific in producing dukes as it was in making wine. The flow of dukes stopped, however, with the Treaty of Arras in 1482, when Louis XI, through a series of connivances, once more annexed Burgundy to the French crown. Louis XIV revived the title of Duke of Burgundy for a short time in 1682, but it didn't last. In recent years the fame of the dukes has been sustained for a time by the vocal efforts of Dennis King, an American singer who has probably said "to hell with Burgundy" more times than the defenders of the French crown whom the Burgundians were attacking. But even the militant air has lost its identity. It is now being sung as a rallying song by the cadets of the United States Military Academy at West Point under the ignominious title of "Slum and Gravy." The perpetuation of the glory of Burgundy rests with its grape-covered hills.

*"A girl who would say 'yes,' says yo-yo!"*

# 13. ALSACE

ALSACE is like somebody's cousin who has just come home from a far-off land where he has been visiting for a long time. He's the same boy all right—it's just because he has picked up so many foreign ways that you begin to wonder. Alsace and Lorraine, of course, have been over there, staying with the Germans, four years this last trip, and a good deal longer the time before that.

Not that this is something voluntary with the provinces, nor even something new. The Alsatians' destiny with the German boot dates all the way back to the first century before Christ. On and off, for over 2,000 years, German legions have battered Alsatian cities, and have treated the citizens with a curious mixture of persecution and patronization. The end result among the population is a marked respect for German efficiency methods, a bitter hatred of German character, and a secret, hopeless wish to be, like Luxembourg, a tiny, independent republic.

Of all the provincial groups that make up France, Alsace is perhaps the most closely knit, the most nationalistic, the most bound by language, custom, and common hardship.

Alsatians never inherited the austerity, the fierceness, the cruelty, the organization, the ambition, or the subservience of the German. Like the French, they enjoy living. Whatever German they have inherited has all been the whimsical oompah associated with beer bellies and German bands. Their language is a hopeless hodge-podge of

French, German, and who-knows-what, spoken at an incredible clip with a certain off-beat, hot-potato quality. A good many Alsatians don't speak anything else but the patois, although whole French and German words and phrases are substituted at will. One can hear a girl finishing a telephone conversation saying, "Ja, ja, ja, ja—merci." If an Alsatian asks someone to have a drink, that's *aner drinke*. A fellow who lives in old Strasbourg is *d'Steckelburger*. And if he exclaims, "Is that possible!" he says, "Allewaj!" A girl who says "yes" in Alsace says *yo-yo,* and *yo-yo* bounces all over the conversation like "uh-huh," "I'll say!" "Sure thing," and "o.k."

There is nothing an Alsatian likes better than a big, heaping platter of frankfurters and sauerkraut, which latter goes under the Gallic appellation of *choucroute*. Place names vary from towns as French as Ste. Marie aux Mines to such Teutonic handles as Abreshweiler, Molsheim, Marckolsheim, and Geispolsheim. A street in Colmar goes under the schizophrenic signpost of Rue Camille Schlumburg.

In Alsatian villages the houses are built with plaster, inlaid with old wooden beams. Pointed roofs keep off the heavy snows, and under the overhanging eaves the farmers dry great, yellow shocks of corn. One of the biggest exports of Alsace is pâté de foie gras, which is put up in clay tureens and sent all over the world. The Alsatian method of pâté manufacture would give the A.S.P.C.A. a mighty bad turn. Farmers have evolved a systematic method of force-feeding geese, holding the birds between their legs and cramming corn kernels down their throats. The pâté derives from the sick liver which the goose develops from overeating.

On Sundays in Alsace the villagers dress up in folk costumes, the round, chubby maidens in big, colorful headdresses, fringed shawls, flowered aprons, and white gloves, the boys in flat, black hats, brass-button jackets and white duck trousers. In Catholic villages the girls' hats are red, in Protestant villages, green.

Reading from north to south, the three main cities of Alsace are

*Sunday in Alsace—"like somebody's cousin"?*

Strasbourg, Colmar, and Mulhouse, which lie more or less along the course of the river Rhine. Mulhouse, pronounced to rhyme with "full ooze," is a big industrial city which manufactures potash. It was badly wrecked during the war. There is an airport at Mulhouse, and the city is serviced by Air France. The best hotel of those left standing is the Parc, the best restaurant the Guillaume Tell, from whose windows one can see a stone head with protruding tongue, formerly hung around the necks of gossiping women. The head hangs on the wall of the town hall.

Colmar, which gave its name to the famous Colmar Pocket in the second World War, was itself spared any extensive damage. It remains a provincial town, strung with a few canals, soft willow trees, and old washboats where women still do their laundry in the open air.

Strasbourg, the tourist city of Alsace, was founded during Celtic times, and knew Germanic tribes even before the Roman era. When the Romans took over, after the end of the first century B.C., the city became an important commercial center, and a forum was located on the present site of the cathedral. By the end of the third century A.D. a German tribe called the Alamanni was on the march again, and overthrew the Roman rule. The Emperor Julian defeated the Alamanni in 357 A.D., and the Romans managed to withstand further invasions for a period of fifty years. Then, in a record not much worse than what we have established today, Strasbourg was invaded by the Huns in 407, the Burgundians in 417, the Huns again in 455, and the Alamanni in 495. Later, under the Merovingians, Christianity found root, the city developed and became the seat of a bishop. Ultimately, the people became jealous of the bishops, who had been granted the rights of lords, and in 1262 revolted against church domination, and established Strasbourg as a free city.

In 1348 the city suffered heavily from an epidemic of the plague, and the following year the Christians decided to persecute the Jews. These two debâcles left Strasbourg in a tottering state. The citizens

*Colmar—in the middle of the famous pocket, it was spared any damage.*

became adherents of the principles of Martin Luther, which were adopted in 1529.

During the Thirty Years' War the small German Protestant states huddled around the French king for protection. As a result, by the Treaty of Westphalia, in 1648, Alsace was awarded to France as a reward for protecting the German Protestant princes during the war. For some two centuries thereafter, Alsace, including Strasbourg, lived as part of the French nation, and it was during those years that the province became French in heart and spirit.

By August, 1870, the Germans were pounding at the gates again, and this time subjected the city to a seven-week siege that set fire to the great Strasbourg library, damaged the cathedral, and ruined most of the civic buildings. On the 27th of September, 1870, Strasbourg capitulated to the Germans.

A mass exodus towards the interior of France followed after 1870, but the city developed under German rule, nonetheless. After forty-eight years as a German state, Alsace again became French on November 22, 1918, and stayed that way for twenty-two years, until the Germans went on the march again in 1940.

Under Hitler, the Germans meant business. Alsace was really German, said the Germans, and they made it an offense against the law to speak French. Not only were French street names changed, but people were obliged to change their names, too. Girls who had been christened Denise were obliged to call themselves Annamaria. Families named Dubois were obliged to translate it into Von Holtz. Worse yet, young Frenchmen of Alsace and Lorraine were pressed into German military service, and forced to fight against the only homeland they ever knew. Over 10,000 of them are either dead or still prisoners inside Russia. Those who returned were repatriated as French citizens, and if they can prove they entered German service against their will their time is being counted as if they had served in the French Army.

*Strasbourg's cathedral—every day a chariot, every hour a cock.*

Not all the Alsatians fought for Germany. Some escaped into the French Army, and at least one caused the German garrison at Strasbourg a mighty embarrassing day. As the Allied army advanced, in the fall of 1944, a column of the Second French Armored Division, attached to the American Seventh Army, reached Saverne, at the foot of the Vosges, forty-two kilometers from Strasbourg. A liaison officer with the French division, an Alsatian who could speak German, phoned the German commander at Strasbourg, told him he was the German commander at Saverne, and asked his compatriot to send down reinforcements. The Strasbourg commander said he had none to send, but the ruse was successful, because when the first French tanks arrived in Strasbourg shortly afterwards, German soldiers were still riding on the trolley cars. The liberation date was November 23, 1944, the first time the French had been required to liberate Strasbourg since November 22, 1918.

The second World War severely damaged Strasbourg, but spared the city's great cathedral, built of rose-colored sandstone, which was completed in 1439. The structure was found capable of supporting only one tower, and a tiny cottage settles at the base where the second tower might have been started. Inside the cathedral is the famous astronomical clock built in 1842. It is constructed of carved figures which usher in various times of the day with mechanical movements. Each quarter hour is struck, in turn, by a baby, a youth, an adult, and an old man. A figure of death sounds the hours by beating on a bell with a bone. Each day a new chariot heaves into view, and every noon a figure of Christ blesses the apostles, all twelve of whom then bow ceremoniously. A cock appears, every hour on the hour, flaps his wings, and crows three times. Some lions used to roar every now and then, but they've slipped into disrepair. All this clockwork goes off all year long with just one winding, every December 31.

Near the clock hangs a plaque erected shortly after the war, "In

*Strasbourg still has "old-time laundry barges where women come down to do their wash in the shadow of . . . imposing buildings."*

Memory of the American Officers, Noncommissioned Officers and Soldiers Who Gave Their Lives to Free Alsace, 1944-1945."

Souvenir shops in Strasbourg sell the famous gray-and-blue Betchdorf pottery made by the peasants, dolls in Alsatian costumes, and three-dimensional inlaid wood carvings, all of which seem to be products of the heavy Teutonic hand. Lorraine is noted for crystal, and the Soufflenheim pottery works supplies the local market from its plant just north of Strasbourg.

Cook's has a travel agency on the Rue Kléber, and offers motor tours of the city and half-day and full-day excursions to St. Odile, the castle of Kaiser Wilhelm II, and the Donon-Vallée de la Bruche. The last named trip includes a visit to a Roman temple perched on one of the highest mountains of the northern Vosges.

In spite of the fact that it is a large and important city, Strasbourg has retained enough of its old ways, traditions, and architecture to give it atmosphere. Canals ribbon through the city, and here, too, are the old-time laundry barges where women come down to do their wash, often in the shadow of the large, imposing public buildings of the new world which is ever encroaching upon the old.

In an ancient courtyard, in the center of town, the Hôtel de Corbeau, built in 1360, still stands on its tired, creaking foundations. A sign in front of the building lists all the prominent visitors who have come by, from Duc Jacob de Deux-Ponts et Bitsch in 1570 to General Keyes of the United States Seventh Army in 1945.

A towering topheavy ornate building with a middle-age façade, across from the cathedral, houses Maison Kammerzell, one of the best restaurants in town. Valentin-Sorg is also good, and there are any number of big, heavy-handed beer halls like Zimmer's (French pronunciation: "Seemair"), the Palais de la Bière, and L'Aubette. The *vin du pays* is Alsatian white wine, strong and dry.

There is no argument about which is the best hotel in Strasbourg. The Maison Rouge, though no George V, takes the title hands down. Bombs took a heavy toll of the city's hotels, but the newest establishment, called, naturally enough, Le Nouvel Hôtel, still stands. It has no restaurant, but is, all the same, proud of the fact that it has a bath for every room. There are a dozen other places in town from which to choose, and travelers seeking moderate-price comfortable accommodations are likely to find them at the Monopole-Métropole run by a round little man named Siegel. In addition to setting a mighty fine table, he also speaks a sort of English, a faculty of his which has gotten rather an extensive exercising lately from the occupation troops in the American zone who came over to his hotel on leave. He still

"A towering, topheavy, ornate building with a middle-age facade . . . houses
Maison Kammerzell. . . ."

maintains the habit, however, of beginning every sentence with "Of course," and ending it with "huh?" "You want a single room with bath?" he's likely to say. "Of course, we have a single room with bath, three hundred francs a night, huh?"

# FACTS AND FIGURES IN FRANCE AND AMERICA

|                     | AMERICAN | FRENCH |              | AMERICAN | FRENCH |
|---------------------|----------|--------|--------------|----------|--------|
| Men's collar sizes  | 14       | 36     | Dress sizes  | 12       | 38     |
|                     | 14½      | 37     |              | 14       | 40     |
|                     | 15       | 38     |              | 16-34    | 42     |
|                     | 15½      | 39     |              | 18-36    | 44     |
|                     | 16       | 40     |              | 38       | 46     |
|                     | 16½      | 41     |              | 40       | 52     |
|                     | 17       | 42     |              |          |        |

|            | AMERICAN | FRENCH |             | FAHRENHEIT | CENTIGRADE |
|------------|----------|--------|-------------|------------|------------|
| Shoe sizes | 4        | 37     | Temperature | 101        | 38.3       |
|            | 5        | 38     |             | 100        | 37.8       |
|            | 6        | 39     |             | 99         | 37.2       |
|            | 7        | 40     |             | 70         | 21.1       |
|            | 8        | 41     |             | 60         | 15.6       |
|            | 9        | 42     |             | 32         | 0          |
|            |          |        |             | 0          | 17.8       |
|            |          |        |             |            | (below)    |

## THE BEST YEARS IN WINE

1947. An exceptional year, especially in white wines.

1946. The red and white Burgundy is excellent, the white Bordeaux, poor.

1945. Considered a great year. Connoisseurs compare the Bordeaux and Burgundy to 1929, some white wines with 1921. Tasters with long memories are hearkening back to 1869.

1943. As great as 1937.

1942. Not that good, but not bad all the same. Fine in white Bordeaux and red Burgundy.

1940. Good in Bordeaux, fair in Burgundy.

1938. Fair but not fabulous.

1937. Great all over, but likely to be expensive.

1934. Likewise.

# HOTELS and RESTAURANTS

# Hotels and Restaurants
# of France

### Abridged and translated from the

### GUIDE MICHELIN

THIS directory is reprinted through the courtesy of the Michelin Tire Company, publishers of the *Guide Michelin* and other regional handbooks and maps of France. Michelin inspectors have visited 10,000 hotels, and have included 8,000 in the *Guide Michelin;* however, only the listings for resorts and principal cities of tourist interest have been included here.

The classification of hotels and restaurants follows in all cases the designation awarded by the *Service de Tourisme Michelin*. Because of possible price changes and the fluctuation of the franc, no costs are listed. However, the French government awards its own classification to each hotel (which in many cases corresponds to the Michelin designation), and maintains an official price ceiling according to grade. Price lists, arranged by categories, are available from the *Commissariat General au Tourisme*, 8 Ave. de l'Opéra, in Paris, and in the provinces, from the local tourist information bureaus.

# *How to Use the Directory*

## HOTELS

☆☆☆☆☆ Palace hotel with de luxe appointments.

☆☆☆☆ Well appointed hotel with all modern improvements.

☆☆☆ Very comfortable hotel with modern and modernized equipment.

☆☆ Partly modernized or new hotel with good, average comfort.

☆ Simple, but well kept hotel.

## RESTAURANTS

☆☆☆ De luxe restaurant.

☆☆ Restaurant of standard type.

☆ Simple, but well kept restaurant.

Dates in parenthesis indicate the opening and closing dates of hotels and restaurants operating on a seasonal basis.

The words "tourist information" preceding addresses and telephone numbers indicates in most cases the location of the Syndicat d'Initiatives, (popularly known as ESSI), a local tourist development board which maintains a tourist information bureau.

Distances to nearby cities are given in kilometers. A kilometer is five-eighths of a mile.

"Service charge 15%" indicates an additional charge which, according to continental custom, is added to the bill in lieu of voluntary tipping.

## Aix-en-Provence

Distance (in kilometers) to: Paris 747; Arles 74; Avignon 75; Marseille 29; Nîmes 107. Spa (March to December). Casino, Blvd. Sextius (closed Mondays). Swimming Pools; Mineral Baths; Nine-hole Golf Course. (For information, telephone National 1793 in Marseille.) Tourist Information (closed Sundays) Pavillon Tourisme, Place Libération, Tel. 293.

### HOTELS

☆☆☆☆ROY RENE, 14 Blvd. Roi René, Tel. 302 and 574. Specialties: Thon frais à la mode provencale, Poulet sauté "Roy René," Medaillon de veau à la façon du chef (certain days only). Wines: Les Arcs-sur-Argens. Service 15%. 70 Rooms. Garage. ☆☆☆THERMES SEXTIUS, 55 Cours Sextius, Tel. 118 and 154. Overlooking park. Service charge 15%. 50 Rooms. Garage. ☆RIVIERA, at the Pigonnet, 800 meters from the Place Libération. Tel. 352. Overlooking park; quiet. Specialties: Bouillabaisse, Langouste a l'américaine, Poulet Riviera. Wines: Meyereuil, Eguilles. Service charge 15%. 20 Rooms. Garage. ☆☆NEGRE COSTE, 33 Cours Mirabeau, Tel. 122. Service charge 15%. 40 Rooms. Garage. ☆☆MODERNE, 32-34 Av. V.-Hugo, Tel. 516. Service charge included. 29 Rooms. ☆PROVENCE, 23 Rue Espariat, Tel. 339. Restaurant (closed Saturdays). 15 Rooms. ☆RELAIS ST-CHRISTOPHE, 2 Av. V.-Hugo, Tel. 124. Service charge 15%. 25 Rooms. Garage. ☆RÉGENCE HOTEL (no restaurant), 16 Rue Espariat, Tel. 604. 15 Rooms.

☆LOUVRE (no restaurant), 1 and 3 Rue Masse, Tel. 217. 20 Rooms. Free garage.

### RESTAURANTS

☆☆LE VENDOME, Place Libération, Tel. 100. ☆BRASSERIE DU CASINO, 8 Pl. Jeanne d'Arc, Tel. 401. Service charge 15%. ☆GLACIER, Place Libération, Tel. 195. ☆BRASSERIE DES MARRONNIERS, 14 Pl. Jeanne d'Arc, Tel. 726. Service charge 15%.

## Aix-les-Bains, Savoy-Alps

Distance (in kilometers) to: Paris 530; Annecy 33; Chamonix 129; Evian 120; Geneva 76; Grenoble 71; Lyon 126. Spa (winter sports at Mt. Revard). Casinos: Grand Cercle, Petit Casino (summer). Beach, Swimming Pool; Mineral Baths (closed Mondays). Eighteen-Hole Golf Course (May to September; for information telephone 197). Tourist Information: Place Thermes, Tel. 197.

### HOTELS (in town)

☆☆☆☆☆SPLENDIDE, ROYAL, and EXCELSIOR (May to September). Rue Georges I, Tel. 423. Overlooking park, quiet. Service charge 15%. 250 Rooms. ☆☆☆☆REGINA-H. BERNASCON (summer), Boulevard Roche-du-Roi, Tel. 456, 558 and 660. View of town, lake, mountain; quiet. Service charge 15%. 180 Rooms. Garage. ☆☆☆GD.H. ALBION (summer), Av. Albion, Tel. 020. Overlooking park; quiet. Service charge 15%. 110 Rooms. Garage. ☆☆☆ASTORIA (summer), Pl.

Thermes, Tel. 228 and 693. Service charge 15%. 130 Rooms. ☆☆☆☆*GRAND HOTEL D'AIX*, (Whitsunday to end of September), 3 Pl. Revard, Tel. 093 and 672. Service charge 15%. 200 Rooms. ☆☆☆*ILES BRITANNIQUES* (May to October), Rue Davat, Tel. 002 and 007. Quiet. Service charge 15%. 90 Rooms. Garage. ☆☆☆*INTERNATIONAL RIVOLLIER*, Av. Gare, Tel. 100 and 676. Specialties: Terrine de paté truffé, Filet de lavaret savoyarde, Volaille aux crêpes du Revard et à la crème. Wines: Crépy, Morestel. Service charge 15%. 65 Rooms. ☆☆☆*VILLA VICTORA* (May to September) (no restaurant), Av. Fleurs, Tel. 105. Service charge 15%. 75 Rooms. ☆☆☆*SEVIGNE* (May 1 to October 15), 1 Rue Lamartine, Tel. 351 and 353. Service charge 15%. 115 Rooms. ☆☆*ETABL'T THERMAL* (April to October), 2 Rue Davat, Tel. 000. Service charge 15%. 75 Rooms. Garage. ☆☆*BRISTOL* (opening date indefinite), 8 Rue Casino, Tel. 114. 110 Rooms. ☆☆ *LOUVRE ET SAVOY* (April to October), 19-21 Av. Gare, Tel. 089. Service charge 15%. 100 Rooms. ☆☆*CONTINENTAL ET PRINCES*, 2-6 Rue Chambéry, Tel. 067. Service charge 15%. 65 Rooms. ☆☆*BERGUES* (May to October), Av. Gare, Tel. 090. Service charge 15%. 65 Rooms. ☆☆ *FOLLIET-FRANCE* (May to October), 4-6 Rue Lamartine, Tel. 189. Service charge 15%. 90 Rooms. ☆☆*PARC* (summer), 28 Rue Chambéry, Tel. 072. 44 Rooms. ☆*WINDSOR* (1st May to 30 September), 17 Rue Davat, Tel. 183. 32 Rooms. ☆*COSMOPOLITAIN* (May to October), 27 Av. Gare, Tel. 101. 52 Rooms. ☆*TERMINUS* (summer), 25 Blvd. Wilson, Tel. 107. 60 Rooms. ☆*CHATEAU-DURIEUX* (May to September), 3 Blvd. Côtes, Tel. 192. View of garden. Service charge 15%. 60 Rooms. Free Garage. ☆*MODERNE* (opening date indefinite), 26 Av. Petit-Port, Tel. 822. 19 Rooms. ☆*BEAU-LIEU*, 29 Av. Gare, Tel. 102. 40 Rooms. ☆*PAIX* (opening date indefinite), Rue Lamartine, Tel. 210. 60 Rooms. ☆*PARIS* (May to September), 9 Rue Daquin, Tel. 190. Service charge 15%. 55 Rooms. ☆*NOUVEL HOTEL DES THERMES* (opening date indefinite), 16 Rue Georges I, Tel. 371. 30 Rooms. ☆*GALLIA BEAU SEJOUR* (opening date indefinite), 24 Blvd. Berthollet, Tel. 279. 40 Rooms. ☆*CECIL*, 20 Av. Victoria, Tel. 412. Service charge 18%. 20 Rooms.

### RESTAURANTS

*GRAND CERCLE* (opening date indefinite), Rue Casino, Tel. 094 and 398. *AMBASSADEURS* (Whitsunday to September), 3 Pl. Revard, Tel. 093, 251 and 672. Service charge 15%. *QUATRE VALETS* (closed Wednesdays), 12 Square A. Boucher, Tel. 110. 30 Rooms. Free Garage. *REVERDY* (opening date indefinite), 26 Av. Petit-Port, Tel. 822. *PROSPER* (April to October), 82 Rue Genève, Tel. 1064. *BRASSERIE DU PAVILLON*, Pl. Gare, Tel. 104.

### At the "Grand Port"

#### HOTEL

☆*LAC* (April to October), Tel. 159. View of the Lake. 17 Rooms. Free Garage.

RESTAURANTS

☆☆*LILLE,* on the Lake Shore, Tel. 422. View of the lake. ☆☆*LES BELLES RIVES* (May to October), Tel. 161. View of the lake.

*At the "Petit Port"*

☆*PLATANES* (opening date indefinite), Tel. 760. 19 Rooms. Garage.

### Ajaccio, Corsica

Distance (in kilometers) to: Bastia 153; Calvi 163. Watering place and winter resort. Casino. Airport of Campo del Oro. Tourist Information: Ajaccio and Corsica, Hôtel de Ville, Pl. Foch, Tel. 287.

HOTELS

☆☆☆*GRAND HOTEL CONTINENTAL,* 22 Cours Grandval, Tel. 016. Service charge 15%. 60 Rooms. Free Garage. ☆*SOLFERINO,* 8 Cours Napoléon, Tel. 052. Service included. 34 Rooms.

RESTAURANTS

☆*PALMIERS,* 3 Pl. Foch, Tel. 245. Service included.

### Amboise; Chateaux de la Loire

Distance (in kilometers) to: Paris 207; Chaumont 17; Loches 35; Orléans 91; Tours 27. Tourist Information (closed Sunday afternoons, and Monday): Librairie Dupont, 30 Rue Nationale, Tel. 165.

HOTELS

☆☆*LE CHOISEUL,* 49 Quai Violettes, Tel. 281. View of the Loire. Specialties: Filets de sole Duc de Choiseul, Brochettes Pompadour, Grillades. Wine: Lussault. 10 Rooms. Free Garage. ☆☆*LION D'OR* (restaurant closed Tuesdays), Quai Charles-Guinot, Tel. 023. View of the Loire. 11 Rooms. Garage. ☆*LA BRECHE,* 34 Rue Poce, Tel. 151. View of garden; quiet. 10 Rooms. Free Garage. ☆*FRANCE ET CHEVAL BLANC,* 5 Quai Mail, Tel. 044. 20 Rooms. Garage. ☆*ST. VINCENT,* Rue Poce, Tel. 201. 16 Rooms. Garage.

RESTAURANTS

☆☆*AUBERGE DU MAIL,* Quai Mail, Tel. 104. (Closed January, also Sunday evenings in November, December, and February). Specialties: Tête de veau Choiseul, Geline de Touraine sauce lochoise, Paté de foies de Touraine. Wines: Nazelles, Montlouis. 14 Rooms.

### Annecy, Savoy

Distance (in kilometers) to: Paris 542; Aix-les-Bains 33; Chamonix 96; Evian 81; Geneva 43; Grenoble 102; Lyon 159; Mégève 60. Casino (summer) Beach. Tourist Information: Pl. Hôtel-de-Ville, Tel. 033, and Club Alpin Francais, Automobile Club du Mt. Blanc, Rue Camille Dunant, Tel. 912.

HOTELS (in town)

☆☆☆*SPLENDID HOTEL,* 4 Quai E.-Chappuis, Tel. 858. 52 Rooms. ☆☆☆*GRAND HOTEL ET ANGLETERRE,* 9 Rue Royale, Tel. 001 and 1329. 61 Rooms. ☆☆☆*CARLTON* (no restaurant), 5 Rue St.-François-de-Sales et des Glières, Tel. 775. Service charge 15%. 42 Rooms. ☆☆*VERDUN* (opening date indefinite), Pl.

Libération. Tel. 010. 60 Rooms. Garage. ☆☆*JEANNE D'ARC* (summer), 26 Rue Vaugelas, Tel. 247. 36 Rooms. ☆☆*NOUVEL HOTEL* (no restaurant), 37 Rue Vaugelas, Tel. 578. 32 Rooms. ☆*VILLA MARY* (opening date indefinite), 3 Rue 30 Infanterie, Tel. 310. 60 Rooms. ☆*SEVIGNE* (no restaurant), 5 Rue Royale, Tel. 118. 14 Rooms. ☆*LAC* (opening date indefinite), 1 Rue Archives. Tel. 166. 35 Rooms. ☆*LA REGENCE*, 17 Rue Royale, Tel. 591. 20 Rooms. Garage. ☆*FRANCE* (restaurant closed Mondays), 23 Rue Sommeiller, Tel. 234. 39 Rooms. Free Garage. ☆*ALPES* (no restaurant), 12 Rue Poste, Tel. 456. 26 Rooms. Garage. ☆*TERMINUS* (no restaurant), 6 Rue Sommeiller, Tel. 028. 52 Rooms. ☆☆*TAVERNE DE SAVOIE* (closed Wednesdays), 4 Quai E.-Chappuis, Tel. 260. Specialties: Dodine de caneton, Omble chevalier du lac. Wines: Crepy, Roussette de Montmélian. ☆☆*PACCARD* (closed Fridays in winter), Pl. Libération, Tel. 689. Extensive view of the Mountain. ☆*AUBERGE DE SAVOIE* (closed Fridays), 1 Pl. St.-Francois, Tel. 305. Meals à la carte. Specialties: Terrine maison, Pâté de gibier, Grillades. Wine: Crépy. ☆ *BRACHON ET HOTEL COMMERCE ET POSTE* (June to November), 13-15 Rue Royale, Tel. 012. 30 Rooms. Garage. ☆*MODERNE*, Rue Sommeiller, Tel. 211.

### On the Lake Shore

HOTELS

☆☆☆☆*IMPERIAL PALACE* (summer), Av. Albigny, Tel. 980. Extensive view of the lake; quiet. Service charge 15%. 240 Rooms. Free Garage.

### On Route 508, 2 kilometers from Annecy

HOTELS

☆☆☆*BEAU RIVAGE* (opening date indefinite), Route Sevrier, Tel. 003 and 004. Extensive view of the Lake. 100 Rooms. Garage. ☆☆*REGINA* (Easter to September), Route Albertville, Tel. 415. Extensive view of the Lake and the Mountain; quiet. Specialties: Omble chevalier au porto, Poularde en vessie, Terrine maison. Wines: Apremont, St-Jean-de-la-Porte. 32 Rooms. Garage.

### On the Puva (Slope South of Main Group). Post Office in Annecy

HOTEL

☆☆*TRESOMS ET FORET* (opening date indefinite), Blvd. Corniche, Tel. 384 in Annecy. Extensive view of Lake and Mountain; quiet. 45 Rooms. Garage.

### At the Barrattes, 3 kilometers on Route 509. Post Office in Annecy

HOTEL

☆*PARISIANA* (opening date indefinite), Route Talloire, Tel. 3 in Annecy. View of garden; quiet. 22 Rooms. Garage. ☆*MAVERIA* (Easter to October), Tel. 12 Annecy-le-Vieux. Quiet. Free Garage.

### At Chavoire, 4 kilometers on Route 509. Post Office in Veyrier-du-Lac

RESTAURANT

☆☆*PAVILLON ERMITAGE* (opening date indefinite), Tel. 114 in Annecy. Extensive view of Lake. 28 Rooms. Garage.

*At Albigny, 1 kilometer on Route 509. Post Office and Telegraph Office in Annecy*

### HOTELS

☆PETIT PORT (March to October), Tel. 843 Annecy. View of lake. 20 Rooms. Free Garage. ☆DES MUSES (Easter to October), Tel. 733 in Annecy. 20 Rooms. Garage.

### Antibes, Maritime Alps.

Distance (in kilometers) to: Paris 912; Cannes 11; Grasse 22; Juan-les-Pins 2; Monte Carlo 40; Nice 21. Watering place and winter resort. Casino Antipolis. 18-hole Golf Course (for information, Tel. 408.35). Tourist Information: 12 Pl. Général-de-Gaulle, Tel. 408.35.

### HOTELS

☆☆ROYAL (opening date indefinite), Blvd. James-Wyllie, Tel. 403.09. View of ocean. 32 Rooms. ☆ANTIPOLIS, 7 Av. Libération, Tel. 404.68. View of ocean. 36 Rooms. Garage. ☆MODERN HOTEL, 6 Rue République, Tel. 403.05. 26 Rooms. ☆MER, Blvd. James-Wyllie, Tel. 411.00. View of ocean. 24 Rooms.

### RESTAURANTS

☆☆TAVERNE PROCENCE, 8 Av. Soleau, Tel. 406.73. Service charge 15%. ☆LA COCARDE, 31 Blvd. Albert I. Tel. 416.15. ☆CHEZ FELIX, 50 Blvd. Aiguillon, Tel. 401.64. View of port. Specialties: Bouillabaisse, Soufflé Grand Marnier. Wine: Caradeau.

*1 Kilometer South*

### HOTEL

☆☆☆JOSSE, Blvd. Cap, Tel. 417.24. View of ocean and park; quiet. Service charge 15%. 36 Rooms. Free garage.

*A la Brague, 4 kilometers. Post Office in Antibes.*

### RESTAURANT

☆☆☆LA BONNE AUBERGE (closed October to December), Route Nationale, Tel. 406.65 in Antibes. View of Ocean. A la carte.

### Arles, Provence

Distance (in kilometers) to: Paris 717; Aix-en-Provence 74; Avignon 40; Marseille 90; Nimes 31. Roman Arena, Antique Theater, the Alyscamps. Tourist Information: Archevêché, Pl. République, Tel. 335.

### HOTELS

☆☆☆JULES CESAR (March 15 to November 15), Blvd. des Lices, Tel. 2.76. Service charge 15%. 68 Rooms. ☆☆NORD-PINUS, Pl. Forum, Tel. 026. ☆☆FORUM (restaurant closed Tuesdays), 10 Pl. Forum, Tel. 024. Beautiful frescos. 55 Rooms. Garage. ☆TOURING (no restaurant), 26 Rue Sauvage, Tel. 375. Garage. ☆MUSEE, 6 bis Rue Reattu.

### Arromanches-les-Bains,

### Calvados, Normandy

Distance (in kilometers) to: Paris 250; Bayeux 10; Caen 29. Watering place. See the artificial harbor (June 6, 1944, landing). Tourist Information: 2 Rue Fresné.

### HOTELS

☆*MARINE*, Tel. 19. View of Port Winston. 25 Rooms. Garage. ☆*OASIS* (Easter to October), Route Bayeux, Tel. 14. View of Port Winston. 32 Rooms. Free garage. ☆*LE MULBERRY* (Easter to All Saint's Day), 4 Rue Fresné, Tel. 5. Garage.

### Avignon, Provence

Distance (in kilometers) to: Paris 677; Aix-en-Provence 75; Arles 40; Marseille 95; Nimes 42; Orange 27. See the Popes' Palace. Bridge St.-Benezet (called Pont d'Avignon). Tourist Information (closed Sunday): Tourelle Porte République, Tel. 511; Automobile Club Vauclusien, 2 Rue République, Tel. 087.

### HOTELS

☆☆☆*EUROPE*, 12-14 Pl. Crillon, Tel. 136 and 19.36. Service charge 15%. 70 Rooms. ☆☆☆*CRILLON*, 43 Cours Jean-Jaurès, Tel. 056 and 129. Service charge 15%. 80 Rooms. Garage. ☆☆☆*TERMINUS*, 44 Cours Jean-Jaurès, Tel. 214, 503 and 29.50. Service charge 15%. 90 Rooms. Garage. ☆☆*REGINA* (no restaurant), 6 Rue République, Tel. 449. Service charge 15%. 35 Rooms. Garage. ☆*AUBERGE DE FRANCE* (restaurant closed Tuesdays), 28 Pl. Clemenceau, Tel. 886. 25 Rooms. ☆*CENTRAL HOTEL* (no restaurant), 31 and 33 Rue République, Tel. 597. 30 Rooms. ☆*LOUVRE*, 23 Rue St.-Agricol (Chapelle des Templiers), Tel. 281. 40 Rooms. Garage.

*Hotels and Restaurants (see also Villeneuve-les-Avignon)*

### RESTAURANTS

☆☆*HIELY* (closed Fridays), 1 Rue Frères-Brian, Tel. 335. Wine: Gigondas. ☆*RICH-TAVERN*, Pl. Préfecture, Tel. 092. ☆*DE L'OLIVIER "CHEZ MARLIER"*, Pl. Jerusalem, Tel. 10.02.

### Ax-les-Thermes, Pyrenees

Distance (in kilometers) to: Paris 805; Andorra (via Soldeu) 65; Carcassonne 105; Lourdes 22; Luchon 80; Pau 60; Toulouse 146. Spa (May-October) and winter sports resort. Casino (summer). Tourist Information (May to October): Av. Th.-Delcassé, Tel. 064.

### HOTELS

☆☆☆☆*GRAND HOTEL CASINO* (opening date indefinite), Av. Th.-Delcassé, Tel. 041. 80 Rooms. ☆*ROSE-MARGUERITE*, 15-17 Av. Docteur-Gomma, Tel. 018. View of mountain. Service charge 16%. 30 Rooms. Garage. ☆*LE GRILLON*, Chemin St.-Udau, Tel. 077. View of Valley; quiet. 13 Rooms. ☆*BEAUSITE* (June to October), Av. Docteur-Gomma, Tel. 061. View of Valley. 26 Rooms. Free Garage. ☆*MODERNE*, 20 Av. Docteur-Gomma, Tel. 024. Service charge 14%. 30 Rooms. Free Garage. ☆*CARRIERE*, 5 Av. Docteur-Gomma, Tel. 050. 22 Rooms. Free Garage. ☆*LE TEICH*, Av. Turrel, Tel. 019. View of park; quiet. 25 Rooms. Garage free. ☆*BELLEVUE* (March to November), 810 Av. A. Authier, Tel. 078. Quiet.

Specialties: Truites, Jambon de pays, Isard. Wines: Maury, Thuirs. 17 Rooms. Free Garage.

### Azay-Le-Rideau; Chateaux de la Loire

Distance (in kilometers) to: Paris 262; Chinon 21; Tours 25. See the Castle.

#### HOTELS

☆☆*GRAND MONARQUE,* 10 Rue Nationale, Tel. 8. 25 Rooms. ☆*COMMERCE* (closed in October), Rue Nationale, Tel. 22. 14 Rooms. Garage.

### Bastia, Corsica

Distance (in kilometers) to: Ajaccio 153; Calvi 93; Ile Rousse 69. Watering place and winter resort. Tourist Information: 33 Blvd. Paoli, Tel. 204.

#### HOTELS

☆☆*ILE DE BEAUTE,* Rue Gare, Tel. 329. Service charge 15%. 30 Rooms. ☆*NORMANDIE* (no restaurant), 13 Av. Carnot, Tel. 422. Service charge 15%. 17 Rooms.

#### RESTAURANTS

☆*LA CHAUMIERE,* 19 Rue César Campinchi. ☆*LAVEZZI,* Rue St.-Jean.

### Baule (La), Brittany

Distance (in kilometers) to: Paris 473; Nantes 77; Rennes 131. Seashore. Casino (summer). 18-hole Golf Course (Easter to October 31). (For information Tel. 40.77). Tourist Information: Maison Tourisme, Pl. Victoire, Tel. 28.20. Automobile Cub, 31 Av. Gen.-de-Gaulle, Tel. 20.01.

#### HOTELS

☆☆☆☆*HERMITAGE* (June 25 to end of September), Espl. Casino, Tel. 2022, 2218, 2273. View of beach. Service charge 15%. 200 Rooms. ☆☆☆☆*CASTEL MARIE-LOUISE* (Easter to October), Espl. Casino, Tel. 2061. Service charge 15%. 33 Rooms. ☆☆☆*MAJESTIC,* Espl. Casino, Tel. 2486. View of beach. 78 Rooms. ☆☆☆*PLAGE ET GOLF* (March to September), Espl. Bénoit et Av. Lilas, Tel. 2002. View of beach; quiet. Service charge 15%. 100 Rooms. Garage. ☆☆☆*LES PLEIADES* (summer), Av. Lombarde, Tel. 2024. Quiet. Service charge 15%. 40 Rooms. Garage. ☆☆☆ *GRAND HOTEL* (summer), Blvd. Armor, Tel. 2007. View of beach. Service charge 15%. 84 Rooms. Garage. ☆☆☆*TOQUE BLANCHE* (Easter to end of September), Av. St.-Saëns. Tel. 2274. View of beach. 33 Rooms. Garage. ☆☆*SPLENDID HOTEL* (Easter, and June to October), Blvd. Darlu, Tel. 2019. View of beach. Service charge 15%. 20 Rooms. Garage. ☆☆*LA ROSERAIE,* 20 Av. Drevet, Tel. 2045. 50 Rooms. Garage. ☆☆*BRETAGNE,* Pl. Chapelle, Tel. 2192. Service charge included. 24 Rooms. ☆☆*WELCOME* (Easter to October), Allée Manette, Tel. 2307. 19 Rooms. ☆*ATLANTIC,* Av. Flandre. 21 Rooms. ☆☆ *ARMORIC,* Blvd. Armor, Tel. 2183. View of beach. 54 Rooms. Garage. ☆*ADELPHI* (April to September), Av. Concorde, Tel. 2358. Quiet. 40 Rooms. ☆☆*NOTRE-DAME-DU-PORT* (March to Sepember), Quai Rageot-de-la-Touche, Tel. 2445. View of port. 40 Rooms. Garage free. ☆☆

*HELIOS* (Easter to September), 7 Blvd. Armor, Tel. 2238. View of beach. Service charge 18%. 35 Rooms. ☆*SABLES D'OR*, Blvd. Armor, Tel. 2326. View of beach. 45 Rooms. Garage. ☆*BELLEVUE-PLAGE*, Blvd. Ocean, Tel. 2855. View of beach. 28 Rooms. ☆*BEAUSE-JOUR* (Easter to October), 23 Blvd. Darlu, Tel. 2307. View of beach. 20 Rooms. *RIVIERA* (Easter to October), 12 Av. Lilas, Tel. 2897. Service charge included. 21 Rooms. ☆ *DUNES*, 283 Av. Paris, Tel. 2104. Service charge 15%. 50 Rooms. Garage. ☆*LA CHAUMIERE*, Pl. Dryades, Tel. 2343. 13 Rooms. Garage. ☆*LES CLEMATITES* (Easter to September), Allée Bouleaux. Tel. 2259. 40 Rooms. ☆*TERRASSE*, 21 Av. Gen.-de-Gaulle, Tel. 2144. 25 Rooms. ☆*SELECT* (March to October), Av. Paris, Tel. 2528. 27 Rooms.

## Baux (Les), Provence

(Post Office, Maussane).

Distance (in kilometers) to: Paris 708 ; Tarascon 18.

### HOTEL

☆*REINE JEANNE*, Tel. 6. View of Val d'Enfer; quiet. 25 Rooms. Garage free.

### RESTAURANT

☆☆*BAUMANIERE*, Tel. 7. Service charge 15%. Specialties: Cervelas truffé, Gratin de Langouste, Poulet flambé à l'Armagnac. Wines: Clairette de Bellegarde, Les Baux.

## Bayeux, Calvados, Normandy

Distance (in kilometers) to: Paris 248; Arromanches 10; Caen 27; Cherbourg 93; St. Lô 35. Tourist Information: 1 Rue Cuisiniers.

### HOTELS

☆☆*LION D'OR*, 71 Rue St. Jean, Tel. 031. 37 Rooms. Garage free. ☆*NOTRE-DAME*, 48 Rue Cuisiniers, Tel. 256. 24 Rooms. Garage free. ☆*LUXEMBOURG*, 25 Rue Bouchers, Tel. 004. 36 Rooms. Garage.

### RESTAURANT

☆*ST. PATRICE*, 12 Rue Alain-Chartier, Tel. 142.

## Beaulieu-Sur-Mer, Riviera

Distance (in kilometers) to: Paris 943; Cannes 43; Monaco 11; Nice 10. Seashore and winter resort. Casino (summer and winter). Tourist Information: 57 Blvd. Gen.-Leclerc, Tel. 202.21.

### HOTELS

☆☆☆☆*BRISTOL* (July to September, and winter), Tel. 200.35 and 200.37. Quiet. Service charge 15%. 200 Rooms. ☆☆☆*LA RESERVE*, 56 Blvd. Gen.-Leclerc, Tel. 200.02. Sea view. Quiet. Specialties: Loup Reserve (poisson du pays), Quartier d'agneau Polignac, Gâteau grand succes. Wines: Château de Selles, Londes-les-Maures. Service charge 15%. 20 Rooms. Garage free. ☆☆*BOND'S HOTEL*, 1 Av. Anglais, Tel. 201.12. View of garden; quiet. Service charge 15%. 45 Rooms. ☆☆*VICTORIA*, 1 Blvd.

Marinoni, Tel. 201.08 and 202.20. View of garden. Service charge 15%. 80 Rooms. Garage. ☆☆*SAVOY*, Tel. 203.31. View of garden and beach; quiet. Service charge 15%. 35 Rooms. Garage. ☆*FRISIA*, 2 Av. Gen.-Leclerc, Tel. 201.04. View of port. 30 Rooms. ☆*HOST. BEAU SITE*, Montée Lucioles, Tel. 202.08. Quiet. 10 Rooms. ☆*BEAULIEU-RICHMOND*, 21 Blvd. Marinoni, Tel. 200.73. View of garden; quiet. 30 Rooms. ☆*FLORA*, 6 Av. Edith Cavell, Tel. 202.01. View of garden; quiet. 25 Rooms. ☆*MARCELLIN*, Av. Albert I, Tel. 201.69. Service charge 15%. 25 Rooms.

## Beaune, Burgundy

Distance (in kilometers) to: Paris 323; Dijon 38. See the Hôtel-Dieu. Tourist Information: Rue de l'Hôtel Dieu, Tel. 513.

### HOTELS

☆☆*POSTE*, 5-7 Blvd. Clémenceau, Tel. 077. Service charge 15%. 30 Rooms. Garage. ☆*CLOCHE ET GRAND ST.-JEAN* (restaurant closed Tuesdays), 42 Pl. Madeleine and 18 Rue Fg. Madeleine, Tel. 182 and 343. 33 Rooms. Garage free.

## Beausoleil, Riviera (Monaco)

Mail address: Beausoleil. Casino.

### HOTELS

☆☆*DIANA* (no restaurant), 17 Blvd. René-Volat, Tel. 212.61, at Beausoleil. Service charge 15%. 33 Rooms. ☆ *OLYMPIA*, Blvd. René-Volat, Tel. 212.95, at Beausoleil. Service charge 15%. 40 Rooms. ☆*COSMOPOLITE*, 19 Blvd. Volat, Tel. 210.24, at Beausoleil. Service charge 15%. 22 Rooms.

### RESTAURANTS

☆*BRASSERIE PARISIANA*, 1 Av. Gen.-de-Gaulle, Tel. 212.91, at Beausoleil. ☆*PASCAL* (closed Tuesdays), 13 Blvd. René-Volat, Tel. 212.54.

## Beg-Meil, Brittany

(Post Office in Fouesnant).

Distance (in kilometers) to: Paris 570; Concarneau 19; Quimper 21. Seashore.

### HOTEL

☆☆*DUNES ET GRAND HOTEL* (summer), Tel. 005 and 007 in Fouesnant. View of beach; quiet. 75 Rooms. Garage.

### RESTAURANT

☆*BRETAGNE* (opening date indefinite), Tel. 104. 25 Rooms. Garage.

## Biarritz, Pyrenees

Distance (in kilometers) to: Paris 748; Bordeaux 183; Hendaye 30; Lourdes 153; Pau 114; St.-Jean-de-Luz 17. Watering place, winter resort and spa. (April to October); Casino Municipal; Casino Bellevue (summer); Swimming Pool; Chambre d'Amour-Angleterre. 18-hole Golf Course (for information, Tel. 414.12). Tourist Information: Av. Edouard VII, Tel. 420.24. Touring Club de France, Maison du Tourisme, 1 Av. Edouard VII, Tel. 424.16.

## HOTELS

☆☆☆☆☆*PALAIS* (Easter to October), Av. Edouard VII, Tel. 409.40. Extensive view of ocean; quiet. Service charge included. 250 Rooms. ☆☆☆☆☆ *MIRAMAR* (Easter, and June to September), Rue Vagues, Tel. 404.40. Extensive view of ocean; quiet. Service charge 15%. 200 Rooms. ☆☆☆☆☆ *CARLTON*, Av. Reine-Victoria, Tel. 409.00. Extensive view of ocean. Service charge 15%. 253 Rooms. ☆☆☆☆*VICTORIA*, Av. Edouard VII, Tel. 414.20. Extensive view of ocean. Service charge 15%. 100 Rooms. ☆☆☆*PLAZA*, Av. Edouard VII, Tel. 404.00. Service charge 15%. 56 Rooms. ☆☆☆*CHESTER*, Av. Reine-Nathalie, Tel. 424.26 and 424.38. Service charge 15%. 40 Rooms. ☆☆☆ *PAIX* (open in season only), 1 Pl. Libération, Tel. 400.98. 60 Rooms. ☆☆☆*CHATEAU DES FALAISES*, Perspective de Miramar, Tel. 419.25. View of ocean. Service charge 15%. 45 Rooms. ☆☆*WINDSOR*, Blvd. Grande Plage, Tel. 408.52. Service charge included. 38 Rooms. ☆☆ *BRITANNIA*, 90 Av. Reine-Victoria, Tel. 402.51. 35 Rooms. Garage. ☆☆*ARRANOA*, Rue L.-Barthou, Tel. 420.47. Service charge 15%. 24 Rooms. ☆☆*MALOUTHEA HOTEL*, Av. Jardin-Public, Tel. 406.00. 21 Rooms. ☆☆*EUROPE*, 5 Rue Helder, Tel. 409.55. 50 Rooms. ☆☆*BRISTOL*, Blvd. Grande Plage, Tel. 408.75. Sea view. 55 Rooms. ☆☆*EL MIRADOR*, 8 Pl. Ste.-Eugénie, Tel. 413.81. Extensive view of sea. 40 Rooms. ☆☆ *EXCELSIOR*, Rue Gardères, Tel. 409.48. Extensive view of sea. 50 Rooms. ☆☆*LES CHARDONS*, Av. Reine-Nathalie, Tel. 404.24. Service charge included. 30 Rooms. ☆ *ROCHER DE LA VIERGE*, 15 Rue Port Vieux, Tel. 411.74. Service charge 15%. 20 Rooms. Garage. ☆ *FLORIDA* (Easter to November), 3 Pl. Ste.-Eugénie, Tel. 401.76. 40 Rooms. ☆*COMMINGES*, 19 Av. Carnot, Tel. 410.46. 15 Rooms. ☆ *EDOUARD VII*, 21 Av. Carnot, Tel. 407.20. 16 Rooms. ☆*ST. JULIEN*, 20 Av. Carnot, Tel. 420.39. Service charge 20%. 30 Rooms. ☆*OCEAN* (April to November), 9 Pl. Ste.-Eugénie, Tel. 403.27. ☆*TOKI-ONA*, Rue Helder, Tel. 420.03. 14 Rooms. ☆*COTE DES BASQUES*, 62 Rue Gambetta, Tel. 421.38. 17 Rooms Garage. ☆*NARTUS*, Pl. Atalaye, Tel. 400.75. 20 Rooms. ☆*ST. PIERRE*, Av. Maréchal-Foch, Tel. 420.89. Quiet. 14 Rooms. ☆*WASHINGTON*, 34 Rue Mazagran, Tel. 410.80. 20 Rooms.

## RESTAURANTS

☆☆*CAFE DE PARIS*, Pl. Bellevue, Tel. 419.53. View of beach. A la carte. ☆☆*PAVILLON ROSE*, Av. Reine-Victoria, Tel. 412.61. ☆☆*LA CREMAILLERE*, Av. Edouard VII, Tel. 404.00. Telegraph address: Plaza. ☆☆*AU PETIT VATEL* (closed Wednesdays in winter), Rue Gardères, Tel. 412.05. Sea view. A la carte. ☆*CHEZ ELIAS*, Av. Hotel-de-Ville, Tel. 416.47. ☆*AMBASSADE DE BOURGOGNE*, Rue Alcedo, Tel. 406.89. Specialties: Filets de sole Ambassade, Homard à l'américaine, Poulet basquaise (summer). Wines: Salies. Service charge 15%. 12 Rooms. Garage free.

## Blois, Chateaux de la Loire

Distance (in kilometers) to: Paris 172; Chambord 16; Chenonceaux 42; Tours 60. See the Castle. Tourist Information: 16 Rue Porte-Côte, Tel. 649. Automobile Club de l'Ouest, 23 bis Rue Denis-Papin, Tel. 321.

### HOTELS

☆☆*FRANCE ET GUISE*, Pl. Victor-Hugo, Tel. 023. Wine: Vouvray. Service charge 16%. 50 Rooms. Garage. ☆☆*CHATEAU* (no restaurant), 22 Rue Porte-Côte, Tel. 024. Service charge 15%. 40 Rooms. Garage. ☆*GARE ET TERMINUS* (no restaurant), 6 Av. Victor-Hugo, Tel. 257. 30 Rooms. Garage. ☆*GERBE D'OR*, 1 Rue Bourg-Neuf, Tel. 088. 20 Rooms. Garage. ☆*LE MONARQUE* (restaurant closed Wednesdays except during July, August, and September), 61 Rue Porte-Chartraine, Tel. 235. Service charge 14%. 10 Rooms. Garage ☆*RABIER* (temporarily no restaurant), 1 Rue A.-Poulain, Tel. 415. 24 Rooms. Garage.

### RESTAURANTS

☆☆*FRANCOIS I* (closed October 15 to November 15, and Mondays), 20 Rue Porte-Côte, Tel. 219. Specialties: Croustade de champignons, Andouillette de Blois grillée, Ecrevisses à la nage. Wine: Vouvray. ☆*TOURNE BRIDE* (closed Wednesdays), 1 to 7, Mail Clouseau, Tel. 479. ☆*COMMERCE*, 35 Rue Porte-Chartraine, Tel. 545.

### On Route 152

### RESTAURANTS

☆☆*VAL DE LA LOIRE*, 119 Quai Ulysse-Besnard, Tel. 901. View of the river Loire. Service charge 13%. 4 Rooms. Garage free.

*At St. Denis-sur-Loire, 6 kilometers on Route 152. Post Office address: Menars*

### HOTEL

☆*MEDICIS*, Tel. 1 at Chaussée St. Victor. View of park; quiet. 10 Rooms.

## Bonifacio, Corsica

Distance (in kilometers) to: Ajaccio 134; Porto Vecchio 27. Watering place.

### RESTAURANTS

☆*VOYAGEURS*, Quai J.-Comparetti, Tel. 16. 10 Rooms. Garage. ☆*LA PERGOLA*, Tel. 22.

## Cabourg, Calvados, Normandy

Distance (in kilometers) to: Paris 205; Caen 24; Deauville 18. Watering place. Casino (summer). Tourist Information (summer): Jardins du Casino, Tel. 097.

### HOTELS

☆☆☆*DUCS DE NORMANDIE* (Whitsunday to September 25), Tel. 052. Extensive view of sea. Service charge 15%. 82 Rooms. Garage. ☆☆*CHAT BOTTE* (Easter to September), Av. Casino Ouest, Tel. 201. Quiet. Service charge 15%. 31 Rooms. ☆☆*DU CASINO* (summer), 2 Av. Mer, Tel. 031. 60 Rooms. ☆☆ *PARIS*, 43 Av. Mer, Tel. 037. 19 Rooms. ☆☆*LA COUR NORMANDE* (opening date indefinite), Av. Piat, Tel. 137. 50 Rooms. ☆☆GRAND BALCON, Av. Roi-Albert I and Av. Jean-Mermoz, Tel. 078. 25 Rooms. Garage. ☆DEUX MONDES (Easter to September), Av. Président R. Poincaré, Tel. 089. 24 Rooms. Garage.

## Caen, Calvados, Normandy

Distance (in kilometers) to: Paris 221; Arromanches 29; Avranches 100; Bayeux 27; Cherbourg 119; Courseulles 18; Deauville 42. Tourist Information: Chez M. Goupil, 1 Pl. Sépulcre, Tel. 47.93. Automobile Club de l'Ouest, 10 Pl. République, Tel. 27.35.

### HOTELS

☆GOURMETS, 94 Blvd, Alliés, Tel. 36.75. 10 Rooms. ☆STRASBOURG, 5 Rue Bras, Tel. 48.97. 15 Rooms.

### RESTAURANTS

☆☆CHANDIVERT, 77 Blvd. Alliés, Tel. 41.34. Service charge 13%. ☆BUFFET GARE ETAT, Tel. 24.58. ☆LABBE, 5 ter. Av. Albert-Sorel, Tel. 31.95. ☆ALCIDE, 1 Pl. Courtonne, Tel. 30.01.

## Cannes, Riviera

Distance (in kilometers) to: Paris 901; Antibes 11; Grasse 17; Marseille 170; Monte Carlo 51; Nice 32. Seashore, summer swimming, warm winters. Casinos: Municipal (winter), Palm Beach (summer), Sporting Club (winter). Swimming pool, Palm Beach. Tourist Information: Tel. 908.08. Automobile Club, Tel. 938.-94.

### HOTELS

☆☆☆☆☆CARLTON, 60 Blvd. Croisette, Tel. 921.90. Ocean front. ☆☆☆☆☆MIRAMAR, 64 Blvd. Croisette, Tel. 924.70. Ocean front. ☆☆☆☆☆LE GRAND HOTEL, 49 Blvd. Croisette, Tel. 929.35. ☆☆☆☆☆ MARTINEZ, Blvd. Croisette, Tel. 925.21. Ocean front. ☆☆☆☆☆MAJESTIC, Blvd. Croisette, Tel. 947.92. Ocean front. ☆☆☆☆SPLENDID (no restaurant), 7 Rue Félix-Faure, Tel. 902.47. ☆☆☆☆GONNET ET REINE, 44 Blvd. Croisette, Tel. 902.64. Ocean front. ☆☆☆☆GRAY ET ALBION, Rue Antibes, Tel. 906.66. ☆ ☆☆☆MONTANA, Rue Pasteur, Tel. 926.72. ☆☆☆SAVOY, Rue Plage, Tel. 917.74. ☆☆☆SUISSE, Av. Cercle Nautique, Tel. 903.67, 939.97. ☆☆☆VICTORIA-WALSDORFF, 100 Rue Antibes, Tel. 908.23. ☆☆☆ ROYAL, Blvd. Croisette, Tel. 901.04. Ocean front. ☆☆☆CAVENDISH HOTEL (no restaurant), 11 Blvd. Carnot, Tel. 906.95. ☆☆☆MONDIAL (no restaurant), 61 Rue Antibes, Tel. 928.70. ☆☆ALEXANDRA, 69 Blvd. Carnot, Tel. 910.25. ☆☆UNIVERS (no restaurant), 2 Rue Maréchal-Foch, Tel. 900.43. ☆☆SELECT (no restaurant), 12 Rue Vagliano, Tel. 931.78. ☆☆WESTMINSTER, 55 Blvd. Alsace, Tel. 906.47. ☆☆ILES BRITANNIQUES, 9 Blvd. Alsace, Tel. 905.85. ☆☆AMIRAUTE (no restaurant), 17 Rue Maréchal-Foch, Tel. 910.53. ☆☆LA RESIDENCE (temporarily no restaurant), 100 Rue Antibes, Tel. 912.44. ☆☆NEGOCIANTS ET COLONIES (no restaurant), Pl. de la Gare, Tel. 900.37. ☆☆NOUVEL HOTEL (no restaurant), 5 Pl. de la Gare, Tel. 903.11.

☆☆*WAGRAM,* 106 Rue Antibes, Tel. 915.53.

### North and East of Center

☆☆☆☆☆*CALIFORNIE* (December to May, and July to September), Chemin Californie, Tel. 922.41. Overlooking ocean. ☆☆☆☆*GALLIA PALACE* (summer and winter), Blvd. Montfleury, Tel. 905.07. ☆☆☆☆*MONT FLEURY* (summer, and November to May), Blvd. Montfleury, Tel. 904.76. ☆☆*REGINA,* Ave. Antibes, Tel. 905.43. ☆☆*LES SABLONS,* 4 Av. Sablons, Tel. 900.27. ☆*INSULINDE,* Av. Antibes, Tel. 93.241.

### West of Center

☆☆☆☆*MEDITERRANEE* (no restaurant), 1 Blvd. Jean Hibert, Tel. 918.52. On the Port. ☆☆☆*MONT-MORENCY,* 9 Route Fréjus. Tel. 931.61. Ocean front. ☆☆*ATLAN-TIDE,* Plage Midi, Tel. 905.36.

**RESTAURANTS**

☆☆☆*AMBASSADEURS* (winter), 2 Blvd. Croisette. In the Municipal Casino, Tel. 934.66. ☆☆☆*DRAP D'OR,* 61 Blvd. Croisette, Tel. 93.179. Ocean front. ☆☆*LA JETEE,* Les Alliés, Tel. 93.921. On the port. ☆☆*BRASSERIE LAMOUR,* 33 Rue Antibes, Tel. 901.49, 938.09. ☆☆ *CAFE DE PARIS,* 7 Blvd. Croisette, Tel. 914.51. ☆☆*LA VOILE AU VENT,* 17 Quai St. Pierre, Tel. 92.784, 91.512. On the port. ☆☆ *BERTHON* (closed Fridays in winter), 12 Rue Mace, Tel. 932.56. ☆☆*LA MARJOLAINE,* Plage Midi,

Tel. 928.26. Ocean view. ☆☆*OS-CAR'S* (closed November and December), 3 Quai St. Pierre, Tel. 922.-56. On the port. ☆☆*REINE PE-DAUQUE* (closed Mondays), Rue Maréchal Joffre. ☆☆*LE BISOU,* 3 Rue St. Honoré, Tel. 901.78.

### Cap d'Ail, Riviera

Distance (in kilometers) to: Menton 12; Monte Carlo 3; Nice 18. Seashore, summer swimming, warm winters. Tourist Information: Tel. 220.-13.

**HOTELS**

☆*EDMOND'S HOTEL,* Route Nationale, Tel. 220.48. ☆*NEPTUNE,* Route Nationale, Tel. 220.80.

### Cap d'Antibes, Riviera

Distance (in kilometers) to: Antibes 14; Cannes 14. Seashore, summer swimming, warm winters.

**HOTELS**

☆☆☆☆*CAP D'ANTIBES* (March to September), Blvd. George V, Tel. 400.43. Ocean front. ☆☆*LA GA-ROUPE,* Blvd. Cap, Tel. 409.01. ☆*GRAND VATEL,* Blvd. Cap, Tel. 403.43.

**RESTAURANT**

☆☆☆*EDEN ROC* (summer), Tel. 406.63. Faces ocean.

### Cap Ferrat, Riviera

Mail address: St. Jean-Cap-Ferrat. Distance (in kilometers) to: Paris 946; Menton 24; Nice 15.

## HOTEL

GRAND HOTEL CAP FERRAT (summer), Tel. 250.20 at St. Jean-Cap-Ferrat. Overlooking sea; quiet. Service charge 15%. 85 Rooms. Garage.

### Carcassonne, Pyrenees

Distance (in kilometers) to: Paris 774; Font-Romeu 131; Lourdes 264; Luchon 222; Toulouse 92. See the fireworks spectacle. Tourist Information (closed Mondays): Jardin des Plantes, Tel. 704.

## HOTELS

☆☆☆☆CITE (April to October), Tel. 334. View of ramparts; beautiful inside decorations; quiet. Specialties: Cassoulet de la Cité; on certain days, Tournedos Rossini; Filets de sole. Wines: Tuchan, Rieux Minervois. Service charge 15%. 55 Rooms. Garage. ☆☆☆TERMINUS, 2 Av. Maréchal-Joffre, Tel. 434 and 13.17. Service charge 15%. 115 Rooms. Garage. ☆☆MODERNE ET COMMERCE, 16 Rue Armagnac, Tel. 2.00. 45 Rooms. Garage. ☆☆BRISTOL (restaurant closed Sundays), 5-7 Av. Maréchal-Foch, Tel. 7.24. 45 Rooms. Garage. ☆CENTRAL HOTEL (restaurant closed Mondays), 27-29 Blvd. Jean Jaurès, Tel. 3.84. 30 Rooms. Garage. ☆AURIOL (temporarily no restaurant), 54 Rue 4 Septembre, Tel. 11.97. 22 Rooms.

## RESTAURANT

☆☆AUTER, 22 Rue Courtejaire, Tel. 152.

### Chamonix, Mont Blanc, Savoy Alps

Distance (in kilometers) to: Paris 625; Aix-les-Bains 129; Annecy 96; Evian 116; Geneve 86; Grenoble 153; Mégève 35. Winter sports; ski tows. Casino du Mt. Blanc (summer, winter). Excursions: Montenvers, outstanding view; Sea of Ice, take cog railway; The Glaciers, take funicular; Le Brevent, outstanding view, take funicular. Nine-hole Golf Course (May to September) (for information, Tel. 0.28); beach. Tourist Information: Pl. Eglise, Tel. 024; Club Alpin Francais, Pl. Gare; Touring Club de France (June to September), Av. Gare, Tel. 083.

## HOTELS

☆☆☆☆MAJESTIC (summer and winter), Tel. 335. View of Chaine des Aiguilles and Mont Blanc; quiet. Service charge 15%. 210 Rooms. ☆☆☆SAVOY (summer and winter), Tel. 029 and 211. View of Mont Blanc; quiet. Service charge 15%. 100 Rooms. Garage. ☆☆☆ALPES (December to October), Rue Dr. Paccard, Tel. 027. View of Mont Blanc. Specialties: Fera farcie à la savoyarde, Brochettes de campagne, Coq en pâté. Wines: Roussette de Seysse, Crépy. Service charge 15%. 103 Rooms. ☆☆☆CARLTON HOTEL (summer and winter), Av. Foch, Tel. 092. Service charge 15%. 50 Rooms. Garage. ☆☆BEAU SEJOUR ET RICHEMOND (summer and winter), Rue Dr. Paccard, Tel. 085. 90 Rooms. ☆☆BEAU RIVAGE (closed in November), Tel. 005. View of Mont Blanc. 25 Rooms. Garage. ☆☆NOU-

VEL HOTEL UNIVERS (summer and winter), Pl. Gare, Tel. 009. 60 Rooms. Garage. ☆☆BELLEVUE (October to December), Tel. 008. View of mountain. 37 Rooms. ☆☆ MONT BLANC (summer), Pl. Eglise, Tel. 034. View of Mont Blanc. 80 Rooms. ☆☆SAPINIERE (June to September, and December to Easter), Rue Vallot, Tel. 153. View of Mont Blanc. Quiet. 23 Rooms. ☆☆BELVEDERE, Tel. 17. Extensive view of Aiguilles and Mont Blanc; quiet. 50 Rooms. Garage. ☆☆ BEAULIEU (Whitsunday to October, and December to March), Tel. 010. View of mountain. 50 Rooms. ☆☆ETRANGERS, Pl. Gare, Tel. 031. View of mountain. 45 Rooms. Garage. ☆LA ROSERAIE (summer and winter), Tel. 287. View of mountain; quiet. Wines: Seyssel, Crépy. 22 Rooms. ☆ALLOBROGES (summer), Rue Lyret, Tel. 045 and 445. View of Mont Blanc; quiet. 87 Rooms. Garage. ☆ASTORIA ET POSTE (summer and winter), Pl. Saussure, Tel. 006. 70 Rooms. ☆ CROIX BLANCHE (Easter to October), Rue J. Vallot, Tel. 011. 45 Rooms. Garage free. ☆ALBERT I ET MILAN (summer and winter); near the Station, Tel. 109. View of mountain. ☆SUISSE ET CHA-MONIX, Pl. Jacques Balmat, Tel. 058. 45 Rooms. ☆GOURMETS, Rue Lyret, Tel. 038. 30 Rooms. ☆SA-VOISIEN, Rue J. Vallot, Tel. 282. 35 Rooms. ☆CENTRAL (opening date indefinite), (no restaurant), Pl. Jacques Balmat, Tel. 167. 46 Rooms. ☆TERMINUS (May to January), (no restaurant), Tel. 007. 25 Rooms.

☆ARCADES, Av. Foch, Tel. 116. 10 Rooms.

RESTAURANTS

☆BRASSERIE ALSACIENNE, Av. Foch, Tel. 214. ☆LA POULARDE, Rue J. Vallot, Tel. 307. Service charge 15%. ☆LION D'OR, Rue Dr. Paccard, Tel. 309.

Montenvers (take cog railway). Altitude 1.909 Meters. Post Office in Chamonix.

HOTEL

☆MONTENVERS (opening date indefinite), Tel. 033 in Chamonix. Extensive view of sea of ice and mountains. 32 Rooms.

Planpraz (funicular from Brevent). Altitude 2.062 Meters. Post Office in Chamonix.

RESTAURANT

☆PAVILLON (June to September, and December to April), (breakfast only), Tel. 245 Chamonix. Extensive view of Mont Blanc.

## Chantilly, Oise

Distance (in kilometers) to: Paris 41. See the Castle, the Museum (Easter to October 15; afernoons only, except Mondays and Fridays). Beaches: Boran (9 kilometers from Chantilly); Toutevoie (5½ kilometers west of Chantilly). 18-hole Golf Course (closed Wednesdays). For information: Tel. 1.00 Lamorlaye (6 kilometers from Chantilly). Tourist Information: (April to October, Thursdays, Sundays, and holidays), Pl. Gare.

## HOTELS

☆☆☆*PARC*, 24 Av. Maréchal-Joffre, Tel. 280. View of garden; quiet. 23 Rooms. ☆☆*LA FORET*, 36 Av. Maréchal-Joffre, Tel. 439. View of park; quiet. Service charge included. 30 Rooms. Garage. ☆*ANGLETERRE* (closed Tuesdays in winter), 5 Pl. Omer Vallon, Tel. 059. 9 Rooms. Garage.

## RESTAURANTS

☆☆*TIPPERARY* (closed Thursdays), 2 Av. Maréchal-Joffre, Tel. 048. ☆*CHATEAU*, 22 Rue Connétable, Tel. 225.

*Gouvieux, 4 kilometers from Chantilly, via Route 309. Post Office in Gouvieux*

## HOTEL

☆☆*CHATEAU DE LA TOUR*, Tel. 39 Gouvieux. Quiet. Garage free.

## Chateauneuf-du-Pape, Provence

Distance (in kilometers) to: Paris 662; Avignon 16; Marseilles 111.

## RESTAURANTS

☆☆*LA MULE DU PAPE*, Tel. 30. ☆*CHEZ LA MERE GERMAINE*, Pl. Fontaine, Tel. 5. View of valley of the Rhone.

## Chaumont-Sur-Loire, Chateaux de la Loire

Distance (in kilometers) to: Paris 189; Tours 42.

## HOTELS

☆*CHATEAU ET BELLE VUE REUNIS* (March to November), Tel. 4. 36 Rooms. Garage. ☆*MANOIR DU MOUTIER ST.-MARTIN*, Route Nationale, Tel. 13. 8 Rooms. ☆*PRIEURE ST.-MARTIN*, Grande Rue, Tel. 8. 10 Rooms. Garage.

## Chenonceaux, Chateaux de la Loire

Distance (in kilometers) to: Paris 214; Tours 35.

## HOTEL

☆*BON LABOUREUR ET CHATEAU*, 12 Route Nationale No. 76, Tel. 2. Specialties: Omelette Bon Laboureur (no extra charge), Escalope Medicis à la crème, Homard à l'américaine (certain days only). Wines: Chenonceaux, Vouvray. 22 Rooms. Garage free.

## Cherbourg, Normandy

Distance (in kilometers) to: Paris 341; Bayeux 93; Caen 119. Tourist Information (closed Sundays and Monday mornings): 2 Quai Alexandre III, Tel. 110; Automobile Club de l'Ouest, 12 Quai Alexandre III, Tel. 544.

## HOTELS

☆☆*NORD ET PAIX* (no restaurant), 32 Rue Paix, Tel. 314. Service charge 15%. 30 Rooms. Garage free. ☆☆*LOUVRE ET MARINE*, 28 Rue Paix, Tel. 228. 40 Rooms. Garage. ☆☆*ETOILE ET NORMANDIE*, 7 Rue Gambetta, Tel. 172. Garage. ☆☆*ATLANTIQUE* (no restaurant),

Rue Dom Pedro, Tel. 259. Service charge included. 90 Rooms. Garage. ☆*GRAND HOTEL* (no restaurant), 42-44 Rue Marine, Tel. 426. Service charge 15%. 33 Rooms.

### RESTAURANTS

☆*GRAND BALCON*, 51 Rue Maréchal-Foch, Tel. 041. View of "Bassin du Commerce." A la carte. ☆ *CAFE DU THEATRE*, Pl. Général-de-Gaulle, Tel. 114. Restaurant à la carte.

### Chinon, Chateaux de la Loire

Distance (in kilometers) to: Paris 283; Azay-le-Rideau 21; Tours 46. Tourist Information (summer): 8 Quai Jeanne d'Arc, Tel. 156.

### HOTELS

☆☆*FRANCE*, 47 Pl. Hôtel de Ville, Tel. 046. 23 Rooms. Garage. ☆ *BOULE D'OR*, 66 Quai Jeanne d'Arc, Tel. 055. 26 Rooms. Garage. ☆ *HOST. GARGANTUA*, 73 Rue Voltaire, Tel. 197. Specialties: Anguille Rabelaisienne, Omelette Gargantua. Wines: Chinon, Brèze. Garage free.

### RESTAURANT

☆*VER LUISANT* (Easter to October), Entrée Château, Tel. 176. View of castle.

### Colmar, Alsace

Distance (in kilometers) to: Paris 442; Mulhouse 39; Strasbourg 67. Tourist Information: 1 Pl. Gare, Tel. 22.23; Automobile Club d'Alsace, Rue Messimy, Chamber of Commerce, Tel. 31.56.

### HOTELS

☆☆*GRAND HOTEL BRISTOL*, 7 Pl. Gare, Tel. 20.38. Service charge 15%. 80 Rooms. Garage. ☆☆ *CENTRE* (no restaurant), 2 Pl. Cathédrale, Tel. 40.83. 100 Rooms. Garage. ☆*RHIN ET DANUBE* (no restaurant), 26 Av. République, Tel. 3144. View of Champ de Mars. Service charge 15%. 30 Rooms. Garage. ☆*MUSEE* (restaurant closed Mondays), 25 Rue Kléber, Tel. 2015. 40 Rooms. Garage. ☆*PARC* (restaurant closed Wednesdays), 54 Av. République, Tel. 34.80. 25 Rooms. Garage free. ☆*NOUVEL HOTEL*, 1 Av. République, Tel. 21.72. 19 Rooms. ☆*A LA VILLE DE REIMS*, 27 Rue Rapp, Tel. 28.19. 15 Rooms. Garage.

### RESTAURANTS

☆☆*MAISON DES TETES* (closed Fridays), 19 Rue Têtes, Tel. 2110. Seventeenth-century house. ☆*CENTRAL*, 8 Av. République, Tel. 24.42. ☆*BUFFET GARE*, Tel. 21.26. ☆ *MEISTERMANN*, 2 Av. République, Tel. 26.35. ☆*CHEZ ALFRED* (closed Mondays), 2 Rue Logelbach, Tel. 3023.

### Concarneau, Brittany

Distance (in kilometers) to: Paris 552; Quimper 23. Watering place.

### HOTELS

☆☆*CORNOUAILLES* (Easter to October), Plage Sables Blancs, Tel. 056. View of Baie de la Forêt. Service charge included. 100 Rooms. Garage. ☆*GRAND HOTEL*, 1 Av.

Pierre Gueguen, Tel. 028. View of port. 35 Rooms. ☆*ATLANTIC HOTEL* (opening date indefinite), Pl. Croix, Tel. 045. View of sea. Garage. ☆*BEAU RIVAGE* (Easter to October), Rue Brizeux in Minez, Post Office and Telegraph address; Tel. 142, in Concarneau. 22 Rooms. Garage. ☆ *SABLES BLANCS* (opening date indefinite), Plage Sables Blancs, in Beuzec-Conq, Tel. 139, in Concarneau. Extensive view of Baie de la Forêt; quiet. 22 Rooms. Garage. ☆ *COMMERCE*, 1 Av. Gare in Beuzec-Conq. Tel. 088, in Concarneau. 20 Rooms. Garage.

### RESTAURANT

☆*CHEZ ARMANDE*, 15 Quai Perenoff, Tel. 076. View of port.

## Courseulles-Sur-Mer, Calvados, Normandy

Distance (in kilometers) to: Paris 239; Bayeux 22. Watering place. See the artificial harbor (invasion of June 6, 1944.) Tourist Information: Pl. 6 Juin.

### HOTELS

☆*PARIS* (closed December and January), Pl. 6 Juin, Tel. 7. 20 Rooms. ☆*NORMANDY*, 56 Rue Maréchal-Joffre, Tel. 12. 20 Rooms. Garage free. ☆*LES GENETS*, 10 Rue Arthur Leduc. View of garden. 10 Rooms. Garage free.

### RESTAURANT

*PARC AUX HUITRES* (closed Mondays from October to June), Pl. 6 Juin, Tel. 18.

## Deauville, Calvados, Normandy

Distance (in kilometers) to: Paris 200; Cabourg 18; Caen 42; Le Havre 51. Watering place. Casino (Easter to September). 18- and 9-hole Golf Course, "New Golf" (Whitsunday to September); for information, Tel. 29.55 and 21.43. Tourist Information: Mairie, Tel. 21.43.

### HOTELS

☆☆☆☆☆*NORMANDY* (Whitsunday to September), Rue Jean Mermoz (on the beach), Tel. 29.21. 500 Rooms. ☆☆☆☆☆*ROYAL* (Whitsunday to September), (on the beach), Tel. 29.41. 400 Rooms. ☆☆*LA CAMARGO*, Rue Edmond Blanc, Tel. 33.30. 7 Rooms. ☆☆*CONTINENTAL* (Easter to September), 1 Rue Désiré le Hoc, Tel. 21.06. Service charge 15%. 60 Rooms. ☆☆*METROPOLE*, 17 Rue Désiré le Hoc, Tel. 22.45. Service charge 15%. 22 Rooms. ☆*LE MORNY* (Easter to September), Pl. Morny, Tel. 33.42. 27 Rooms. ☆*ATLANTIC* (Easter to end of September), 118 bis Av. République, Tel. 20.50. 40 Rooms. ☆*FRASCATI*, 2-4 Av. République, Tel. 20.95. 18 Rooms. Garage. ☆*TERMINUS SPORTING* (restaurant closed Thursdays), 12 Av. République (across from the station), Tel. 20.24. 30 Rooms. ☆*CHAUMIERE NORMANDE*, 15 Av. République, Tel. 32.60. 11 Rooms.

### RESTAURANTS

☆☆*CHALET NORMAND* (Easter to September), 26 Rue Gontaut-Biron, Tel. 23.49. 7 Rooms. ☆☆*LUIGI'S*

BAR (Easter to end of September), 68 Rue Désiré le Hoc, Tel. 20.22. ☆SIECLE (closed Wednesdays in winter), 37 Rue Désiré le Hoc, Tel. 20.10. A la carte. Specialties: Bisque de Homard, Homard à l'américaine, Sole normande. ☆BAZILLE (Easter to September), 60 Rue Désiré le Hoc, Tel. 23.08. ☆HOLLYWOOD, 13 Rue A. Fracasse, Tel. 34.83. A la carte. ☆PETIT VATEL, 129 Av. République, Tel. 21.56.

*Au Nouveau Golf:*

☆☆☆☆☆GOLF (Whitsunday to September), Tel. 29.01. Quiet. 250 Rooms.

## Dijon, Burgundy

Distance (in kilometers) to: Paris 323; Beaune 38; Geneva 197; Lausanne 202; Lyon 197; Nancy 192. Tourist Information: for Dijon et Côte-d'Or, 34 Rue Forges, Tel. 18.54. Automobile Club de Bourgogne, 1-3 Pl. Bossuet, Tel. 23.23. Touring Club de France, 22 Rue Préfecture, Tel. 47.90.

HOTELS

☆☆☆☆CLOCHE (restaurant closed Sundays), 14 Pl. Darcy. Service charge included. 220 Rooms. Garage. ☆☆☆ CENTRAL, 10 Rue Château, Tel. 22.41 and 22.43. 100 Rooms. Garage. ☆☆MOROT ET GENEVE (restaurant closed Wednesdays), 17 Av. Maréchal-Foch, Tel. 189 and 482. Service charge included. 93 Rooms. ☆☆BOURGOGNE (no restaurant), 7 Pl. Darcy, Tel. 017. 54 Rooms. Garage. ☆☆☆TERMINUS (restaurant Grande Taverne, closed Fridays), 20 Av. Maréchal-Foch, Tel. 13.93. Serv-

ice charge 15%. 30 Rooms. ☆☆CHAPEAU ROUGE, 5 Rue Michelet, Tel. 530. 60 Rooms. ☆☆☆NORD (restaurant closed Mondays), 2 Rue Liberté. 41 Rooms. ☆☆JURA (no restaurant), 14 Av. Maréchal-Foch, Tel. 071. 60 Rooms. Garage. ☆POSTE (restaurant closed Mondays), 5 Rue Château, Tel. 30.20. 41 Rooms. ☆CONTINENTAL (restaurant closed Sundays), 7 Rue Docteur-Remy, Tel. 551. 33 Rooms.

RESTAURANTS

☆☆TERMINUS ET GRANDE TAVERNE (closed Fridays), 20 Av. Maréchal-Foch, Tel. 12.93. Service charge 15%. ☆AU CHATEAUBRIANT, 3 Av. Maréchal-Foch, Tel. 355. ☆PRE AUX CLERCS (closed Wednesdays), 11-13 Pl. Libération, Tel. 221. ☆BUFFET GARE, Tel. 051.

*Chenove: 4 kilometers from Dijon, altitude 374. Post Office address: Chenove*

HOTELS

☆ESCARGOTIERE (restaurant closed Thursdays), 96 Route Beaune, Tel. 5 Chenove. 6 Rooms. Garage free.

## Dinard, Brittany

Distance (in kilometers) to: Paris 400; La Baule 204; Cancale 14. Watering place. Casinos in summer. Swimming Pools, Casino Balneum, Open air pools, A la Grande Plage and A la Plage du Prieuré. Golf Club, 12-hole Golf Course (for information, Tel. 310.08 St. Briac), near St. Briac (6½ kilometers). Tourist Information: 5 Rue Casino, Tel. 382.54.

## HOTELS

☆☆☆☆LE GRAND HOTEL (summer), 46 Av. George V, Tel. 380.28 and 381.89. View of Baie de la Vicomté. 130 Rooms. ☆☆☆GRAND HOTEL PLAGE (June to October), 3 Blvd. Wilson, Tel. 385.43. Sea view. 70 Rooms. Garage. ☆☆☆CRYSTAL (Whitsunday to October), 15 Rue Malouine, Tel. 380.59. Extensive view of beach. Service charge 15%. 200 Rooms. ☆☆MER (summer), Rue Villas-de-la-Mer, Tel. 382.48. View of beach; quiet. Service charge 15%. 200 Rooms. Garage free. ☆☆DUNES, 5 Rue G.-Clémenceau, Tel. 382.72. Service charge 15%. 34 Rooms. ☆☆PRINTANIA (Easter to September), 5 Av. George V, Tel. 383.07. View of Rance. 55 Rooms. ☆☆EMERAUDE PLAGE (July to September), 1 Pl. Joffre, Tel. 385.79. Service charge 15%. 52 Rooms. ☆☆DINARD HOTEL, 5 Rue Levavasseur, Tel. 383.10. View of Rance. 19 Rooms. ☆☆EDEN, 14 Blvd. Féart, Tel. 383.69 and 384.48. Service charge 15%. 38 Rooms. ☆☆ MICHELET (summer) (restaurant at the Hôtel de la Mer), 46 Blvd. Albert-Lacroix, Tel. 380.22. Service charge 15%. Garage free. ☆CHATEAUBRIAND (April to October), 16 Av. George V, Tel. 382.52. 28 Rooms. Garage. ☆ALTAIR (opening date indefinite), 18 Blvd. Féart, Tel. 383.58. 33 Rooms. ☆CORBIERES (Easter to September), 10 Rue Corbières, Tel. 383.51. 23 Rooms. ☆ EDOUARD VII, 10 Av. Edouard VII, Tel. 382.26. 23 Rooms. ETRANGERS, 70 Rue St. Enogat, Tel. 384.37. 40 Rooms. ☆BELLEVUE (summer), 9-11 Av. George V, Tel. 380.66. View of Rance. Service charge 15%. 38 Rooms. ☆PANORAMA (Easter to September), 1 Av. George V, Tel. 383.86. View of Rance. 33 Rooms. ☆MODERNE ET TERMINUS, Pl. Gare, Tel. 380.65. 25 Rooms. Garage.

## RESTAURANTS

☆☆AU CHAPON FIN (summer), 8 Rue G.-Clémenceau, Tel. 384.85. View of beach.

*Outside the city: A la Richardais, 3 kilometers SE of Dinard. Post Office, à la Richardais.*

☆AU PETIT ROBINSON, Tel. 384.82 Dinard. Specialties: Homard Newburg, Poulet sauté Vicomte, Petit Robinson. Service charge 15%. 4 Rooms.

*A la Landriais, 9 kilometers SE of Dinard. Post Office in Minihic-sur-Rance.*

☆LA LANDRIAIS, Tel. 6 Minihic-sur-Rance.

## Dives-Sur-Mer, Calvados, Normandy

Distance (in kilometers) to: Paris 203; Cabourg 2; Deauville 16.

## RESTAURANT

☆☆☆HOST. GUILLAUME-LE-CONQUERANT (opening date indefinite), Rue Hasting, Tel. 4.08. Beautiful interiors.

## Evian-Les-Bains, Savoy Alps

Distance (in kilometers) to: Paris 585; Geneva 42; Lausanne 61. Spa (summer), Casino (summer), Beach. Swimming Pool, Av. Sources. 18-hole Golf Course (June to September) (for information, Tel. 0.15). Tourist Information (summer), 29 Rue Nationale, Tel. 0.88.

## HOTELS (in town)

☆☆☆☆SPLENDIDE (summer), near the spring "Source Cachat," Tel. 069, 8 and 214. View of lake; quiet. 150 Rooms. ☆☆☆AMBASSADEURS (summer), Av. Gen.-Dupas, Tel. 161 and 240. View of lake. Service charge 15%. 70 Rooms. ☆☆PLAGE (opening date indefinite), Av. Gen.-Dupas, Tel. 270. 48 Rooms. ☆☆ BELLEVUE (June to October), 6 Rue Levant, Tel. 114. View of lake. Service charge 15%. 60 Rooms. ☆☆ CHATEAU DE FONBONNE (June to October), Pl. Port, Tel. 113. Service charge 15%. 40 Rooms. ☆☆AL-BERT I (May to September), Pl. Port, Tel. 196. View of lake. 55 Rooms. ☆☆ETRANGERS (Restaurant Marceau), (May 15 to October), 69 Rue Nationale, Tel. 046. 50 Rooms. Garage. ☆☆BEAU SITE ET DU LAC (summer) (no restaurant), Quai Baron-de-Blonay, Tel. 129. Service charge 15%. 45 Rooms. Garage. ☆☆CONTINENTAL, 65 Rue Nationale, Tel. 081. Service charge 15%. 40 Rooms. ☆☆MIRABEAU (opening date indefinite), Blvd. Jean-Jaurès, Tel. 092. View of lake. 48 Rooms. ☆☆PARIS (summer), Quai Baron-de-Blonay, Tel. 033. View of lake. Service charge 15%. 35 Rooms. Garage free. ☆☆SAVOY HOTEL (summer), Quai Baron-de-Blonay, Tel. 035. View of lake. Service charge 15%. 70 Rooms. ☆ALPES (opening date indefinite), Rue Nationale, Tel. 099. ☆NOAILLES, 12 Rue Nationale, Tel. 027. 40 Rooms. ☆BON SEJOUR (April to October), Av. A.-de-Noailles, Tel. 179. 40 Rooms. Garage free. ☆TOURISTES (opening date indefinite) (no restaurant), 2 Av. Gare, Tel. 183. 30 Rooms.

## RESTAURANTS

☆☆DU CASINO (opening date indefinite), Au Casino, Tel. 152. Extensive view of lake. ☆REGENCE (opening date indefinite), 2 Pl. Port, Tel. 175. View of port. 24 Rooms. ☆MARCEAU (May to October), 69 Rue Nationale, Tel. 046.

### Hotels outside the city

☆☆☆☆☆ROYAL (summer), Tel. 400. View of the lake; quiet. 200 Rooms. Garage. ☆☆☆☆LA VERNIAZ (Easter to October), Post Office address: La Verniaz. Tel. 055 and 168 Evian. View of lake and mountain; quiet. Specialties: Truites au bleu, Ecrevisses. Wines: Crépy, Douvaine, Crépy-Marignan. Service charge 15%. 70 Rooms. Garage. ☆☆☆ERMITAGE (summer), Tel. 042. View of lake and mountain; quiet. Service charge 15%. 110 Rooms. ☆☆☆PARC (June to September), Quai Paul-Leger, Tel. 330. View of lake; quiet. Service charge 15%. 84 Rooms. Garage. ☆☆GALLIA (summer), au Rond Point: 1 kilometer from Evian-les-Bains. Tel. 004. Altitude 435. View of lake and mountain. Service charge 15%. 56 Rooms. Garage. ☆☆☆ LUMINA (May to September), Maxilly-Petite-Rive, 3 kilometers from Evian-les-Bains. Post Office address:

Evian-les-Bains, Tel. 140 and 468 Evian. Specialties: Paupiettes de truite en croute au champagne, Fera à l'oseilles, Poulet grillé Lumina. Wines: Publier, Crépy. View of lake and mountain. Service charge 15%. 70 Rooms. Garage.

## Fontainebleau

Distance (in kilometers) to: Paris 60. Beach at Thomery. Open-air Swimming Pool. 18-hole Golf Course (closed Tuesdays; information, Tel. 22.95). Tourist information (closed mornings out of season), 38 Rue Grande, Tel. 25.68.

### HOTELS

☆☆☆*AIGLE NOIR*, 27 Pl. Denecourt, Tel. 20.27. Service charge 15%. 40 Rooms. Garage. ☆☆*LÉGRIS ET PARC* (Easter to November), 36 Rue Parc, Tel. 24.24. Gardens; quiet. 40 Rooms. ☆☆*ALBE*, 9-11 Rue Royale, Tel. 23.42. Gardens. Service charge 15%. 30 Rooms. Garage. ☆☆*PALAIS*, 25 Place Denecourt, Tel. 21.11. Service charge 15%. 24 Rooms. Garage. ☆☆*MORET ET ARMAGNAC*, 16 Rue Château, Tel. 21.28. 32 Rooms. Garage. ☆*TOULOUSE* (May to October), 183 Rue Grande, Tel. 22.73. Service charge 15%. 16 Rooms. Garage. ☆*CYGNE* (restaurant closed Wednesdays), 30 Place F-Roosevelt, Tel. 25.99. 12 Rooms. ☆ *MODERNE ET ANCIENS COURRIERS*, 48 Rue France, Tel. 24.33. Gardens; restaurant. 25 Rooms. Garage. ☆*LAUNOY* (Easter to October), (no restaurant), 37 Blvd. Magenta, 20 Rooms.

### RESTAURANTS

☆☆*FILET DE SOLE* (closed Wednesdays), 5 Rue Coq-Gris, Tel. 25.05. Specialties: Filet de Sole, Jambonneau en croute, Soufflé du Filet de Sole. ☆☆*A L'ILE DE BEAUTE*, 53 Rue France, Tel. 29.43. Specialties: Truite au Champagne, Terrine Maison, Châteaubriand pommes soufflés (certain days). ☆*LES CHOUPETTES* (closed Mondays), 3 Rue Royale, Tel. 24.68. A la carte. ☆*CERF NOIR* (closed Mondays), 4 Rue France, Tel. 23.64. A la carte.

## At Avon

### HOTELS

☆☆*FORET*, 79 Av. Pres. Roosevelt, Tel. 59.26 at Fontainebleau. Gardens; quiet. 32 Rooms. Garage. ☆☆*CASCADES ET BEAUSEJOUR*, 2 Rue Gambetta, Mail address: Avon. Tel. 58.10 at Fontainebleau. Forest; quiet. 30 Rooms. Garage. ☆☆*DES CHASSES* (March to November), Route Thomery, Mail address: Avon. Tel. 58.11 at Fontainebleau. Gardens; quiet. 20 Rooms. Garage free. ☆ *CHATEAU DU VAL* (March-November), 2 Rue Basses-Loges, Mail address: Avon. Tel. 59.61 at Fontainebleau. Large grounds; quiet. 14 Rooms. Garage free. ☆*DE FRANCHARD*, Tel. 29.69 at Fontainebleau. Forest. Aux Gorges de Franchard, 5 kilometers on N837. Mail address: Fontainebleau.

## Font-Romeu, Pyrenees

Distance (in kilometers) to: Paris 874; Ax-les-Thermes 68; Carcassonne 127; Toulouse 192. Mountain resort, winter sports. Casino (winter and summer), 9-hole Golf Course (July 1 to September 15) (for information, Tel. 4 and 33). Tourist Information: Place Casino, Tel. 70.

## HOTELS

☆☆☆☆GRAND HOTEL ET GOLF (summer and winter), Tel. 4 and 33. Quiet. Service charge 15%. 150 Rooms Garage free. ☆☆BELLEVUE ET BEAUSITE (summer and winter) (restaurant), Av. Egat, Tel. 16 and 43. Quiet. 50 Rooms. Garage. ☆☆ VILLA ST. PAUL (closed May and November), Tel. 81. Quiet 25 Rooms, Garage free. ☆☆PYRENEES, Tel. 49. 40 Rooms. ☆REGINA, Tel. 19. Garage free. ☆BON ACCUEIL, Tel. 27. 35 Rooms. Garage.

## Geneva, Switzerland

Distance (in kilometers) to: Paris 520; Aix-les-Bains 76; Annecy 43; Berne 154; Chamonix 86; Lyon 154; Nice 484. Municipal Casino (May to September). Beaches: Geneve-Plage; Plage des Paquis. 18-hole Golf Course at Onex (March to December; for information, Tel. 8.70.33 and 26.920). Automobile Club of Switzerland, 18 Rue Croix d'Or, Tel. 5.50.16. Touring Club of Switzerland, 9 Rue P. Fatio, Tel. 4.33.44.

## HOTELS (in town)

☆☆☆☆LES BERGUES, 33 Quai Bergues, Tel. 2.66.45. On lake. 110 Rooms. ☆☆☆☆BEAU RIVAGE, 13 Quai Mont-Blanc, Tel. 2.04.50. Lake. Service charge 15%. 180 Rooms. ☆☆☆☆PAIX, 9 and 11 Quai Mont-Blanc, Tel. 2.61.59. On lake. Service charge 15%. 115 Rooms. ☆☆☆☆

RICHEMOND, Jardin Brunswick, Tel. 2.71.20. On lake. Garden. Service charge 15%. 100 Rooms. ☆☆☆☆ CORNAVIN (no restaurant; breakfast and service charge included), Place Cornavin, Tel. 2.04.30. 135 Rooms. ☆☆☆RUSSIE (no restaurant), 1 Quai Mont-Blanc, Tel. 2.65.54. On lake. Service charge 15%. 80 Rooms. ☆☆☆BERNINA (no restaurant; breakfast included), 22 Pl. Cornavin, Tel. 2.81.77. 76 Rooms. ☆☆☆REGINA, 7 Quai Mont-Blanc, Tel. 2.61.74. On lake. 40 Rooms. ☆☆☆ANGLE-TERRE, 17 Quai du Mont-Blanc, Tel. 2.81.88. 85 Rooms. ☆☆INTER-NATIONAL ET TERMINUS, 20 Rue Alpes, Tel. 2.80.95. 70 Rooms. ☆☆FAMILLES, 14 Rue Lausanne, Tel. 2.60.29. Service charge 15%. 70 Rooms. ☆☆SUISSE (no restaurant), 23 Rue Mont-Blanc, Tel. 2.66.30. 55 Rooms. ☆☆STRAS-BOURG ET UNIVERS, 10 Rue Pradier, Tel. 2.81.44. 40 Rooms. ☆ BRISTOL, 10 Rue Mont-Blanc, Tel. 2.91.50. Service charge 15%. 35 Rooms. ☆SIECLE (no restaurant), 12 Pl. Cornavin, Tel. 2.80.50. 50 Rooms.

## RESTAURANTS

☆☆BUFFET GARE CORNAVIN, Pl. Cornavin, Tel. 2.60.02. ☆☆AU-BERGE MERE ROYAUME, 9 Rue des Corps-Saints. A la carte.

## Left Bank, Business Center

### HOTELS

☆☆☆☆LA RESIDENCE, 11 Route Florissante, Tel. 4.13.88. Quiet. Service charge 15%. 160 Rooms. ☆☆☆ECU, 2 Pl. Rhone, Tel. 4.23.24.

On River Rhone. Service charge 15%. 55 Rooms. ☆☆*VICTORIA*, 11 Rue Pierre Fatio, Tel. 4.83.40. On lake. Service charge 15%. 50 Rooms. ☆*TOURING BALANCE* (breakfast included), 13 Place Longemalle, Tel. 5.13.80. 65 Rooms. ☆ *BALMORAL*, 23 Rue Ferdinand-Bodler, Tel. 5.33.56. 35 Rooms.

### RESTAURANTS

☆☆*PLAT D'ARGENT*, 4 Grande Rue, Tel. 4.27.37. ☆☆*E. FAVRE* (Cercle des Arts), 4 Quai Poste, Tel. 5.20.92. ☆☆*LE GLOBE*, 1 Pl. Lac, Tel. 5.53.60 and 69. ☆*LE PRADO*, 1 Rue Purgatoire, Tel. 5.28.44.

### North of the City

#### HOTEL
☆☆*MON REPOS*, 131 Rue Lausanne, Tel. 2.65.69. 50 Rooms. Garage.

### RESTAURANT
☆☆*PERLE DU LAC* (March to December), 128 Rue Lausanne, Tel. 2.75.20. On lake; large grounds.

### East of the City

#### RESTAURANTS
☆☆*CAFE DES MARINS*, 28 Quai Gustave-Ador, Tel. 4.49.55. ☆☆*PARC DES EAUX-VIVES* (March to November), 82 Quai Gustave-Ador, Tel. 4.54.38. ☆*SIMPLON*, 5 Route de Chène, Tel. 4.26.66.

### South and Southwest of the City

#### RESTAURANTS
☆☆*LONGCHAMP* (closed Wednesdays), Stand St. Georges, Tel. 4.70.50. Specialties: Aspic de foie gras, Quenelles à a mode de Bugey, Soufflé maison. Wine: Morges. ☆☆*INTERNATIONAL* (closed Wednesdays), Place Cirque, Tel. 4.07.29. ☆☆*LA BONNE AUBERGE*, 19 Blvd. G.-Favon, Tel. 4.10.03.

### Environs of Geneva

#### HOTELS
☆*LE PAVILLON*, Tel. 8.50.32 at Versoix. On lake. Service charge 15%. 8 Rooms. Garage free. ☆*LAC GRANDE RUE*, Tel. 8.60.18 at Coppet. Post Office address: Coppet. On lake. 12 Rooms. ☆*CERF*, Tel. 8.37.24 at Hermance. Garden; quiet. 14 Rooms. Garage.

#### RESTAURANTS
☆*LE CREUX DE GENTHOD*, Tel. 8.40.06 at Bellevue. On lake. ☆*PORT*, Tel. 8.20.54 at Collonge. On lake.

### Gets (Les), Savoy-Alps

Distance (in kilometers) to: Paris 591. Mountain resort. Winter sports. (December to May, July to October).

#### HOTELS
☆*BEAU SITE* (summer and winter), Tel. 1. 32 Rooms. Garage. ☆*NATIONAL*, Tel. 2. 28 Rooms. Garage free. ☆*LION D'OR*, Tel. 6. 22 Rooms. Garage. ☆*WEEK-END* (summer and December; Easter), Tel. 17. 35 Rooms. Garage. ☆*REGINA* (summer and winter), Tel. 16. 10 Rooms.

### Grenoble

Distance (in kilometers) to: Paris 557; Aix-les-Bains 71; Annecy 118; Geneva 147; Lyon 106; Marseilles 277; Nice 337.

## HOTELS

☆☆☆*MODERNE ET TROIS DAU-PHINS*, 2 and 4 Rue Felix-Poulat, Tel. 2.71 and 12.29. Service charge 15%. 160 Rooms. Garage. ☆☆☆ *SAVOIE* (no restaurant), 52 Av. Alsace-Lorraine, Tel. 0.21, 2.21, and 37.21. Service charge 15%. ☆☆ *TERMINUS* (no restaurant), 10 Pl. Gare, Tel. 18.80. Service charge 15%. 45 Rooms. Garage. ☆☆*SUISSE ET BORDEAUX*, 6 Pl. Gare, Tel. 10.72 and 47.97. 89 Rooms. ☆☆ *SPLENDID HOTEL* (no restaurant), 22 Rue Thiers, Tel. 33.12. Service charge 15%. 25 Rooms. ☆☆*BRISTOL* (no restaurant), 11 Av. Félix-Viallet, Tel. 23.18. Service charge 15%. 65 Rooms. Garage. ☆☆*ANGLETERRE* (no restaurant), 5 Pl. Victor-Hugo, Tel. 7.42. Service charge 15%. 64 Rooms. ☆☆ *TOURING* (no restaurant), 26 Av. Alsace-Lorraine, Tel. 24.32. Service charge 15%. 50 Rooms. Garage. ☆☆*LUX HOTEL* (no restaurant), 6 Rue Crépu, Tel. 41.89. 27 Rooms. ☆☆*ROYAL* (no restaurant), 2 Rue Gabriel Peri, Tel. 3.79. 40 Rooms. ☆☆*NAPOLEON*, 7 Rue Montorge, Tel. 33.31. 50 Rooms. ☆☆*EUROPE*, 22 Pl. Grenette, Tel. 16.94. 50 Rooms. ☆☆*GLORIA* (no restaurant), 12 Rue A-Berges, Tel. 12.93. Service charge 15%. ☆☆*STANDARD* (no restaurant), 5 Rue Docteur-Mazel, Tel. 21.44. Service charge 15%. 32 Rooms. ☆*CONDORCET-ARMES DAUPHINOISES* (temporarily without restaurant), 8 Rue Condorcet, Tel. 20.64. 20 Rooms. ☆*AU VAUTOUR*, 9 Rue Arago, Tel. 12.13. 12 Rooms. Garage.

## RESTAURANTS

☆☆*BEC FIN*, 11 Pl. Victor-Hugo, Tel. 4.86. ☆☆*LE REFUGE*, 5 Pl. Victor-Hugo, Tel. 7.94. ☆*FALCONNET*, 1 Rue République, Tel. 28.52. ☆*PHILIPPE*, 4 Pl. Grenette, Tel. 17.99. ☆*BRASSERIE DE LA PAIX*, 42 Av. Alsace-Lorraine, Tel. 29.22. ☆*UNIVERS*, 49 Av. Alsace-Lorraine, Tel. 35.80. ☆*POULARDE BRESSANE*, 25 Rue Docteur-Mazet, Tel. 39.43.

## *Outside the City*

## HOTEL

☆*LESDIGUIERES*, 122 Cours Libération, Tel. 15.56. Grounds; quiet. Service charge 15%. 40 Rooms. Garage.

## RESTAURANT

☆*BEAUSEJOUR* (closed Wednesdays), 62 Cours Libération, Tel. 12.52.

## Grasse, Alpes-Maritimes

## (near Côte d'Azur)

Distance (in kilometers) to: Paris 854; Antibes 22; Cannes 17; Nice 37. See the perfume factories. Tourist information: Pl. de la Foux, Tel. 3.56. Automobile Club de Nice et Côte d'Azur, 3 Blvd. Jeu-de-Ballon, Tel. 3.43.

## HOTELS

☆☆☆*PARC PALACE HOTEL*, Av. Victoria, Tel. 5.16. Picturesque sea view. Service charge 15%. 45 Rooms. Garage. ☆☆*VICTORIA*, Av. Riou-Blanquet, Tel. 1.24. View of Grasse and sea. 60 Rooms. Garage.

✩✩*BEAU SOLEIL AND BEAU SEJOUR*, 14 Blvd. Crouet, Tel. 1.70. Garden view. Service charge 15%. Garage. ✩*MURAOUR*, 10 Blvd. Jeu-de-Ballon, Tel. 0.45. Service charge 15%. 40 Rooms. Garage. ✩*NEGO-CIANTS*, 33 Blvd. Jeu-de-Ballon, Tel. 3.24. Service charge 15%. 20 Rooms.

## RESTAURANTS

✩✩*BIANCHI*, 6 Cours H.-Cresp., Tel. 1.72. ✩*LA FOUX*, 10 Pl. la Foux, Tel. 4.67. ✩*LES PAPILLONS*, Av. Chiris, Tel. 3.58

## Loches, Chateaux de la Loire

Distance (in kilometers) to: Paris 235; Tours 40. Tourist Information: Rue Ponts, Tel. 0.88.

## HOTELS

✩✩*FRANCE*, 6 Rue Picoys et 6 Rue République, Tel. 0.32. 25 Rooms. Garage. ✩*TOUR ST. ANTOINE*, Rue Moulins, Tel. 1.06. 16 Rooms. Garage. ✩*PALAIS* (restaurant, closed Saturdays Sept. 30-April 1), 35 Rue Picoys, Tel. 1.16. Specialties: Rillettes maison, Sundays, Thursdays; Poulet cocotte grand'mère, Champignons à la lochoise. 16 Rooms. Garage.

## RESTAURANT

✩*CHEZ FRANCOIS* (closed Sundays), 3 Pl. Marché-aux-Légumes, Tel. 3.10.

## Lourdes, Pyrenees

Distance (in kilometers) to: Paris 798; Biarritz 153; Bordeaux 233; Luchon 103; Pau 39; Toulouse 174. Grand National Pilgrimage, August 18 to 25. Tourist Information: 18 Rue du Bourg, Tel. 6.11.

## HOTELS

✩✩✩*IMPERIAL* (Easter to October), Av. Paridis, Tel. 6.30. Service charge 15%. 120 Rooms. ✩✩✩*MODERNE* (March to October), Rue Ste. Marie, Tel. 0.32. Service charge 15%. 100 Rooms. ✩✩✩ *CHAPELLE ET PARC* (Easter to October), 21 Av. Bernadette-Soubirous, Tel. 0.10. Park. Service charge 15%. 95 Rooms. ✩✩*GROTTE* (March to November), 66-68 Rue Grotte, Tel. 0.50. Service charge 15%. 100 Rooms. Garage. ✩✩*BE-THANIE*, Rue Docteur-Boissarie, Tel. 0.28. View of Basilica; quiet. 70 Rooms. ✩✩*AMBASSADEURS*, 66 Blvd. de la Grotte, Tel. 0.16. View of mountains and river. Service charge 15%. 50 Rooms. ✩✩*NEVERS*, 6 Av. Baron-Maransin, Tel. 1.69. 45 Rooms. ✩✩*LONDRES ET GALLIA* (April to November), 26 Av. Bernadette-Soubirous, Tel. 0.14. View of park. Service charge 15%. 60 Rooms. Garage. ✩✩*TERMINUS TOUR-ING*, 19 Av. IV-République, Tel. 0.22 Service charge 15%. 50 Rooms. ✩✩*PANORAMIC HOTEL*, 2 Av. IV-République, Tel. 1.08. 70 Rooms. Garage. ✩✩*EUROPE* (Easter to October), 34 Av. Peyramale, Tel. 1.50. 47 Rooms. ✩✩*BELLEVUE* (February to November), 58 to 62 Rue Grotte, Tel. 0.78. Service charge 15%. 60 Rooms. Garage free. ✩✩*JEANNE D'ARC* (Easter to October), 5 Av. Alsace-Lorraine, Tel. 1.07. Quiet. Service charge 15%. 100 Rooms. Garage free. ✩✩*SPLENDID BEAU*

SEJOUR, opposite station, Tel. 0.18. Service charge 15%. 40 Rooms. Garage free. ☆☆ANGLETERRE, 12 Rue Ste. Marie, Tel. 0.15. 50 Rooms. ☆☆METROPOLE, Rue Carrières-Peyramale, Tel. 0.47. Garage. ☆ BASILIQUE (Easter to October), 158 Av. Bernadette-Soubirous, Tel. 1.66. Service charge 15%. 40 Rooms. ☆EXCELSIOR, 83 Blvd. Grotte, Tel. 2.05. Service charge 15%. 50 Rooms. ☆HEINS ET BOULEVARD (April to October), 20 Av. Bernadette-Soubirous, Tel. 0.63. Service charge 15%. 60 Rooms. ☆ST. LOUIS DE FRANCE (April to October), Av. Paradis, Tel. 0.99. Service charge 15%. 80 Rooms. ☆ESPAGNE (Easter to October), 13 Av. Paradis, Tel. 1.02. Quiet. Service charge 15%. 105 Rooms. Garage. ☆MAJESTIC, 10 Av. Baron-Maransin, Tel. 7.23. 30 Rooms. ☆ST. MARIE-MADELEINE (Easter to October), 9 Rue St. Felix, Tel. 3.19. Service charge 15%. 65 Rooms. ☆ST. ETIENNE (Easter to October), 61-63 Blvd. de la Grotte, Tel. 2.03. Service charge 20%. 80 Rooms. ☆ NOTRE DAME DE FRANCE (Easter to October), 8 Av. Peyramale, Tel. 0.77. Service charge 15%. 30 Rooms. Garage free. ☆LECUYER (Easter to November), 8 Rue Docteur-Boissarie, Tel. 7.09. Quiet. Service charge 15%. 40 Rooms. Garage free. ☆LA ROTONDE, 59 Rue de la Grotte, Tel. 4.16. 44 Rooms. ☆ST. FRANCOIS-D'ASSISE, 14 Av. Peyramale, Tel. 0.79. 60 Rooms. Garage. ☆VATICAN (Easter to October), 95 Rue de la Grotte, Tel. 0.21. Service charge 15%. 36 Rooms. ☆MYOSOTIS, Av. Reine-Astrid, Tel. 4.02. 30

Rooms. ☆MARANSIN, 5 Av. Baron-Maransin, Tel. 2.84. Service charge 15%. 13 Rooms. ☆BEAU RIVAGE, 18 Av. Peyramale, Tel. 0.53. 56 Rooms. ☆CENTRAL (Easter to October), 3 Rue Massabielle, Tel. 1.49. Service charge 15%. 90 Rooms. Garage free. ☆BASILIA, 37 Rue Bagnères, Tel. 2.62. Service charge 15%. 20 Rooms. Garage. ☆SACRE COEUR ET ST. PIERRE (Easter to October), 65 Blvd. de la Grotte, Tel. 0.61. Service charge 15%. 70 Rooms. ☆ VICTORIA, Rue Massabielle, Tel. 40 Rooms. Garage.

**RESTAURANT**

☆ROTISSERIE MARSEILLAISE, 44 Rue de la Grotte, Tel. 1.32. Service charge 15%.

## Luchon, Pyrenees

Distance (in kilometers) to: Paris 818; Montrejeau 38; Toulouse 135. Mountain resort; winter sports; casino (summer). For information, Tel. 0.87. Open-air Swimming Pool. 6-hole Golf Course (summer; for information, Tel. 2.70). Tourist Information: Maison du Tourisme, 18 Allées Etigny, Tel. 0.83.

**HOTELS**

☆☆☆☆PYRENEES PALACE (summer), 2 Rue Sylvie and Blvd. Tron, Tel. 0.63. Service charge 15%. 130 Rooms. ☆☆☆☆SACARON (June to October), 65 Allées Etigny, Tel. 0.48. Service charge 15%. 93 Rooms. ☆☆☆☆ANGLETERRE (summer and winter), 24 Allées Etigny, Tel 0.60. Service charge 15%. 80 Rooms. Garage free. ☆☆☆BRISTOL, 12-14

Allées Bains Tel. 0.14. 50 Rooms. ☆☆*POSTE ET GOLF*, 29 Allées Etigny, Tel. 0.40. 80 Rooms. Garage. ☆☆*RICHELIEU ET THERMES* (no restaurant), Cours Quinconces, Tel. 0.44. 30 Rooms. ☆☆ *ROYAL HOTEL* (summer), 9 Cours Quinconces, Tel. 0.62. 36 Rooms. ☆☆*BORDEAUX*, 15 Allées Etigny, Tel. 0.19. 70 Rooms. Garage free. ☆☆*CONTINENTAL* (summer), 22 Allées Etigny, Tel. 0.38. 65 Rooms. Garage free. ☆☆*LE GRAND HOTEL* (June to September; December to February), 79 Allées Etigny, Tel. 0.46. 65 Rooms. ☆☆*VILLA CORNEILLE* (summer), 5 Av. Alexandre-Dumas, Tel. 0.22. Quiet. Specialties: Foie gras, Dinde truffée à la gelée. 30 Rooms. ☆☆*FRANCE* (closed October to December), 10 Allées Etigny, Tel. 1.44. 58 Rooms. ☆*LE BON GITE*, 21 Allées Bains, Tel. 1.13. 30 Rooms. ☆☆*PYRENEES*, 2 Allées Etigny, Tel. 0.80. 60 Rooms. Garage free. ☆*CAVE MODERNE*, 12 Allées Etigny, Tel. 0.69. 20 Rooms. ☆☆*BAINS*, 75 Allées Etigny, Tel. 0.58. 50 Rooms. Garage. ☆*PARIS*, 17 Cours Quinconces, Tel. 1.34. 45 Rooms. Garage. ☆*HENRI SORS* (summer), 3 Av. Carnot, Tel. 0.47. 15 Rooms. ☆*BELLEVUE*, 3 Allées Etigny, Tel. 1.65. 25 Rooms. Garage free. ☆*PARC* (summer), 33 Cours Quinconces, Tel. 1.58. 24 Rooms.

## Lyon

Distance (in kilometers) to: Paris 472; Aix-les-Bains 126; Annecy 159; Dijon 197; Geneva 154; Grenoble 106; Marseilles 323. Swimming pools (closed Tuesdays), 221 Garibaldi; open-air pool, 70 Quai de Serin. 12-hole Golf Course, Montlouis (for information, Tel. 36 St. Genis-Laval). Airport: Bron, Tel. Parmentier 93.16 and 101.81. Tourist Information: Pavillon du Tourisme, Pl. Bellecour, Tel. Franklin 30.39. Touring Club de France, Tel. 33.44. Automobile Club of the Rhone, 7 Rue Grolée, Tel. Franklin 51.01.

HOTELS

☆☆☆*CARLTON*, Pl. République, Tel. F56.51. Service charge 15%. 120 Rooms. Garage. ☆☆☆*GRAND NOUVEL HOTEL* (restaurant, closed Sundays), 11 Rue Grolée, Tel. F56.21. Service charge 15%. 160 Rooms. Garage. ☆☆☆*ROYAL HOTEL* (no restaurant), 20 Pl. Bellecour, Tel. F57.31. 98 Rooms. ☆☆☆ *TERMINUS* (Gare Perrache), 12 Cours Verdun, Tel. F58.11. 160 Rooms. ☆☆☆*BEAUX-ARTS* (temporarily without restaurant), 73-75 Rue Hôtel-de-Ville, Tel. F52.48. 80 Rooms. ☆☆☆*CITY* (no restaurant), 16 Rue République, Tel. F56.11. Service charge 15%. 89 Rooms. Garage. ☆☆☆*ANGLETERRE*, 22 Pl. Carnot, Tel. F55.48. 80 Rooms. Garage. ☆☆☆*BRISTOL* (no restaurant), 28 Cours Verdun (Gare Perrache), Tel. F55.93. Service charge 15%. 140 Rooms. ☆☆☆*BORDEAUX ET PARC* (no restaurant), Cours Verdun, Tel. F46.64 and 58.73. Service charge 15%. 90 Rooms. ☆☆☆*CONTINENTAL*, 17 Pl. Carnot, Tel. F56.58. 100 Rooms. ☆☆☆*GLOBE ET CECIL* (restaurant, closed Sundays), 15-21 Rue Gasparin, Tel. F58.95. Service charge 15%. 70 Rooms. ☆☆*RUSSIE* (temporarily without restaurant), 4-

6-8 Rue Gasparin, Tel. F53.44. Service charge 15%. 80 Rooms. ☆☆*DUBOST* (no restaurant), 19 Pl. Carnot, Tel. F05.46. 50 Rooms. ☆☆*VICTORIA* (no restaurant), 3 Rue Delandine, Tel. F57.61. 53 Rooms. ☆☆*NATIONAL* (no restaurant), 15 Cours de Verdun, Tel. 04.11. 44 Rooms. ☆☆*PIOLAT ET LUETIA,* 114 Blvd. Belges, Tel. L27.79 and 44.68. 72 Rooms. ☆☆*REGINA* (no restaurant), 21 Rue Bat d'Argent, Tel. B32.76. Service charge 15%. 35 Rooms. ☆☆*PARIS ET NORD* (no restaurant), 16 Rue Platière, Tel. B00.95, Service charge 15%. 35 Rooms. ☆☆*CELTIC HOTEL* (no restaurant), 10 Rue François Vernay, Tel. B01.12. 40 Rooms. Garage. ☆*NORMANDIE* (no restaurant), 3 Rue Belier (Gare Perrache), Tel. F05.61. 40 Rooms. ☆*DAUPHINE,* 3 Rue Duhamel, Tel. F24.19. 40 Rooms. ☆*ETRANGERS* (no restaurant), 5 Rue Stella, Tel. F01.56. 60 Rooms. ☆*TOURING HOTEL,* 37 Cours Verdun, Tel. F39.03. 22 Rooms. ☆*VERDUN,* 82 Rue Charité, Tel. F34.71. 30 Rooms. ☆*TERMINUS-BROTTEAUX* (no restaurant), 97 Blvd. Belges, Tel. L44.13. 22 Rooms.

**RESTAURANTS**

☆☆*MORATEUR* (closed Sundays), 14 Rue Grolée, Tel. F36.76. A la carte. Specialties: Quenelles Nantua, Langouste truffée, Poulet de Bresse des gourmets. ☆☆*LE MOLIERE* (closed Sundays), 18 Pl. Morand, Tel. L14.42. A la carte. Specialties: Quenelles de brochet, Langouste maison, Rulet de Bresse aux aubergines. Wines: Brouilly, Chaintre. ☆☆*MERE BRAZIER* (closed Sundays, May 1 to September 30), 12 Rue Royale, Tel. B15.49. A la carte. Specialties: Quenelles au gratin, Volaille à Mère Brazier, Fonds d'artichauts au foie gras. Wines: Pouilly-Fuisse, Brouilly. ☆☆*MERE GUY* (March to October) (closed Mondays in winter), 35 Quai J. J. Rousseau, Tel. F129.02. Garden; river view. Service charge 15%. ☆☆ *FRANCOTTE* (closed Saturdays in summer), 8 Pl. Celestine, Tel. F38.64. A la carte. ☆☆*MERE FILLIOUX* (closed Saturdays), 73 Rue Dequesne, Tel. L03.19. A la carte. ☆☆*FARGE,* 1 Pl. Cordelière, Tel. F37.64. ☆☆ *FOILLARD FRERES* (closed Saturdays), 5 Rue Stella, Tel. F29.84. A la carte. ☆☆*RESTAURANT DU CAFE NEUF, VETTARD* (closed Mondays, July to September), 7 Pl. Bellecour, Tel. F07.59. A la carte. Specialties: Quenelles de brochet, Côte de marcassin Grand-Veneur, Poularde maison. Wines: Pouilly-Fuisse, Fleurie. ☆☆*FILET DE SOLE* (closed Mondays), 34 Rue Ferrandière, Tel. F44.06. A la carte. ☆☆*GARCIA* (closed Mondays), 11 Rue Algerie, Tel. B18.58. A la carte. ☆☆*LA COUPOLE* (closed Saturdays), 3 Pl. Terreaux, Tel. B12.12. ☆☆*LAMOUR,* 19 Pl. Tolozan, Tel. B35.77. A la carte. ☆*RIVIER* (closed Sundays), 1 Pl. Terreaux, Tel. B02.35. ☆*NANDRON* (closed Sundays), 26 Quai Retz, Tel. F03.28. Specialties: Filets de sole, Volaille Jaquard, Chateaubriant Béarnaise. Wines: Pouilly-Fuisse, Brouilly. ☆*CHEZ JEAN,* 22 Rue Palais-Grillet, Tel. F05.79. ☆ *VIGNARD JOSEPH* ("Chez Juillete"), (closed Sundays and in August), 23 Rue Arbre-Sec, Tel. B64.06. A la carte. ☆*LE CAPITOLE*, 22 Blvd. Brotteaux, Tel. L76.47. ☆*MERE BIGOT*, 3 Rue Chavanne, Tel. B30.96. ☆*CHATEAUBRIAND* (closed Sundays), 3 Pl. Kléber, Tel. L63.83. ☆*BRASSERIE DU NORD*, 18 Rue Neuve, Tel. B24.54.

## Marseilles

Distance (in kilometers) to: Paris 776; Aix-en-Provence 29; Arles 90; Avignon 104; Bordeaux 660; Nice 202. Nine-hole Golf Course (for information, call N17.93). Boat service to Corsica via Fraissinet Co., 3 Rue Beauvau, Tel. D68.57. Flights via Air France. Tourist Bureau, 4 Canebière, Tel. C69.20. Auto Club, 27 Cours Pierre-Puget, Tel. D33.61. Touring Club, 4 and 6 Canebière, Tel. C35.84.

### HOTELS

☆☆☆☆*LE GRAND HOTEL*, 66-68 Canebière, Tel. C09.38. Service charge 15%. 40 Rooms. ☆☆☆☆ *L'ARBOIS*, Blvd. Charles-Nedelec, Tel. N45.35. Service charge 15%. 150 Rooms. Garage free. ☆☆☆☆*NO-AILLES*, 64 Canebière, Tel. C69.97. Service charge 15%. 130 Rooms. ☆☆☆☆*SPLENDIDE HOTEL*, 31 Blvd. Athènes, Tel. C69.77. Service charge 15% 170 Rooms ☆☆☆☆ *TERMINUS*, P.L.M. (Gare St. Charles), Tel. N38.47. Service charge 15%. 105 Rooms. ☆☆☆*BEAUVAIS* (no restaurant), 4 Rue Beauvau, Tel. C0849. Service charge 15%. 93 Rooms. ☆☆☆*LA MEDITERRANEE* (no restaurant), 15 Quai Belges, Tel. F14.33. 71 Rooms. ☆☆☆*GENEVE*, 3 Rue Reine-Elizabeth, Tel. C03.46. 65 Rooms. ☆☆☆*ASTORIA* (no res-

taurant), 10 Blvd. Garibaldi, Tel. C32.78. Service charge 15%. 65 Rooms. ☆☆☆*PARIS* (no restaurant), 11-13-15 Rue Colbert, Tel. C32.78. Service charge 15%. 65 Rooms. ☆☆ *SELECT HOTEL* (no restaurant), 4 Allées Léon-Gambetta, Tel. N41.26. Service charge 15%. 61 Rooms. ☆☆ *POSTE* (no restaurant), 2 Rue Colbert, Tel. C08.15 and 18.46. Service charge 15%. 135 Rooms. ☆☆*ROME ET ST. PIERRE* (no restaurant), 7 Cours St. Louis, Tel. C29.52. 66 Rooms. ☆☆*PETIT LOUVRE* (no restaurant), 19 Canebière, Tel. C16.27. Service included. 37 Rooms. ☆☆ *CALIFORNIE*, 60 Cours Belsunce, Tel. C07.39. Service charge 15%. 102 Rooms. ☆☆*LUX HOTEL* (no restaurant), 120 Canebière, Tel. L04.22. Service charge 15%. 25 Rooms. ☆☆*MODERN HOTEL* (no restaurant), 5 Canebière, Tel. C15.60. 50 Rooms. ☆☆*GLOBE* (no restaurant), 26 Rue Colbert, Tel. C17.63, 51.13. Service charge 15%. 60 Rooms. *BELLEVUE*, 34 Quai Port, Tel. C24.72. 16 Rooms. ☆*ROYAL HOTEL* (no restaurant), 29 Blvd. Dugommier, Tel. C04.11. Service charge 15%. 24 Rooms. ☆*REX* (no restaurant), 25 Blvd. Dugommier, Tel. C67.08. 30 Rooms. ☆*PRINCES* (no restaurant), 12 Pl. Bourse, Tel. C65.15. Service charge 15%. 60 Rooms. ☆ *GRAND HOTEL PREFECTURE* (no restaurant), 9 Blvd. Salvator, Tel. L65.70. Service charge 15%. 42 Rooms. ☆*UNIVERSEL* (no restaurant), 44 Cours Belsunce, Tel. C13.03. ☆*BAINS DE LA COR-NICHE* (no restaurant), 1 Blvd. Felix-Fregier, Tel. D84.09. 20 Rooms. Garage free.

**RESTAURANTS**

☆☆☆*LA RESERVE*, 317 Promenade Corniche, Tel. D02.01. On the ocean. A la carte. ☆☆☆*ISNARD*, 4 Rue Thubaneau, Tel. C14.44. Service charge 15%. ☆☆*BRASSERIE FLOR-IDA*, 15 Quai Belges, Tel. D07.31. Service charge 15%. ☆☆*STRAS-BOURG*, 11 Pl. Bourse, Tel. C14.17. A la carte. Specialties: Bouillabaisse, Loup flambé sur fenouil, Gibier des Alpes. ☆☆*CAMPA*, 9 Rue Euthy-mènes, Tel. D45.96. A la carte. ☆☆ *GARDANNE*, 28 Rue Pavillon, Tel. C09.25. Specialties: Supreme de sole Normande, Bouillabaisse, Poissons flambés au fenouil. Wine: Cassis. ☆☆*PASCAL*, 27 Pl. Thiars, Tel. D20.76. ☆☆*MONT VENTOUX*, 1 Quai Belges, Tel. C59.33. Situated on old harbor. A la carte. ☆☆*LE COL-BERT*, 7 Rue Colbert, Tel. C10.67 and 78.86. ☆*JAMBON DE PARME* (closed Sundays in summer), 47 Rue La Palud, Tel. C59.66. ☆*LA CAS-CADE MENELIK*, 5 Quai Rive-Neuve, Tel. D46.37. A la carte. ☆ *LA RASCASSE* (closed Sundays), 6 Quai Rive-Neuve, Tel. D49.82.

**Menton, Riviera**

New Municipal Casino.

**HOTELS**

☆☆☆☆*ROYAL AND WESTMINS-TER* (winter), 28 Av. Félix-Faure, Tel. 300.60. 60 Rooms. ☆☆☆☆ *ORIENT HOTEL* (November to April), 1 Rue République, Tel. 300.10. Gardens. Service charge 15%. 100 Rooms. ☆☆☆☆*VENISE ET CONTINENTAL*, Rue Partoun-eaux, Tel. 300.12 and 300.54. Gar-dens. Service charge 15%. 180 Rooms. Garage. ☆☆☆☆*GRAND HO-TEL DU LOUVRE*, 66 Av. Boyer, Tel. 302.94. Service charge 15%. 80 Rooms. Garage. ☆☆☆*REGINA* (October to May), 34 Av. Félix-Faure, Tel. 301.11. On the ocean; gardens. Service charge 15%. 80 Rooms. ☆☆☆ *BALMORAL*, 38.40 Av. Félix-Faure and Promenade du Midi, Tel. 301.56. On the ocean. Service charge 15%. 80 Rooms. ☆☆☆*PARC*, 11 Av. Ver-dun, Tel. 301.74. Service charge 15%. 90 Rooms. Garage free. ☆ *NOUVEL HOTEL*, 19 Av. Verdun, Tel. 301.71. Service charge 21%. 28 Rooms. Garage. ☆*GLOBE*, 49 Av. Verdun, Tel. 303.103. Service charge 15%. 30 Rooms.

**RESTAURANT**

☆☆☆*NOUVEAU*, Casino Municipal (opening date not yet announced), Tel. 308.36.

## West Quarter (La Madonne)

**HOTELS**

☆☆*PRINCESS*, 14 Av. Madonne, Tel. 304.97. Quiet. Service charge 15%. 51 Rooms. Garage free. ☆*EXCEL-SIOR*, 3 Av. Carnot, Tel. 304.07. Service charge 15%. 40 Rooms.

## East Quarter (Garavan)

**HOTELS**

☆☆☆*ANGLAIS*, 28 Quai Laurent, Tel. 300.69. Service charge 15%. 60 Rooms. Garage free.

**Monte Carlo, Monaco**

Distance (in kilometers) to: Paris 952; Beaulieu 11; Menton 9; Nice (coast road) 21. Principality of Monaco, capital of the Principality. 18-hole Golf Course at Mt. Agel (year-round; for information, Tel. 019.31 and 219.01). Swimming pool on the ocean; Monte Carlo beach. Prince's Palace. Oceanographic Museum. National Tourist office: 24 Blvd. Moulins, Tel. 019.01.

## HOTELS

☆☆☆☆*PARIS*, Pl. Casino, Tel. 018.11. Specialties: Mostèle valentinoise, Volaille sautée Alexandra, Souffle glace au Grand Marnier. Service charge 15%. 300 Rooms. ☆☆☆☆☆ *METROPOLE*, Av. Grande Bretagne, Tel. 017.41. Service charge 15%. 280 Rooms. ☆☆☆☆*HERMITAGE*, Square Beaumarchais, Tel. 017.31. On the sea. 300 Rooms. Garage. ☆☆☆☆ *MONTE-CARLO PALACE*, 5 Blvd. Moulins, Tel. 018.01. Service charge 15%. 250 Rooms. Garage free. ☆☆☆☆*MIRABEAU*, 2 Av. Citronniers, Tel. 017.51. Service charge 15%. 100 Rooms. ☆☆☆*WINDSOR*, 10 Blvd. Princesse-Charlotte, Tel. 018.75. Quiet. Service charge 15%. 150 Rooms. Garage free. ☆☆☆*HELDER* (no restaurant), 6 Av. Madonne, Tel. 023.07. Service charge 15%. 70 Rooms. ☆☆☆*BEAU RIVAGE*, 9 Av. Monte-Carlo, Tel. 023.96. On harbor. Service charge 15%. 76 Rooms. ☆☆☆*ROYAL HOTEL*, 15 Blvd. Pereira, Tel. 022.15. On harbor; quiet. Service charge 15%. 75 Rooms. ☆☆☆ *ANGLAIS ET ST. JAMES*, 5 Av. Princesse-Alice, Tel. 018.65. Service charge 15%. 65 Rooms. ☆☆☆*ALBION ET LITTORAL*, 38 Blvd. Moulins, Tel. 023.53. On the ocean. Service charge 15%.

60 Rooms. ☆☆☆*NOUVEL HOTEL LOUVRE*, 16 Blvd. Moulins, Tel. 023.25. On the ocean. Service charge 15%. 45 Rooms. ☆☆☆*LA RESERVE*, 7 Blvd. Bas-Moulins, Tel. 022.44. Service charge 15%. 45 Rooms. ☆☆*REGINA*, 13 Blvd. Moulins, Tel. 023.60. 30 Rooms. ☆☆*PRINCES*, 7 Av. Monte-Carlo, Tel. 025.98. Service charge 15%. 75 Rooms. ☆☆ *SPLENDID*, 4 Av. Roqueville, Tel. 025.93. Service charge 15%. 40 Rooms. ☆☆*RUSSIE* (no restaurant), 25 Av. Costa, Tel. 022.66. Service charge 15%. 43 Rooms. ☆☆*VILLA DES FLEURS*, 27 Blvd. Princesse-Charlotte, Tel. 026.84. Service charge 15%. 20 Rooms. ☆*COLONIES*, 2 Rue Scala, Tel. 024.64. Service charge 15%. 35 Rooms.

## RESTAURANTS

☆☆☆☆*CAFE DE PARIS*, Pl. Casino, Tel. 017.81. Service charge 15%. ☆☆*OSCARS*, 11 Av. Grande-Bretagne, Tel. 024.16. ☆☆*BEC ROUGE*, 12 Av. St. Charles, Tel. 014.91. A la carte. Service charge 15%. ☆☆*ROTISSERIE DU CHAPON FIN*, 6 Av. Madonne, Tel. 023.07. A la carte. ☆☆*RE*, 3 Av. St.-Charles, Tel. 023.11. ☆☆*QUICK'S*, 1 Quai Plaisance, Tel. 029.39. On harbor.

## Mont St. Michel, Normandy

Distance (in kilometers) to: Paris 328; Avranches 27; Pontsoron 9; Rennes 66. Tourist Information (summer): Maison de l'Arcade, Tel. 19.

## HOTELS

☆☆*POULARD*, Tel. 1. On bay; quiet. Specialties: Omelette Mère Poulard,

Côte d'agneau de pre-sale au feu de bois. 51 Rooms. Garage free. ☆TERRASSES POULARD (March to November), Tel. 9. On bay; quiet. 12 Rooms. ☆CONFIANCE (March to November), Tel. 7. Quiet. 20 Rooms. ☆CROIX BLANCHE ET BELLE VUE (March to October), Tel. 4. On bay; quiet. 35 Rooms. ☆MOUTON BLANC (March to November), Tel. 8. On bay; quiet. 16 Rooms. ☆ST. PIERRE, Grande Rue, Tel. 3. Quiet. 22 Rooms.

**RESTAURANTS**

☆DUQUESCLIN, Tel. 10. On bay. ☆CHEVAL BLANC, Tel. 6 and 25.

### Morlaix, Finistere, Brittany

Distance (in kilometers) to: Paris 523; Quimper 81; Roscoff 28; St. Brieuc 86. Tourist Information: Tel. 3.02.

**HOTELS**

☆☆EUROPE, 1-3 Rue d'Aiguillon, Tel. 0.58. 70 Rooms. ☆CENTRAL (no restaurant), 22 Rue Brest, Tel. 0.94. 25 Rooms. Garage.

**RESTAURANT**

☆TOUR D'ARGENT (closed Tuesdays), 2 Rue Lavoirs, Tel. 3.83. A la carte.

### Nice, Riviera

Distance (in kilometers) to: Paris 933; Aix-en-Provence 186; Antibes 21; Beaulieu 10; Cannes 32; Grasse 37; Grenoble 337; Juan-les-Pins 23; Marseilles 202. Beach and winter resort. Casinos: Casino de la Méditerranée, Nouveau Casino and Casino Municipal. Airport California (6.5 kilometers from Nice), Tel. 759.36. Boat service to Corsica by Compagnie Fraissinet, 7 Rue Antoine-Gautier, Tel. 62.21. Tourist information: 13 Pl. Masséna, Tel. 847.89. Automobile Club de Nice and Côte d'Azur, 7 Rue Massenet, Tel. 899.17 and 899.18. Club Alpin Français, 15 Av. Victoire, Tel. 895.41. Touring Club de France, 5 Rue Liberté, Tel. 818.95.

### At the Beach and in Town

**HOTELS**

☆☆☆☆☆NEGRESCO, 37 Promenade Anglais, Tel. 839.52 and 840.32. View of sea. Service charge 15%. 400 Rooms. ☆☆☆☆☆RUHL, 1 Promenade Anglais, Tel. 879.32. View of sea. Service charge 15%. 300 Rooms. Garage. ☆☆☆☆PLAZA DE FRANCE (winter), 12 Av. Verdun, Tel. 889.41. 180 Rooms. Garage. ☆☆☆☆ROYAL (temporarily without restaurant), 23 Promenade Anglais, Tel. 840.91. Service charge 15%. 150 Rooms. ☆☆☆☆ANGLETERRE ET GRANDE BRETAGNE, 4 and 6 Jardin du Roi Albert I, Tel. 829.48. 200 Rooms. ☆☆☆☆NAPOLEON (no restaurant from May to November), 6 Rue Grimaldi, Tel. 840.08. Service charge 15%. 100 Rooms. Garage. ☆☆☆☆SPLENDID, 50 Blvd. Victor-Hugo, Tel. 839.66. Service charge 15%. 110 Rooms. Garage free. ☆☆☆☆CONTINENTAL, 12 Rue Rossini, Tel. 879.21. Quiet. 180 Rooms. ☆☆☆☆ALBERT I (no restaurant), 4 Av.Phocéens, Tel. 829.07. Service charge 15%. 80 Rooms. ☆☆☆☆ REGINA (no restaurant), 48 Av. Victoire, Tel. 899.15. 44 Rooms. ☆☆☆☆ WESTMINSTER, 27-29 Promenade Anglais, Tel. 829.44. View of sea.

Service charge 15%. 130 Rooms. ☆☆☆QUEEN'S HOTEL, 15 Blvd. Victor-Hugo, Tel. 829.24. Service charge 15%. 87 Rooms. ☆☆☆☆ LUXEMBOURG, 9 Promenade Anglais, Tel. 839.45. Service charge 15%. 120 Rooms. ☆☆☆FELIX FAURE (no restaurant), 8 Av. Félix-Faure, Tel. 829.18. Service charge 15%. 100 Rooms. ☆☆☆CECIL (no restaurant), 7 Av. Thiers, Tel. 219.18. Service charge 15%. 130 Rooms. ☆☆MONTY (no restaurant), 129 bis Promenade Anglais, Tel. 755.48. Service charge 15%. 60 Rooms. ☆☆☆WEST END, 31 Promenade Anglais, Tel. 879.91. View of sea. Service charge 15%. 105 Rooms. ☆☆☆PAIX (winter), 12 Av. Félix-Faure, Tel. 819.38. 117 Rooms. ☆☆☆TERMINUS (temporarily no restaurant), 9 Av. Thiers, Tel. 889.62. Service charge 15%. 118 Rooms. ☆☆☆MASSENA (no restaurant), 58 Rue Gioffredo, Tel. 889.25. Service charge 15%. 40 Rooms. ☆☆BRICE, 44 Rue Maréchal-Joffre, Tel. 814.44. Service charge 15%. 69 Rooms. ☆☆☆VOLNAY (no restaurant), 8 Jardin du Roi Albert I, Tel. 845.79. Service charge 15%. 35 Rooms. ☆☆☆LITTLE PALACE (no restaurant), 9 Av. Baquis, Tel. 870.49 and 870.70. Service charge included. 35 Rooms. ☆☆☆RIVOLI (no restaurant), 47 Rue Pastorelli, Tel. 825.11. Service charge 15%. 65 Rooms. ☆☆☆FRANCIA, 9-11 Blvd. Victor-Hugo, Tel. 830.28. Service charge 15%. 45 Rooms. ☆☆☆ COLOMBIA (no restaurant), 17 Blvd. Victor-Hugo, Tel. 818.32. Service charge 15%. 40 Rooms. ☆☆☆ ATHENA (no restaurant), 11 Rue Paul-Déroulède, Tel. 803.19. Service charge 15%. 22 Rooms. ☆☆LA MALMAISON, 48 Blvd. Victor-Hugo, Tel. 834.28. Service charge 15%. 42 Rooms. ☆☆UNIVERS (no restaurant), 9 Av. Victoire, Tel. 828.81. Service charge 15%. 80 Rooms. ☆☆FRANCK (no restaurant), 31 Rue Paganini, Tel. 836.77. Service charge 15%. 85 Rooms. ☆☆ WINDSOR (no restaurant), 11 Rue Dalpozzo, Tel. 830.59. Service charge 15%. 58 Rooms. ☆☆COLBERT, 34 Rue Lamartine. 30 Rooms. ☆☆NOUVEL HOTEL (no restaurant), 19 bis Blvd. Victor-Hugo, Tel. 813.60. Service charge 15%. 54 Rooms. ☆☆ BUSBY, 36-38 Rue Maréchal Joffre, Tel. 826.01. Service charge 15%. 78 Rooms. ☆☆ST. GEORGES, 7 Av. G.-Clemenceau, Tel. 817.33. Service charge 15%. 30 Rooms. ☆☆RICHELIEU (no restaurant), 30 Rue Assalit, Tel. 838.00. Service charge 15%. 31 Rooms. Garage free. ☆ TRIANON (restaurant closed Sundays), Pl. Mozart and 15 Av. Auber, Tel. 830.69. Service charge 15%. 32 Rooms. ☆BRITANNIQUE (no restaurant), Rue France, Tel. 830.38. 35 Rooms. Garage. ☆TROIS EPIS (no restaurant), 51 Promenade Anglais, Tel. 851.42 (Breakfast included). Service charge 15%. 18 Rooms. Garage free. ☆VICHY HOTEL, 22 Rue Assalit, Tel. 818.54. Service charge 15%. 55 Rooms. ☆ST. PIERRE (no restaurant), 2 Av. Fleurs, Tel. 855.20. Service charge 15%. 25 Rooms. ☆PARISIEN, 10 Rue Verniers, Tel. 877.38. 26 Rooms.

RESTAURANTS

☆☆☆RAYNAUD (closed Sundays), 59 Quai Etats-Unis, Tel. 892.90.

View of sea. A la carte. ☆☆*MAISON ROUGE*, 65 Quai Etats-Unis, Tel. 837.21. View of sea. ☆☆*LE CABARET*, 71 Quai Etats-Unis, Tel. 848.92. View of sea.- ☆☆*LE CANETON*, 15 Rue Alexandre-Mari, Tel. 818.59. ☆☆*LE VERDUN*, 4 Av. Verdun, Tel. 859.45. Service charge 15%. ☆☆*ST. MORITZ*, 5 Rue Congrès, Tel. 854.90. Service charge 15%. Specialties: Gateaux au fromage, Coquille St. Jacques amoureuse, Poularde au riz. Wines: Pellet, Château Selle. ☆☆*STERN* (closed Mondays), 4 Rue France, Tel. 801.57. Service charge 15%. ☆☆*LA RIBOTE* (closed Mondays), 5 Av. Bellet, Tel. 756.26. A la carte. ☆☆*PETIT BROUAND* (closed in June, and Mondays), 4 bis Rue Gustave-Deloye, Tel. 825.84. ☆☆*FRANCHIN* (closed Sundays), 10 Rue Massenet, Tel. 803.74. ☆☆*LE PERE CAMUS*, 5 Rue Hôtel-de-Ville, Tel. 821.08. ☆☆*GARAC* (closed Tuesdays), 2 Blvd. Carnot, Tel. 67.36. Service charge 14%. ☆☆*RIVOLI* (closed Mondays), 9 Rue Rivoli, Tel. 812.62. ☆☆*BUFFET GARE*, S.N.C.F., Av. Thiers, Tel. 830.27. Service charge 15%. ☆☆ *TAVERNE ALSACIENNE*, 49 Rue Hôtel-des-Postes, Tel. 814.38. Service charge 15%. ☆☆*ADOLPHE*, Cours Saleva, Tel. 874.10. ☆*BONNE AUBERGE*, 9 Rue Chauvin, Tel. 854.86. Service charge 15%. ☆*MANOIR NORMAND*, 32 Rue France, Tel. 842.59. ☆*CHEZ PRINCE*, 58 Quai Etats-Unis, Tel. 805.07. View of sea. ☆*CHEZ JOSEPH*, 6 Cours Saleva, Tel. 843.06. ☆*DA BOUTTAU*, 2 Pl. Fr. Gallo, Tel. 805.20. ☆*MAISON DU ST. EMILION*, 12 Rue Gioffredo, Tel. 826.63.

## North of Nice (Cimiez, Carabacel, etc.)

HOTEL

☆*FLORIDE*, 52 Blvd. Cimiez, Tel. 886.70. Service charge 15%. 22 Rooms. Garage free.

## At the Mont-Boron (Southeast of Nice) Post Office in Nice

HOTEL

☆☆*VILLA D'ORSAY*, 16 Blvd. Mont-Boron, Tel. 649.94 in Nice. View of garden; quiet. Service charge 15%. Garage free.

RESTAURANTS

☆*PRINTEMPS*, Av. Hesperides, Tel. 69.32 in Nice. Panoramic view of Villefranche roads and Cap Ferrat. ☆*LE SITE ENCHANTEUR*, Pl. Mont-Boron, Tel. 66.59 in Nice. Panoramic view of sea and Cap Ferrat.

## Nimes, Provence

Distance (in kilometers) to: Paris 694; Aix-en-Provence 107; Arles 31; Avignon 42; Marseilles 121. Open-air swimming pool, 36 Rue Nôtre-Dame. Tourist information, Nîmes and Gard: Place Comédie (theater), Tel. 29.11. Automobile Club du Gard "Mer-Rhone-Cevennes," 6 Av. Feuchères, Tel. 28.10 and 31.68.

HOTELS

☆☆☆*IMPERATOR*, 15 Rue G.-Boissier, Tel. 30.31. View of garden. Service charge 15%. 60 Rooms. Garage. ☆☆*CHEVAL BLANC*, 1 Pl. Arènes, Tel. 20.03. 53 Rooms. Garage. ☆☆*MIDI ET POSTE*, Square Couronne, Tel. 21.86. Service charge included. 60 Rooms. ☆☆*VICTORY HOTEL*, Blvd. Pierre-Santenac, Tel. 25.81. Service charge 15%. 30 Rooms. ☆☆*ROYAL HOTEL* (no restaurant), 1 Pl. d'Assas, Tel. 28.36. Service charge 15%. 30 Rooms. ☆☆ *PROVENCE* (restaurant, closed Saturdays), 5-7 Square Couronne, Tel. 28.64. Service charge 15%. 40 Rooms. ☆*MODERN* (no restaurant), 10 Rue Roussy, Tel. 29.27.

### RESTAURANTS

☆*LISITA*, 2 Blvd. Arènes, Tel. 29.15. A la carte. ☆*COMBE*, 10 Rue Porte-de-France, Tel. 32.69. A la carte. ☆*CHATEAU*, 3 Pl. Château, Tel. 40.42. ☆*LA BONNE TABLE*, 3 Rue Rangueil, Tel. 55.77.

*Outside the city, 4 kilometers from Nice*

☆☆*MOULIN GAZAY*, Route d'Arles, Tel. 26.22. View of garden. A la carte.

### Orange, Provence

Distance (in kilometers) to: Paris 650; Aix-en-Provence 97; Avignon 27; Nimes 55. Tourist information, Pl. Clémenceau, Town Hall.

### HOTELS

☆☆*PRINCES* (restaurant closed Mondays), 7 Av. Arc-de-Triomphe, Tel. 0.16. 41 Rooms. ☆*LOUVRE ET TERMINUS*, Av. Frédéric-Mistral, Tel. 0.08. 31 Rooms. Garage. ☆ *MODERNE HOTEL PROVENÇAL*, 27 Rue République, Tel. 1.89. Specialties: Terrine aux truffes du Ventoux, Croquettes sauce Perigueux, Soufflé surprise. Vins: Gigondas, Sar-

riano. 12 Rooms. ☆*ARENE*, Pl. Langes and 2 to 6 Rue Victor-Hugo, Tel. 0.95 24 Rooms.

### RESTAURANTS

☆*GRAND CAFE D'ORANGE*, Route Nationale No. 7, Tel. 0.24. Service charge 15%. ☆*CHEZ HENRI*, 23 Rue Victor-Hugo, Tel. 3.14.

### Paris

TOURIST AGENCIES AND INFORMATION OFFICES (All closed Sundays):

National Tourist Bureau and National Union of Tourist Agencies, 127 Av. Champs Elysées, Tel. Bal. 12.80. General tourist information, railway companies. Travelers' Aid Society (weekdays 9 a.m. to 7 p.m., Sundays 9 a.m. to 6 p.m.), 8 Av. Opéra, Tel. Ope. 17.71. Aero Club of France and Association of Private Commercial Airlines (closed Saturday afternoons), 6 Rue Galilée, Tel. Kle. 76.40. Automobile Club of France (closed Saturdays), 6 and 8 Pl. Concorde, Tel. Anj. 34.70. Automobile Club de l'Ile de France (closed Saturdays), 8 Pl. Vendôme, Tel. Ope. 83.10. Automobile Club du Palais, Palais de Justice (closed Saturdays), Tel. Lit. 29.80. Auto-Camping-Caravaning Club de France (open from 2:30 to 5:30 p.m.; closed Saturdays), 15 Rue Faubourg Montmartre, Tel. Pro. 29.81. Camping Club de France (open 2 to 7 p.m. and all day Saturdays; closed Mondays), 218 Blvd. St. Germain, Tel. Lit. 30.03. Camping Club International de France, 69 Rue

Cardinal Lemoine. Club Alpin Français, 7 Rue La Boëtie, Tel, Anj. 54.45. French Federation of Cyclo-Tourism, 10 Rue Lancry, Tel. Bot. 81.79. French Ski Federation (closed Saturday afternoons), 119 Rue Courcelles, Tel. Car. 66.21. French Aeronautic Federation (closed Saturdays), 7 Av. Raymond Poincaré, Tel. Kle. 75.68. Maison de Savoie, 117 Av. Champs Elysées, Tel. Bal. 29.21. Moto-Club of Paris (closed Mondays), 19 Rue Charles V, Tel. Arc. 87.51. Touring Club of France, 65 Av. Grande Armée, (closed Monday mornings), Tel. Pas. 62.65. Trans-Aëro Service (closed Saturday afternoons), 155 Rue Courcelles, Tel. Car. 93.42. National Union of Tourist Associations (closed Saturday afternoons), 8 Rue César Franck, Tel. Sui. 21.73. Union of Tourist Information Federations, 127 Av. Champs Elysées, Tel. Bal. 12.80. French Union of Camping Associations (closed Saturday afternoons), 22 Av. Victoria, Tel. Cen. 12.40. French Union of Youth Hostels (closed Saturday afternoons and Monday mornings), 140 Blvd. Haussmann, Tel. Car. 68.64. Motorcycle Union of France (closed Saturday afternoons), 8 Pl. Concorde, Tel. Anj. 34.70.

## Colonies

Agence Economique des Colonies (closed Saturday afternoons), 20 Rue La Boëtie, Tel. Anj. 26.94. Algeria: Trade and Tourist Offices, 28 Av. Opéra (closed Saturday afternoons), Tel. Ope. 79.40. Morocco: Office of the French Protectorate in Morocco (closed Saturday afternoons), 21 Rue Pyramides, Tel. Ope. 75.63. Tunisia: 9 Rue Pyramides, Tel. Ope. 94.86.

## Foreign Countries

Belgian Tourist Bureau (closed Saturday afternoons), 14 Rue Quatre-Septembre, Tel. Ric. 61.08. Dutch Tourist Bureau (A.N.V.V.), (closed Saturday afternoons), 1 Pl. Opéra, Tel. Ope. 87.50. Norwegian Tourist Bureau, Agence Bennett's, 4 Rue Scribe, Tel. Ope. 40.07. Portugal: Casa de Portugal (closed Saturday afternoons), 7 Rue Scribe, Tel. Ope. 44.71. Swedish Tourist Office (closed Saturday afternoons), 125 Av. Champs Elysées, Tel. Bal. 04.28 and 41.42. Switzerland: (closed Saturday afternoons), 37 Blvd. des Capucines, Tel. Ope. 63.30.

## Air Lines

Air France (Central agency, all destinations; open 9 a.m. to 5 p.m.; Sundays 9 to 11:30 a.m.), 119 to 121 Av. Champs Elysées, Tel. Ely. 26.00 and Bal. 50.29. European flights only (closed Sundays), 2 Rue Scribe, Tel. Ope. 41.00. A.B.A. (Swedish), 125 Av. Champs Elysées, Tel. Bal. 41.42 and 04.28. B.E.A.C. and B.O.A.C. (Great Britain), 38 Av. Opéra, Tel. Tai. 60.50. D.N.L. (Norway), 4 Rue Scribe, Tel. Ope. 81.05. K.L.M. (Holland), 36 bis Av. Opéra, Tel. Ope. 25.84, 19.78, and 09.27. P.A.B. (Brazil), Hotel Plazza, 25 Av. Montaigne, Tel. Ely. 85.23. S.A.B.E.N.A. (Belgium), 37 Rue Caumartin, Tel. Ope. 28.40. SWISSAIR (Switzerland), 33 Rue Paix and 17 Blvd. Capucines, Tel. Ope. 61.21 and 66.08. T.W.A. (U.S.A.), 101 Av. Champs Elysées, Tel. Bal. 10.83.

## Abbreviations of Paris Telephone Exchanges

| | | | | |
|---|---|---|---|---|
| Ale | = Alésia | | Lit | = Littré |
| Anj | = Anjou | | Lon | = Longchamp |
| Arc | = Archives | | Lou | = Louvre |
| Arg | = Argenteuil | | | |
| Aut | = Auteuil | | Mai | = Maillot |
| Avi | = Aviation | | Mal | = Malmaison |
| Avr | = Avron | | Man | = Mansart |
| | | | Mar | = Marcadet |
| Bab | = Babylone | | Men | = Ménilmontant |
| Bac | = Bac | | Mic | = Michelet |
| Bal | = Balzac | | Mol | = Molitor |
| Bel | = Belle-Epine | | Mon | = Montmartre |
| Ber | = Berny | | | |
| Bot | = Botzaris | | Nor | = Nord |
| | | | | |
| Car | = Carnot | | Obe | = Oberkampf |
| Cen | = Central | | Obs | = Observatoire |
| Cha | = Charlebourg | | Ode | = Odéon |
| Cli | = Clignancourt | | Ope | = Opéra |
| Com | = Combat | | | |
| | | | Pas | = Passy |
| Dan | = Danton | | Per | = Pereire |
| Dau | = Daumesnil | | Pig | = Pigalle |
| Def | = Défense | | Pla | = Plaine |
| Did | = Diderot | | Pom | = Pompadour |
| Dor | = Dorian | | Por | = Port-Royal |
| | | | Pro | = Provence |
| Ely | = Elysées | | | |
| Ent | = Entrepôt | | Ric | = Richelieu |
| Eto | = Etoile | | Rob | = Robinson |
| Eur | = Europe | | Roq | = Roquette |
| | | | | |
| Fla | = Flandre | | Sab | = Sablons |
| | | | Seg | = Ségur |
| Gal | = Galvani | | Suf | = Suffren |
| Gam | = Gambetta | | | |
| Gob | = Gobelins | | Tai | = Taitbout |
| Gra | = Gravelle | | Tre | = Tremblay |
| Gré | = Grésillons | | Tri | = Trinité |
| Gut | = Gutenberg | | Tro | = Trocadéro |
| | | | Tru | = Trudaine |
| Inv | = Invalides | | Tur | = Turbigo |
| Ita | = Italie | | | |
| | | | Vau | = Vaugirard |
| Jas | = Jasmin | | Ver | = Versailles |
| | | | Vil | = Villette |
| Kle | = Kléber | | Vol | = Voltaire |
| | | | | |
| Lab | = Laborde | | Wag | = Wagram |
| Lec | = Lecourbe | | | |

## Alphabetical Listing of Paris Hotels and Restaurants

*ARR Arrondissement

## Near the Opéra, Louvre, Palais Royal, Halles, Bourse (1st and 2nd Arrondissements)

### HOTELS

☆☆☆☆☆*RITZ*, 15 Pl. Vendôme, Tel. Ope. 28.30. Quiet. 200 Rooms. ☆☆☆☆☆*MEURICE*, 228 Rue Rivoli, Tel. Ope. 32.40. Service charge 15%. 200 Rooms. ☆☆☆☆*CONTINENTAL*, 3 Rue Castiglione, Tel. Ope. 18.00 and 92.80. Service charge 15%. 400 Rooms. ☆☆☆☆*LOTTI*, 7-9 Rue Castiglione, Tel. Ope. 23.00. 140 Rooms. ☆☆☆☆*WESTMINSTER*, 13 Rue Paix, Tel. Ope. 36.40. Service charge 15%. 123 Rooms. ☆☆☆☆ *VENDÔME*, 1 Pl. Vendôme, Tel. Ope. 48.24. 66 Rooms. ☆☆☆☆*CHATHAM*, 18 Rue Volney, Tel. Ope. 51.30. 150 Rooms. ☆☆☆☆*NORMANDIE*, 7 Rue Echelle, Tel. Ope. 04.80. 145 Rooms. ☆☆☆☆*LOUVOIS*, 1 Rue Lulli, Tel. Ric. 64.41. Service charge 15%. 167 Rooms. ☆☆☆*REGINA* (no restaurant), 2 Pl. Pyramides, Tel. Ope. 74.00. 144 Rooms. ☆☆☆*LOUVRE*, Pl. Théâtre-Français, Tel. Lou. 63.00. Service charge 15%. 250 Rooms. ☆☆*FRANCE ET CHOISEUL* (no restaurant), 239-241 Rue St. Honoré, Tel. Ope. 41.92 and 15.54. 125 Rooms. ☆☆☆*DEUX MONDES* (no restaurant), 22 Av. Opéra, Tel. Ope. 04.75. 167 Rooms. ☆☆☆*SAINTE ANNE* (temporarily without restaurant), 10 Rue Ste. Anne, Tel. Ric. 12.56. 103 Rooms. ☆☆☆*METROPOLITAIN* (no restaurant), 8 Rue Cambon, Tel. Ope. 61.44. 81 Rooms. ☆☆☆*OXFORD ET CAMBRIDGE* (temporarily without restaurant), 11-13 Rue Alger, Tel. Ope. 28.45. 75 Rooms. ☆☆*RHONE* (temporarily without restaurant), 5 Rue J. J. Rousseau, Tel. Gut. 59.00. 93 Rooms. ☆☆*MAITE* (no restaurant), 63 Rue Richelieu, Tel. Ric. 69.67. Service included. 75 Rooms. ☆☆*FRANCE* (no restaurant), 4 Rue Caire, Tel. Gut. 30.98. 70 Rooms. ☆*PERIGORD* (temporarily without restaurant), 2 Rue Grammont, Tel. Ric. 80.31. Service charge 15%. 42 Rooms. ☆*NORMANDIE* (no restaurant), 3 Rue Banque, Tel. Gut. 17.90. Service charge 15%. 50 Rooms. ☆*EMPEREURS* (no restaurant), 20 Rue J. J. Rousseau, Tel. Cen. 88.18. Service charge 18%. 48 Rooms. ☆ *LION D'ARGENT* (restaurant, closed Sundays), 9-11 Rue L. Bellan, Tel. Gut. 31.11 and Lou. 70.12. Service charge 15%. 86 Rooms. Garage free. ☆*FAMILY HOTEL*, 35 Rue Cambon, Tel. Ope. 33.85 and 86.74. Service charge 15%. 28 Rooms.

### RESTAURANTS

☆☆☆*CAFE DE PARIS*, 41 Av. Opéra, Tel. Ope. 82.64. A la carte. ☆☆☆ *PRUNIER* (closed Mondays, and July and August), 9 Rue Duphot, Tel. Ope. 11.40. A la carte. ☆☆☆ *DROUANT*, 18 Rue Gaillon, Tel. Ope. 53.72. A la carte. ☆☆*ESCARGOT* (closed Mondays), 38 Rue Montorgueil, Tel. Cen. 83.51. ☆☆ *AU CANETON* (closed Saturdays), 3 Rue Bourse, Tel. Ric. 59.95. A la carte. ☆☆*GRIFFON* (closed Sundays), 6 Rue d'Antin, Tel. Ope. 66.81. A la carte. ☆☆*ZIMMER BLONDEL*, 27 Rue Ste. Apolline, Tel. Gut. 45.79. Wall paintings. A la carte. ☆ ☆*ESCARGOT D'OR* (closed Mondays), 250 Rue St. Dénis,

Tel. Gut. 01.07. A la carte. ☆☆CI-GOGNE, 17 Rue Duphot, Tel. Ope. 47.91. ☆☆FONTAINE GAILLON (closed Mondays), Pl. Gaillon, Tel. 63.22 and 87.04. ☆☆ZIMMER CHATELET, 1 Pl. du Châtelet, Tel. Cen. 74.03. A la carte. ☆ROY GOURMET (breakfast only) (closed Saturdays and Sundays), 4 Pl. Victoires, Tel. Lou. 30.16. A la carte. ☆PETIT COIN (closed Sundays), 16 Rue Feydeau, Tel. Lou. 00.08. A la carte. ☆ LE RALLYE, 35 Blvd. Capucines, Tel. 70.85 and 81.32.

## Near the Bastille, République, Hôtel de Ville

(3d, 4th and 11th Arrondissements.)

### HOTELS

☆☆☆MODERNE, 8 bis Pl. République, Tel. Obe. 58.20. Service charge 15%. 339 Rooms. ☆☆CHARIOT D'OR ET BELLEVUE (restaurant, closed Thursdays), 39 Rue Turbigo, Tel. Tur. 45.60 and Arc 37.64. Service charge 15%. 71 Rooms. ☆☆LITTLE PALACE, 4 Rue Salomon-de-Caus, Tel. Arc. 08.15 and 60.49. Service charge 15%. 68 Rooms. ☆FERRY HOTEL, 8 Blvd. Jules-Ferry, Tel. Obe. 55.60. Service charge 15%. 50 Rooms.

### RESTAURANTS

☆☆BOFINGER (closed temporarily on Thursdays), 5 Rue Bastille, Tel. Arc. 05.34 and 87.82. A la carte. ☆☆CHEZ JENNY, 39 Blvd Temple, Tel. Arc. 32.50 and 73.22. ☆AU VRAI BEARNAIS, 36 Blvd. Henri-IV, Tel. Arc. 17.09. ☆DUPONT BASTILLE, Pl. Bastille, Tel. Arc. 98.35. ☆QUASIMODO, 42 Quai

Orléans, Tel. Ode. 63.60. ☆CHEZ BENOIT (closed Sundays), 20 Rue St. Martin, Tel. Arc. 25.76. A la carte. ☆TAVERNE NICOLAS FLAMEL (closed Mondays), 51 Rue Montmorency, Tel. Arc. 07.11. A la carte. ☆BRISSAUD, 74 Rue Gravilliers, Tel. Arc. 17.02.

## Latin Quarter, Luxembourg

(5th and 6th Arrondissements)

### HOTELS

☆☆☆☆LUTETIA, 43 Blvd. Raspail, Tel. Lit. 44.10 and 45.10. Service charge 15%. 350 Rooms. ☆☆☆VICTORIA PALACE (temporarily without restaurant), 6 Rue Blaise-Desgoffe, Tel. Lit. 80.40. Quiet. 110 Rooms. Garage. ☆☆LITTRE, 9 Rue Littré, Tel. Lit. 67.71. Quiet. 100 Rooms. ☆☆☆PARIS-DINARD (temporarily without restaurant), 29 Rue Cassette, Tel. Lit. 63.86. 55 Rooms. ☆☆☆ MADISON HOTEL (no restaurant), 143 Blvd. St. Germain, Tel. Dan. 57.12. Service charge 15%. 70 Rooms. ☆☆SAINTS PERES (no restaurant), 65 Rue Sts. Pères, Tel. Lit. 44.45. 45 Rooms. ☆☆CLAUDE BERNARD (no restaurant), 43 Rue Ecoles, Tel. Dan. 78.97. 43 Rooms. ☆☆RECAMIER (no restaurant), 3 bis Pl. St. Sulpice, Tel. Dan. 04.89. Quiet. Service charge 15%. 30 Rooms. ☆☆SUNNY HOTEL (no restaurant), 48 Blvd. Port-Royal, Tel. Gob. 79.86. Service included. 32 Rooms. ☆☆NICE, 4 bis Rue Beaux-Arts, Tel. Dan. 50.06 and 54.05. 34 Rooms. Garage. ☆PAS-DE-CALAIS (temporarily without restaurant), 59 Rue Sts. Pères, Tel. Lit. 78.74. 38 Rooms. ☆STUDIO HOTEL (no restaurant), 4 Rue Vieux-Colombier, Tel. Lit. 31.81. 38 Rooms. ☆*DAG-MAR HOTEL* (no restaurant), 225-227 Rue St. Jacques, Tel. Ode. 52.17. Service charge 15%. 65 Rooms. ☆ *TERMINUS-AUSTERLITZ*, 12 Blvd. Hôpital, Tel. Gob. 08.18. Service charge 15%. 52 Rooms.

### RESTAURANTS

☆☆☆*TOUR D'ARGENT* (closed Mondays), 15 Quai Tournelle, Tel. Ode. 23.32. Roof terrace; View of Nôtre-Dame. A la carte. ☆☆☆*LAPER-OUSE*, 51 Quai Grands-Augustins, Tel. Dan. 68.04. A la carte. ☆☆☆ *ROTISSERIE PERIGOURDINE* (closed Fridays), 2 Pl. St. Michel, Tel. Dan. 70.54. View of Nôtre-Dame. A la carte. ☆☆*ROTONDE MONTPARNASSE*, 103-105 Blvd. Montparnasse, Tel. Dan. 68.84. A la carte. ☆☆*LA COUPOLE*, 102 Blvd. Montparnasse, Tel. Dan. 95.90. ☆☆ *MAGDELEINE*, 61 Quai Tournelle, Tel. Dan. 02.11. ☆☆*LA MEDITER-RANEE*, 2 Pl. Odéon, Tel. Dan. 46.75. ☆☆*CALVET* (closed Sundays, and from August 15 to September 15), 165 Blvd. St. Germain, Tel. Lit. 93.51. A la carte. ☆☆*DUPONT LA-TIN*, 25 Blvd. St. Michel, Tel. Ode. 98.90. ☆☆*BRASSERIE LIPP* (closed Mondays), 151 Blvd. St. Germain, Tel. Lit. 53.91 and 78.64. A la carte. ☆☆*BALZAR* (closed Tuesdays), 49 Rue Ecoles, Tel. Ode. 13.67. A la carte. ☆*CASENAVE*, 7 Pl. Odéon, Tel. Dan. 03.48. ☆*CHEZ DOUCET*, 25 Rue d'Assas, Tel. Lit. 49.50. ☆*LA SOURCE*, 35 Blvd. St. Michel, Tel. Ode. 07.33. ☆*CHEZ MARIE*, 145 Blvd. St. Michel, Tel. Ode. 36.93. ☆*LA BOUTEILLE D'OR* (closed

Mondays), 9 Quai Montebello, Tel. Ode. 52.58. A la carte.

## Faubourg-St.-Germain, Ecole Militaire, Champ-de-Mars, Invalides

## (7th Arrondissement)

### HOTELS

☆☆☆☆*PALAIS D'ORSAY*, 7-9 Quai d'Orsay, Tel. Lit. 59.04. Service charge 15%. 300 Rooms. ☆☆☆☆ *PONT ROYAL*, 7 Rue Montalembert, Tel. Lit. 42.50. Service charge 15%. 120 Rooms. ☆☆☆*MONT-ALEMBERT* (no restaurant), 3 Rue Montalembert, Tel. Lit. 68.11. Service included. 63 Rooms. ☆☆*CAYRE*, 4 Blvd. Raspail, Tel. Lit. 88.41. Service charge 15%. 126 Rooms. ☆☆☆*LA BOURDONNAIS* (temporarily without restaurant), 111-113 Av. La Bourdonnais, Tel. Seg. 24.42. 85 Rooms. ☆☆☆*BOURGOGNE ET MONTANA* (no restaurant), 7 Rue Bourgogne, Tel. Inv. 20.22 and 20.24. 40 Rooms. ☆☆*JEANNE D'ARC* (no restaurant), 59-61 Rue Vaneau, Tel. Lit. 98.37. Service charge 15%. 65 Rooms. ☆*FAMILY HOTEL ST. SI-MON*, 14 Rue St. Simon, Tel. Lit. 35.66. Quiet. Service charge 15%. 24 Rooms. ☆*PRINCE*, 66 Av. Bosquet, Tel. Seg. 85.90. Service charge 15%. 30 Rooms. ☆*ROYAL PARK* (temporarily without restaurant), 71 Av. Bosquet, Tel. Seg. 57.78. 48 Rooms.

### RESTAURANTS

☆☆*CHAULAND* (closed Thursday evenings), 107 Rue Université, Tel. Seg. 30.54. ☆☆*MARIUS*, 9 Rue Bourgogne, Tel. Inv. 79.42. A la carte. ☆☆*LA FLAMBERGE*, 12 Av. Rapp, Tel. Inv. 88.62. ☆☆*CHEZ BEULE-MANS* (closed Sundays), 204 Blvd. St. Germain, Tel. Lit. 73.30. A la carte. ☆☆*BON MARCHE* (dept. stores; lunch only; closed Sunday and Monday), Rue Velpeau. ☆*RELAIS DE SEVRES*, 64 Rue de Sèvres, Tel. Seg. 06.12. ☆*VALENTIN*, 36 Av. Motte-Picquet, Tel. Inv. 24.64. ☆ *TOQUE BLANCHE* (closed Saturdays), 66 Av. Bosquet, Tel. Inv. 12.45. A la carte. ☆*TOUR EIFFEL* (first and second stories of the Tower), Tel. Inv. 19.59 and 44.67. A la carte.

## Near the Champs-Elysées, Concorde, St.-Lazare, Europe (8th Arrondissement)

### HOTELS

☆☆☆☆☆*GEORGE V*, 31 Av. George-V, Tel. Ely. 89.71. Service charge 15%. 250 Rooms. ☆☆☆☆☆*ROYAL MONCEAU*, 35-39 Av. Hoche, Tel. Car. 78.00. 250 Rooms. ☆☆☆☆☆ *PLAZA-ATHENEE*, 25 Av. Montaigne, Tel. Ely. 85.23. 275 Rooms. ☆☆☆☆☆*CRILLON*, 10 Pl. Concorde, Tel. Anj. 24.10. 262 Rooms. ☆☆☆☆ *CLARIDGE*, 74 Av. Champs-Elysées, Tel. Ely. 33.01. Service charge 15%. 280 Rooms. ☆☆☆*WINDSOR ETOILE*, 14 Rue Beaujon, Tel. Car. 73.00. Service charge 15%. 142 Rooms. ☆☆☆☆*REYNOLDS*, 6 Av. Bertie-Albrecht, Tel. 73.00. Service charge 15%. 120 Rooms. ☆☆☆☆ *TERMINUS ST. LAZARE*, 108 Rue St. Lazare, Tel. Eur. 36.80. Service charge 15%. 370 Rooms. ☆☆☆*ASTOR*, 11 Rue d'Astorg, Tel. Anj.

04.31. Service charge 15%. 150 Rooms. ☆☆☆*LINCOLN* (no restaurant), 24 Rue Bayard, Tel. Ely. 62.72. Service included. 45 Rooms. ☆☆☆ *BEDFORD* (temporarily without restaurant), 17 Rue Arcade, Tel. Anj. 40.32. Service charge 15%. 148 Rooms. ☆☆☆*ROBLIN*, 6 Rue Chauveau-Lagarde, Tel. Anj. 57.00. Service charge 15%. 70 Rooms. ☆☆ *ROYAL HOTEL* (no restaurant), 33 Av. Friedland, Tel. Ely. 08.14. Service charge 15%. 54 Rooms. ☆☆ *PRINTEMPS*, 1 Rue Isly, Tel. Eur. 35.44. Service charge 15%. 70 Rooms. ☆☆*BUCKINGHAM*, 42 Rue Mathurins, Tel. Anj. 81.62. Service charge 15%. 57 Rooms. ☆☆*FLORIDA*, 12 Blvd. Malesherbes, Tel. Anj. 72.06. Service included. 45 Rooms. ☆☆*EUROPE* (temporarily without restaurant), 15 Rue Constatinople, Tel. Lab. 80.80. Service charge 15%. 55 Rooms. ☆☆*THEATRES CHAMPS-ELYSEES* (no restaurant), 6 Av. Montaigne, Tel. Ely. 35.57. 35 Rooms. ☆☆*BRADFORD* (no restaurant), 10 Rue St-Phillippe-du-Roule, Tel. Ely. 24.20. 48 Rooms. ☆☆*OPAL*, 19 Rue Tronchet, Tel. Anj. 77.97. 39 Rooms. ☆☆*ALEXANDRA* (no restaurant), 16 Rue Bienfaisance, Tel. Lab. 62.93. 40 Rooms. ☆☆*AVENIDA*, 41 Rue Colisée, Tel. Bal. 46.77. 69 Rooms. ☆☆*WEST-END* (no restaurant), 7 Rue Clement-Marot, Tel. Ely. 79.72. 53 Rooms. ☆☆*ARCADE* (no restaurant), 7-9 Rue Arcade, Tel. Anj. 43.85. 70 Rooms. ☆☆*HAUSSMANN* (no restaurant), 192 Blvd. Haussmann, Tel. Car. 20.07. Service charge 15%. 37 Rooms.

## RESTAURANTS

☆☆☆*LARUE*, 3 Pl. Madeleine, Tel. Anj. 10.10. ☆☆☆*LUCAS-CARTON* (closed Sundays), 9 Pl. Madeleine, Tel. Anj. 22.90. A la carte. ☆☆☆ *FOUQUET'S*, 99 Av. Champs-Elysées, Tel. Bal. 59.54. A la carte. ☆☆☆ *PAVILLON DE L'ELYSEE* (closed Mondays), Carré Marigny, Tel. Anj. 29.60 and 85.10. A la carte. ☆☆*LE CABARET*, Av. F. D. Roosevelt, Tel. Ely. 18.52. A la carte. ☆☆*JEAN CASENAVE* (closed Sundays), 39 Rue Boissy-d'Anglas, Tel. Anj. 10.49. A la carte. ☆☆*CHEZ TANTE LOUISE* (closed Mondays), 41 Rue Boissy-d'Anglas, Tel. Anj. 06.85 and 28.19. A la carte. ☆☆*LA CREMAILLERE* (closed Mondays, and in August), 92 Faubourg St-Honoré, Tel. Anj. 24.41. A la carte. ☆☆*ROTISSERIE DE LA REINE PEDAUQUE*, 6 Rue Pepinière, Tel. Lab. 86.90 and 73.07. A la carte. ☆☆ *ROTISSERIE NORMANDE*, 108 Rue St. Lazare, Tel. Eur. 36.80. A la carte. ☆☆*LE MARIGNAN*, 27-31 Av. Champs-Elysées, Tel. Bal. 43.81. A la carte. ☆☆*CHEZ FRANCIS*, 7 Pl. Alma, Tel. Ely. 79.11. ☆*CHEZ MERCIER* (closed Mondays and in August), 13 Rue Lincoln, Tel. Bal. 40.27. A la carte. ☆*CHEZ DOUCET*, 4 Rue Marbeuf, Tel. Ely. 85.92. ☆*BRASSERIE D'ALSACE*, 1 Rue Isly, Tel. Eur. 35.44. A la carte. ☆*MARTIN ALMA*, 44 Rue Jean-Goujon, Tel. Ely. 28.25. ☆*LA ROCHE VERTE* (lunch only, and closed Sundays), 13 Blvd. Courcelles, Tel. Lab. 16.68. A la carte. ☆*ANDROUET* (closed Sundays), 41 Rue Amsterdam, Tel. Tri. 26.90. A la carte.

## Near the Opéra, Gare du Nord, Gare de L'Est
### (9th and 10th Arrondissements)

### HOTELS

☆☆☆☆*LE GRAND HOTEL*, Pl. Opéra, Tel. Ope. 05.40. Service charge 15%. 600 Rooms. ☆☆☆☆ *SCRIBE*, 1 Rue Scribe, Tel. Ope. 92.70. Service charge 15%. 200 Rooms. ☆☆☆☆*AMBASSADOR*, 16 Blvd. Haussmann, Tel. Pro. 72.21. Service charge 15%. 600 Rooms. ☆☆☆☆*PARIS*, 8 Blvd. Madeleine, Tel. Ope. 03.80. Service charge 15%. 190 Rooms. ☆☆☆☆*COMMODORE*, 12 Blvd. Haussmann, Tel. Pro. 93.00. 180 Rooms. ☆☆☆*GRAND HOTEL, PAVILLON*, 36 Rue Echiquier, Tel. Pro. 17.15. Service included. 200 Rooms. ☆☆☆*FRANCIA*, 100 Rue La Fayette, Tel. Pro. 21.41. 110 Rooms. ☆☆☆*RONCERAY* (no restaurant), 10 Blvd. Montmartre, Tel. Pro. 73.90. Service charge 15%. 104 Rooms. ☆☆☆ *RICHMOND*, 11 Rue Helder, Tel. Tai. 75.27 and Pro. 53.20. Service included. 67 Rooms. ☆☆☆*BERGERE*, 34 Rue Bergère, Tel. Pro. 24.96 and 32.40. Service included. 105 Rooms. ☆☆☆*TERMINUS NORD*, 12 Blvd. Denain, Tel. Tru. 87.54. Service charge 15%. 270 Rooms. ☆☆☆*TERMINUS EST* (no restaurant), 5 Rue Strasbourg, Tel. Bot. 58.50. 217 Rooms. ☆☆*FRANKLIN* (temporarily without restaurant), 19 Rue Buffault, Tel. Tru. 69.40. 70 Rooms. ☆☆*ASTRA* (temporarily without restaurant), 29 Rue Caumartin, Tel. 11.25. Service included. 75 Rooms. ☆☆ *MONDIAL* (no restaurant), 5 Cité Bergère, Tel. Pro. 52.96 and 55.56. Service included. 250 Rooms. ☆☆

GRAND HOTEL HAVRE (no restaurant), 18 Rue Amsterdam, Tel. 15.93. 90 Rooms. ☆☆LAFFON (no restaurant), 25 Rue Buffault, Tel. Tru. 49.91. 48 Rooms. ☆☆GARAGE CITROEN (no restaurant), 272 Faubourg St. Martin, Tel. Nor. 34.63. 74 Rooms. ☆HELIOPOLIS (restaurant closed Sundays), 24 Rue Condorçet, Tel. Tru. 05.82. Service charge 15%. 60 Rooms. ☆OPERA (temporarily without restaurant), 16 Rue Helder, Tel. Pro. 83.91. 40 Rooms. ☆ GARE DU NORD (no restaurant), 31 Rue St. Quentin, Tel. 02.92. Service included. 50 Rooms. ☆BRITANNY (temporarily without restaurant), 3 Rue St.-Lazare, Tel. 44.50 and 48.76. 45 Rooms. ☆REX (no restaurant), 4 bis Cité Rougemont, Tel. Pro. 59.24. Service charge 15%. 33 Rooms. ☆INTERNATIONAL MAGENTA (no restaurant), 49 Blvd. Magenta, Tel. Nor. 62.65. 90 Rooms. ☆FÉNELON (no restaurant), 23 Rue Buffault, Tel. Tru. 32.18. 35 Rooms. ☆METROPOL (no restaurant), 98 Rue Maubeuge, Tel. Tru. 06.44. 47 Rooms. ☆BON GENIE (no restaurant), 9 Rue Douane, Tel. Nor. 48.21. Service charge 15%. 40 Rooms. ☆ALSACE HOTEL (temporarily without restaurant), 13 Rue Deux-Gares, Tel. Nor. 45.23. 52 Rooms. ☆TROIS NATIONS (no restaurant), 13 Rue Chateau-d'Eau, Tel. Bot. 23.27. 20 Rooms. ☆PARADIS (no restaurant), 9 Rue Paradis, Tel. Pro. 18.28. 60 Rooms.

**RESTAURANTS**

☆☆DROUANT EST (closed Saturdays), 79 Blvd. Strasbourg, Tel. Nor. 35.33 and 43.98. A la carte. ☆☆ECU DE FRANCE, 6 Rue Strasbourg, Tel. Nor. 63.82. A la carte. ☆☆DUCS DE BOURGOGNE, 2 Pl. Anvers, Tel. Tru. 35.21. A la carte. ☆☆ANE ROUGE (closed Mondays), 28 Av. Trudaine, Tel. Tru. 23.67. A la carte. ☆☆MADRID, 6 Blvd. Montmartre, Tel. Tai. 97.22. A la carte. ☆☆CHEZ TAILLEVENT, 37 Rue St.-Georges, Tel. Tru. 09.20. Service charge 15%. A la carte. ☆KUNTZ (closed Sundays), 31 Rue Alsace, Tel. Nor. 53.54. A la carte. ☆NICOLAS (closed Sundays), 12 Rue Fidélité, Tel. Pro. 10.72. ☆BRASSERIE FLO (closed Sundays), 7 Cour Petites-Ecuries, Tel. Pro. 13.59. A la carte. ☆CHEZ WEISS, 5-7 Rue Hauteville, Tel. Pro. 61.25. ☆GALERIES LAFAYETTE (in store) (lunch only; closed Sundays and Mondays), Blvd. Haussmann. ☆PRINTEMPS (in store) (lunch only; closed Sundays and Mondays), Blvd. Haussmann. ☆ CHEZ TITIN, 56 Rue La-Bruyère, Tel. Tri. 73.64.

## Near the Gare de Lyon, Gare D'Austerlitz, Gobelins, Bercy

## (12th and 13th Arrondissements)

**HOTELS**

☆☆PARIS-LYON PALACE (temporarily without restaurant), 11 Rue Lyon, Tel. Did. 09.09 and 37.73. 140 Rooms. ☆☆AZUR HOTEL (no restaurant), 5 Rue Lyon, Tel. Did. 88.35. 70 Rooms. ☆☆TERMINUS LYON, 19 Blvd. Diderot, Tel. Did. 24.03. Service charge 15%. 55 Rooms. ☆MODERN' HOTEL (no restaurant), 98 bis Cours de Vincennes, Tel. Did. 11.24. Service charge 15%. 58 Rooms. ☆PALYM (no restaurant), 4 Rue Emile-Gilbert, Tel. Did. 24.48. 47 Rooms. ☆*JULES CESAR*, 52 Av. Ledru-Rollin, Tel. Did. 15.88. 54 Rooms. ☆*IDEAL HOTEL* (no restaurant), 192 Av. Daumesnil, Tel. Did. 41.92. 50 Rooms. ☆*SLAVIA HOTEL* (no restaurant), 51 Blvd. St.-Marcel, Tel. Gob. 15.90. 58 Rooms. ☆*LUX HOTEL* (no restaurant), 8 Av. Corbera, Tel. Did. 42.84. 30 Rooms. ☆*ARTS* (no restaurant), 8 Rue Coypel, Tel. Gob. 22.30. 51 Rooms. ☆*PAIX* (no restaurant), 12 Rue Clisson, Tel. Gob. 05.54. 37 Rooms.

### RESTAURANTS

☆*JAMET*, 48 Blvd. Arago, Tel. Gob. 64.17. ☆*LES MARRONNIERS* (closed Tuesdays and in August), 53 bis Blvd. Arago. A la carte.

*Au Bois de Vincennes*
☆*PLATEAU DE GRAVELLE*, Route Pesage, Tel. Ent. 00.13. View of woods.

## Vaugirard, Montparnasse, Grenelle, Cité Universitaire
## (14th and 15th Arrondissements)

### HOTELS

☆☆☆*LE ROYAL*, 212 Blvd. Raspail, Tel. Dan. 69.20. 55 Rooms. ☆☆☆ *L'AIGLON* (no restaurant), 232 Blvd. Raspail, Tel. Dan. 82.42. 54 Rooms. ☆☆*ORLEANS PALACE* (no restaurant), 187 Blvd. Brune, Tel. Vau. 10.61. Service charge 15%. 109 Rooms. ☆☆*CHATILON'S HOME* (no restaurant), 11 Square Chatillon, Tel. Vau. 31.17. 30 Rooms. ☆☆*TERMINUS ORLEANS* (no restaurant), 197 Blvd.

Brune, Tel. Vau. 22.74. Service charge 15%. 66 Rooms. ☆☆*L'ACROPOLE* (no restaurant), 199 Blvd. Brune, Tel. Vau. 64.17. 40 Rooms. ☆*LE HOME JOLI* (temporarily without restaurant), 237 Rue Convention, Tel. Vau. 49.30. 80 Rooms. ☆*TERMINUS VAUGIRARD* (no restaurant), 403 Rue Vaugirard, Tel. Vau. 18.72. 116 Rooms. ☆*FLORIDOR* (no restaurant), 28 Pl. Denfert-Rochereau, Tel. Dan. 90.73. 48 Rooms. ☆*ROSARIA HOTEL* (no restaurant), 42 Blvd. Garibaldi, Tel. Suf. 20.10. 35 Rooms. ☆*SPLENDID HOTEL* (no restaurant), 54 Rue Fondary, Tel. Suf. 17.73. 47 Rooms.

### RESTAURANTS

☆☆*LA COUPOLE*, 102 Blvd. Montparnasse, Tel. Dan. 95.90. ☆☆ *COUTEAU* (closed Mondays), 32 Av. Orléans, Tel. Seg. 40.16. A la carte. ☆☆*PETIT DUC*, 194 Rue Convention, Tel. Vau. 41.59. ☆☆ *LES CIGOGNES*, 187 Rue Croix-Nivert, Tel. Vau. 42.09. ☆☆*PAVILLON DU LAC*, 20 Rue Gazan, Parc Montsouris, Tel. Gob. 38.52. View of park. ☆☆*LE BOLERO*, 62 Rue Alesia, Tel. Seg. 02.40. ☆*BRASSERIE SCHMITZ*, 55 Av. Motte-Picquet, Tel. Seg. 63.50 and 52.77. A la carte.

## Passy, Auteuil
## (16th Arrondissement)

### HOTELS

☆☆☆☆*RAPHAEL*, 17 Av. Kléber, Tel. Kle. 07.70. 110 Rooms. ☆☆☆☆*LA PEROUSE*, 40 Rue La Perouse, Tel. Pas. 43.68. 46 Rooms. ☆☆☆☆*PRIN-*

CESS HOTEL, 10 Rue Presbourg, Tel. Kle. 91.56. View of Arc de Triomphe. 30 Rooms. ☆☆BALTIMORE, 88 bis Av. Kléber, Tel. Kle. 83.33. Service charge 15%. 100 Rooms. ☆☆REGINA DE PASSY, 6 Rue de la Tour, Tel. Tro. 42.94. 62 Rooms. ☆☆MASSENET (no restaurant), 5 bis Rue Massenet, Tel. Aut. 53.61. 45 Rooms. ☆☆ROYAL VERSAILLES, 31 Rue Le Marois, Tel. Aut. 97.41. 150 Rooms. ☆PASSY (no restaurant), 10 Rue Passy, Tel. Aut. 20.47. Service included. 45 Rooms. ☆POINT DU JOUR (no restaurant), 11 Rue Claude-Terrasse, Tel. Aut. 77.73. 10 Rooms. ☆ALBONI (no restaurant), 22 Quai de Passy, Tel. Jas. 15.57. 45 Rooms.

### RESTAURANTS

☆☆PRUNIER TRAKTIR (closed Mondays), 16 Av. Victor-Hugo, Tel. Pas. 01.45. A la carte. ☆☆KUGLER (closed Mondays), 19 Rue Pompe, Tel. Tro. 26.36. View of garden. ☆☆AUBERGE D'ARBOIS (closed Thursdays and in August), 25 Rue Lesueur, Tel. Pas. 65.53. A la carte. ☆☆RAMPONNEAU (closed Mondays and in August), 21 Av. Marceau, Tel. Pas. 14.31. ☆CHEZ ERNEST (closed Wednesdays), 193 Av. Versailles, Tel. Aut. 03.28. ☆CHEZ DOUCET (closed Mondays), 65 Rue Auteuil, Tel. Jas. 02.65. A la carte. ☆MOUTON BLANC (closed Wednesdays), 40 Rue Auteuil, Tel. Aut. 02.21. A la carte. ☆AU GRAND BEARNAIS (closed Mondays), 90 Av. Victor-Hugo, Tel. Pas. 77.89. A la carte. ☆LE CLOCHER DU VILLAGE (closed Mondays, Tuesdays, and in August), 8 bis Rue Verderet, Tel. Aut. 35.87.

*Au Bois de Boulogne*

☆☆PAVILLON ROYAL (summer only), Carrefour du Rond-Royal (Grand Lac), Tel. Pas. 92.00. View of woods. A la carte.

## Plaine Monceau, Terne, Batignolles

## (17th Arrondissement)

### HOTELS

☆☆☆LES ACACIAS (temporarily without restaurant), 47 Rue Acacias, Tel. Eto. 45.98. Service charge 15%. 90 Rooms. ☆☆MERCEDES (no restaurant), 128 Av. Wagram, Tel. Car. 75.18 and 77.82. Service charge 15%. 50 Rooms. ☆☆SPLENDID, 1 bis Av. Carnot, Tel. Eto. 14.56. 80 Rooms. ☆☆ASTRID (no restaurant), 27 Av. Carnot, Tel. Eto. 56.20. Service charge 15%. 50 Rooms. ☆☆GRAND HOTEL CHICAGO (no restaurant), 99 bis Rue Rome, Tel. 49.52. 56 Rooms. ☆☆TERRASSE ETOILE HOTEL (no restaurant), 74 Av. Grande-Armée, Tel. Eto. 16.00. Service charge 15%. 90 Rooms. ☆NOLLET, 55 Rue Nollet, Tel. Mar. 72.94. Quiet. Service charge 15%. 46 Rooms. ☆VERNIQUET (no restaurant), 3 Rue Verniquet, Tel. Eto. 26.30. 25 Rooms.

### RESTAURANTS

☆☆AUX RELAIS DE FRANCE, 4 Av. de Mac-Mahon, Tel. Eto. 20.96. ☆☆LION D'OR, 72 Av. Villiers, Tel. Wag. 19.22. ☆☆AUX ARMES DE BRETAGNE, 98 Rue Tocqueville, Tel. Wag. 39.97. ☆LE GRILLON, 4 Rue Bremontier, Tel. Wag. 13.39. ☆LE GRAND VENEUR (closed in

August), 6 Rue Pierre-Demours, Tel. Eto. 18.15. ☆*MANOIR TOPSY*, 64 Av. Ternes, Tel. Eto. 16.66 and 33.87. A la carte. ☆*CHEZ JEAN*, 19 Rue Rennequin, Tel. Car. 41.91.

## *Montmartre, La Chapelle, La Villette, Belleville, Menilmontant (18th, 19th, and 20th Arrondissements)*

### HOTELS

☆☆☆*TERRASSE HOTEL*, 12-14 Rue Maistre, Tel. Mon. 72.85. 135 Rooms. ☆☆☆*ALSINA* (no restaurant), 39 Av. Junot, Tel. Mon. 57.85. Service charge 15%. 43 Rooms. ☆☆*BOURGES HOTEL* (no restaurant), 100 Blvd. Rochechouart, Tel. Mon. 27.20 and 99.17. Service charge 15%. 69 Rooms. ☆☆*LE KHEDIVE* (no restaurant), 79 Av. Gambetta, Tel. Men. 61.45. Service charge 15%. 70 Rooms. ☆*UNIC HOTEL* (no restaurant), 6 Rue Dupont-de-l'Eure, Tel. Men. 93.10. Service charge 15%. 40 Rooms.

### RESTAURANTS

☆☆*DAGORNO*, 190 Av. Jean-Jaurès, Tel. Nor. 02.29. ☆☆*COCHON D'OR*, (closed Wednesdays), 192 Av. Jean-Jaurès, Tel. Nor. 23.13 and Bot. 39.81. ☆*TETE DE BOEUF* (lunch only; closed Sundays), 23 Av. Corentin-Cariou, Tel. Nor. 12.74. ☆*ARTISTES* (closed Mondays), 11 Rue Lepic, Tel. Mon. 15.82. A la carte. ☆*BON BOCK* (closed Thursdays), 2 Rue Dancourt.

## Pau, Pyrenees

Distance (in kilometers) to: Paris 760; Biarritz 114; Bordeaux 195; Lourdes 39; Luchon 129. Winter resort. Casinos: Palais d'Hiver, Casino Municipal. 18-hole Golf Course (for information, Tel. 22.33.) Tourist Information: Hôtel de Ville, Pl. Royale, Tel. 22.48. Automobile Club Basco-Béarnais, Palais Aragon, Tel. 35.03. Club Alpin Français, Maison des Jeunes, Palais Pyrénées.

### HOTELS

☆☆☆☆*FRANCE*, Blvd. Pyrénées and Pl. Royale, Tel. 29.62. Panoramic view of Pyrenees. Service charge 15%. 126 Rooms. Garage free. ☆☆☆ *PALAIS ET BEAU SEJOUR*, 3 Rue Louis-Berthou, Tel. 21.07. ☆☆☆*CONTINENTAL*, 2 Rue Maréchal-Foch, Tel. 26.69. Service charge 15%. 100 Rooms. ☆☆*BEAUMONT HOUSE*, 7 Pl. Royale, Tel. 28.80. 45 Rooms. ☆☆*ALBRET*, 7 Rue Gassion, Tel. 27.29. Service charge 15%. 45 Rooms. Garage. ☆☆*BRISTOL*, 3 Rue Gambetta, Tel. 22.98. Service charge 15%. 30 Rooms, Garage free. ☆☆ *RONCEVAUX* (no restaurant), 25 Rue Louis-Barthou, Tel. 25.15. Service charge 15%. 24 Rooms. Garage free. ☆☆*POSTE*, 3 Pl. Gramont, Tel. 20.51. Service charge 15%. 50 Rooms. Garage. ☆*REGINA* (restaurant closed Tuesdays), 18 Rue Gassion, Tel. 27.18. Service charge 15%. 25 Rooms. ☆*PYRENEES*, 1 Pl. Clemenceau, Tel. 22.23. 40 Rooms. ☆ *EUROPE ET MODERNE*, 3 Pl. Clemenceau, Tel. 23.40. Service charge 15%. 50 Rooms. ☆*BEAUPRE*, 9 Av. Thiers, Tel. 22.51. View of park. 23 Rooms. Garage. ☆*CENTRAL*, 15 Rue Léon-Daran, Tel. 22.75. 25 Rooms. ☆*COMMERCE*, 9 Rue Maréchal-Joffre, Tel. 25.02.

Service charge 15%. 55 Rooms. ☆ *NOTRE-DAME*, 36 Rue Montpensier, Tel. 28.39. 22 Rooms. Garage. ☆*BOYER*, 13 Rue Buboue, Tel. 40.-65. 15 Rooms. Garage.

## RESTAURANTS

☆☆*CHEZ PIERRE*, 14-16 Rue Louis-Barthou, Tel. 26.86. A la carte. ☆☆ *ROTISSERIE PERIGOURDINE*, 6 Rue Adoue, Tel. 28.51 A la carte. ☆ *l'ETRIER* (closed Fridays), Pl. Royale, Tel. 25.47. A la carte. ☆*LE ROMANO* (closed Wednesdays), 1 bis Rue Orphelines, Tel. 40.50. A la carte. ☆*BERNARD* (closed Sundays in Winter), 7 Rue Foix, Tel. 40.28. A la carte.

## Pont-Aven, Brittany

Distance (in kilometers) to: Paris 537; Concarneau 15. Excursion in motor boat on the Aven to Port-Manech; 3 to 4 departures each day; takes 45 minutes. For information: M. Jean Dervout, Moulin-Mer-en-Nevez, Tel. 70 in Pont-Aven.

## HOTELS

☆*MIMOSAS* (Easter-September) (temporarily no restaurant), au Port, Tel. 30. Service charge 15%. 12 Rooms. Garage. ☆*POSTE* (restaurant closed Mondays), Rue Gare, Tel. 54. 14 Rooms. Garage free.

## RESTAURANTS

☆☆*MOULIN DE ROSMADEC* (closed Thursdays), Tel. 22. View of garden; beautiful interiors. A la carte. Specialties: Palourdes farcies, Filets de sole normande, Homard au whisky.

## Quimper, Finistere, Brittany

Distance (in kilometers) to: Paris 568; Beg-Meil 20; Brest 91; Concarneau 23; Douarnenez 22; Rennes 205. Tourist Information of Cornouaille, 1 Pl. Résistance and Automobile Club du Finistère, Tel. 4.69.

## HOTELS

☆☆☆*EPEE*, 14 Rue Parc, Tel. 0.14. 100 Rooms. Garage. ☆☆*PAIX ET POSTE*, 36 Rue Reguaires, Tel. 1.76. Service charge included. 40 Rooms. Garage. ☆☆*MODERNE*, 21 Av. Gare, Tel. 4.71. Service charge included. 65 Rooms. Garage. ☆☆*PASCAL FRERES ET TERMINUS*, 15 to 21 Av. Gare, Tel. 0.81. Service charge included. 75 Rooms. Garage.

## RESTAURANT

☆☆*RELAIS ST. CORENTIN*, 10 Rue Parc, Tel. 0.14. Service charge included. A la carte.

## Reims, Marne

Distance (in kilometers) to: Paris, by way of Soissons, 155; Brussels 195; Château-Thierry 62; Lille 197; Soissons 57; Verdun 117. Swimming pools, indoors: 41 Rue Talleyrand; open air: Parc Pommery. 9-hole Golf Course, (for information Tel. 46.98 Reims). Tourist Information, Cours Gare, Tel. 25.69. Automobile Club de Champagne, 23 Cours Lauglet, Tel. 34.76.

## HOTELS

☆☆☆*LION D'OR*, 58 Pl. Drouet-d'Erlon, Tel. 54.28 and 41.59. Service charge 15%. 120 Rooms. Garage.

☆☆☆*BRISTOL* (Restaurant La Coupole), 74 and 76 Pl. Drouet-d'Erlon, Tel. 35.08. Service charge 15%. 50 Rooms. ☆☆*NORD* (Restaurant La Coupole), 73 and 75 Pl. Drouet-d'Erlon, Tel. 39.03. 50 Rooms. ☆☆ *UNIVERS*, 41 Blvd. Foch, Tel. 52.71. Service charge 15%. 45 Rooms. ☆☆*FOCH*, 37 Blvd. Foch, Tel. 48.22. Service charge 15%. 15 Rooms. ☆☆*CECYL* (no restaurant), 24 Rue Buirette, Tel. 57.47. 19 Rooms. ☆☆*ASTOR* (no restaurant), 43 Blvd. Foch, Tel. 35.36. Service charge 15%. 12 Rooms. ☆☆*CRYSTAL*, 86 Pl. Drouet-d'Erlon, Tel. 59.88. Service charge included. 32 Rooms. ☆*LALLEMENT* (no restaurant), 1 Rue Buirette, Tel. 21.79. 30 Rooms. ☆*PAIX*, 25 Pl. Drouet-d'Erlon, Tel. 46.85. 16 Rooms. ☆ *MAJESTY HOTEL*, 45 Rue Libergier, Tel. 42.64. 12 Rooms. Garage. ☆*SPLENDID*, 13 Av. Laon, Tel. 25.22. Service charge 15%. 15 Rooms. Garage free.

### RESTAURANTS

☆☆*LA COUPOLE*, 73 Pl. Drouet-d'Erlon. Tel. 59.38. Service charge 13%. ☆☆*BRASSERIE STRASBOURG*, 24 Rue Etape, Tel. 54.92 and 64.92. Service charge 13%. ☆ *LAMBERT* (closed Sundays), 8 Rue St. Jacques, Tel. 37.35. À la carte. ☆*LE LIDO*, 171 Rue Vesle, Tel. 51.33. ☆*COLBERT* (closed Mondays), 64 Pl. Drouet-d'Erlon, Tel. 55.79. ☆*PETIT VATEL*, 21 Pl. Drouet-d'Erlon, Tel. 47.09.

### St.-Brieuc, Brittany

Distance (in kilometers) to: Paris 437; Dinard 67; Morlaix 86; Rennes 99; St. Malo 69 (by ferry boat). Tourist Information: Pavillon Tourisme, Pl. Champ-de-Mars, Tel. 7.50 and Automobile Club, 6 Pl. Duguesclin, Tel. 4.20.

### HOTELS

☆☆☆*GRAND HOTEL ET ANGLETERRE* (Restaurant, Les Terrasses), Pl. Duguesclin, Tel. 1.29. Service charge 15%. 90 Rooms. Garage. ☆☆*CROIX ROUGE*, 2 Rue Gouedic and Pl. Duguesclin, Tel. 3.61. Beautiful interiors. 45 Rooms. Garage. ☆*MON HOTEL* (no restaurant), 19 Rue Jean-Metairie, Tel. 10.21. 24 Rooms. Garage free. ☆*DUGUESCLIN*, Pl. Duguesclin, Tel. 1.65. 30 Rooms. Garage. ☆*CELTIC*, 7 Blvd. Clémenceau, Tel. 8.79. 18 Rooms.

### RESTAURANTS

☆☆*LES TERRASSES*, Pl. Duguesclin, Tel. 1.29. Beautiful paintings. ☆*MARCHE* (Le Covec), 17 Rue Jouallan, Tel. 5.18. Specialties (certain days): Homard à l'Américaine, Sole meuniere, Poularde de Souvaroff.

### St.-Jean-Cap-Ferrat, Riviera

Distance (in kilometers) to: Paris 945; Beaulieu-sur-Mer 2; Menton 22; Monaco-Monte Carlo 13; Nice 12. Beach and winter resort. Tourist Information, Pl. G.-Clémenceau, Tel. 250.91.

### HOTELS

☆☆*LA VOILE D'OR* (restaurant open February to September), Montée St.-Hospice, Tel. 250.13. View of sea and mountain. Service charge 15%. 25 Rooms. ☆*BELLE AURORE*, Av. D.-Semeria, Tel. 250.85. Service charge 15%.

**RESTAURANTS**

☆☆*CAPPA* (closed Thursdays, and from October 15 to November 15) Rue Jean-Mermoz, Tel. 250.06. View of sea and mountain. Service charge 15%. ☆☆*AU PETIT TRIANON*, Av. Gen.-de-Gaulle, Tel. 251.47. Specialties: Bouillabaisse Langouste Trianon, Poulet saute maison. ☆ *TERMINUS* (chez Giordan) (closed from October 15 to November 15), Pl. Clémenceau, Tel. 251.11. View of sea.

## St.-Jean-de-Luz, Pyrenees

Distance (in kilometers) to: Paris 761; Bayonne 21; Biarritz 17; Hendaye 11. Beach and winter resort. Casino. 18-hole Golf Course in La Nivelle 1 (for information. Tel. 618.99.) 18-hole Golf Course in Chantaco (2½ kilometers from St. Jean de Luz) for information Tel. 614.22. Tourist Information, St. Jean de Luz and Ciboure. Pl. Maréchal-Foch, Tel. 603.16.

**HOTELS**

☆☆☆☆*ATLANTIC* (summer), Blvd. Plage, Tel. 609.50. Service charge 15%. 50 Rooms. ☆☆☆☆*MIRAMAR*, Route Ste-Barbe, Tel. 609.94. View of sea; quiet. 25 Rooms. Garage. ☆☆☆☆*ANGLETERRE* (restaurant closed Wednesdays from October to June), Rue Garat, Tel. 604.17. View of sea; quiet. Service charge 15%. 54 Rooms. ☆☆☆☆*GOLF HOTEL* (may be closed from October to March), Blvd. Thiers, Tel. 604.20. View of sea. Service charge 15%. 100 Rooms. ☆☆☆*BRITANNIA*, 52 Blvd. Victor-Hugo, Tel. 604.60. 100 Rooms. ☆☆☆*EDOUARD VII*, Tel. 614.06. View of garden; quiet. Service charge 15%. 40 Rooms. ☆☆☆ *MODERN HOTEL* (Easter-October; will eventually be open out of season), on the beach, Tel. 600.65. View of sea. 100 Rooms. ☆☆*MADISON*, 25 Blvd. Thiers, Tel. 600.73. Service charge 15%. 30 Rooms. ☆☆*FLOTS BLEUS* (Easter to October) (temporarily no restaurant), Blvd. Thiers, Tel. 605.35. View of sea; quiet. Service charge included. 45 Rooms. ☆☆*MAITAGARRIA*, Blvd. Thiers, Tel. 604.77. View of sea; quiet. Service charge 15%. 52 Rooms. ☆☆*POSTE*, 85 Rue Gambetta, Tel. 604.53. 80 Rooms. ☆☆*GUERNICA*, Rue Vauban, Tel. 603.96. View of sea; quiet. 30 Rooms. ☆*COMMERCE* (temporarily no restaurant), 3 Blvd. Commandant-Passicot, Tel. 600.13. Service charge 15%. 33 Rooms. Garage. ☆*ESKUALDUNA* (temporarily no restaurant), Av. Labrouche, Tel. 600.55. 20 Rooms. ☆*PARIS ET PARC*, 1 Blvd. Commandant-Passicot, Tel. 600.62. Service charge 15%. 17 Rooms. ☆*ST. JEAN* (no restaurant), opening date indefinite, Av. Labrouche, Tel. 600.86. 27 Rooms. ☆*BOULE D'OR*, Route Bayonne, Tel. 605.53. 17 Rooms.

**RESTAURANTS**

☆☆*BAS BASQUE*, 22 Blvd. Thiers, Tel. 604.12. ☆☆*LE CORSAIRE*, 18 Rue Sopite, Tel. 602.00. ☆*PETIT GRILL BASQUE*, 2 Rue St. Jacques, Tel. 603.53. A la carte. ☆*TAVERNE BASQUE*, 6 Rue République, Tel. 601.26. A la carte.

*Chantaco Golf:* 2½ kilometers from St. Jean-de-Luz. Post Office in St. Jean-de-Luz.

### HOTEL

☆☆☆☆*CHANTACO* (Easter to October), Tel. 614.76. St. Jean-de-Luz View of mountain. 24 Rooms. Garage free.

## St. Lo, Normandy

Distance (in kilometers) to: Paris 283; Avranches 56; Bayeux 35; Caen 62; Carentan 28; Cherbourg 78; Coutances 27; Falaise 82. Tourist Information (closed Monday mornings), Carrefour Soleil Levant and Automobile Club de l'Ouest.

### HOTEL

☆*FRANCE*, Route Bayeux, Tel. 178. 18 Rooms.

### RESTAURANTS

☆*UNIVERS,* 13 and 15 Rue Alsace-Lorraine, Tel. 154. Service charge 15%. 4 Rooms. ☆*AUX GOURMETS* (closed Mondays), 28 Route Villedieu, Tel. 2.23. ☆*PAULOU,* Rue O.-Feuillet, Tel. 1.31.

## St. Malo, Brittany

Distance (in kilometers) to: Paris 382; Avranches 69; Cancale 14; Mont St. Michel 52. Cruises on the Rance to Jersey Island and St. Cast; no stops en route; departure from slip at Dinan, St. Malo; 4 hours (for information, Tel. 74.76); salt-water swimming pool: Bon Secours Beach. Tourist Information: Esplanade St. Vincent, Tel. 74.67.

### HOTELS

☆☆☆*FRANCE ET CHATEAUBRIAND,* 1 Pl. Chateaubriand, Tel. 70.48. 100 Rooms. Garage. ☆☆ *DIGUE* (Easter to October), 51 Chaussée Sillon, Tel. 72.28. View of sea. 40 Rooms. Garage. ☆☆*UNIVERS,* Pl. Chateaubriand, Tel. 74.52. 70 Rooms. ☆*JERSEY,* 55 Chaussée Sillon, Tel. 70.41. View of sea. 28 Rooms. Garage free. ☆*CELTIC HOTEL,* 25 Chaussée Sillon, Tel. 72.48. View of sea. 14 Rooms. ☆*TERMINUS,* 6 Blvd. Talard, Tel. 77.38. 27 Rooms. ☆*KER-JO-LEL* (opening date indefinite), 65 Chaussée Sillon, Tel. 70.75 View of sea. 28 Rooms.

### RESTAURANTS

☆*DUCHESSE ANNE,* 5-7 Pl. Chateaubriand, Tel. 75.33. A la carte. ☆*CHEZ CHUCHE,* on the board walk, Tel. 73.58. View of sea. Service charge 12%.

## St. Raphael, Riviera

Distance (in kilometers) to: Paris 869; Cannes 38; Grasse 47; Nice 69. Beach and winter resort. Grand Casino. 18-hole Golf Course in Valescure, 4½ kilometers from St. Raphael. (Open from October to April, and from July to September) (for information, Tel. 1.57 in St. Raphael. Tourist Information, 6 Rue Waldeck-Rousseau, Tel. 0.87.

### HOTELS

☆☆☆☆*BEAU RIVAGE,* Blvd. Gen.-de-Gaulle, Tel. 0.45 and 8.63. View of sea. Service charge 15%. 80 Rooms. Garage. ☆☆☆☆*CONTINENTAL,* (closed from October to December), 25 Blvd. Libération, Tel. 0.14 and 8.51. View of sea. Service charge 15%. 52 Rooms. ☆☆HERMITAGE, Av. Chèvrefeuilles, Tel. 0.48. View of park; quiet. Service charge 15%. 55 Rooms. ☆☆EXCELSIOR, Blvd. Libération, Tel. 2.42. View of sea. 43 Rooms. ☆☆LES ALGUES, Blvd. Gen.-de-Gaulle, Tel. 1.89. View of sea. Garage. ☆GENEVE, 18 Blvd. Félix-Martin, Tel. 3.35. 26 Rooms. ☆TERMINUS, 1 Rue Amiral-Baux, Tel. 2.91. 33 Rooms. ☆SELECT, Rue Boetmann, Tel. 6.22. 18 Rooms. Garage.

### RESTAURANTS

☆☆LA CIGALE, 35 Blvd. Libération, Tel. 2.08. View of sea. Specialties: Bourride Provençale, Bouillabaisse, Escabèche au Loup. Service charge 15%. 12 Rooms. ☆CAFE DES BAINS, 27 Blvd. Libération, Tel. 7.39. View of sea.

*In Valescure*, 2 kilometers North of St. Raphael by Route D 37. Post Office in St. Raphael. Winter resort.

### HOTEL

☆☆☆☆GOLF (from July 15 to September 15, and from December 15 to May 15), Tel. 1.57 and 4.91 in St. Raphael. View of park; quiet. Service charge 15%. 150 Rooms. Garage.

## St. Tropez, Riviera

Beach and winter resort. Casino (summer). Open-air swimming pool at Hotel Latitude 43. Tourist Information, 11 Rue Citadelle, and Automobile Club du Var, La Farigoulette, Tel. 1.75.

### HOTELS

☆☆☆☆LATITUDE 43 (opening in Spring eventually), Tel. 0.05. Quiet. 108 Rooms. ☆☆L'AIOLI, 3 Blvd. Aumale, Tel. 1.07. Quiet. 15 Rooms. ☆MEDITERRANEE (restaurant closed in December and January), Pl. Croix-de-Fer, Tel. 0.44. 15 Rooms. Garage. ☆SPORTING CLUB, Pl. Licés, Tel. 065. 10 Rooms.

### RESTAURANTS

☆ESCALE, Quai Jean-Jaurès, Tel. 0.63. Service charge 15%. ☆AUBERGE DES MAURES, 30 Rue Allard, Tel. 1.50. ☆DE MOUSCARDINS, 40 Rue Allard, Tel. 1.53. Service charge 15%.

*Outside of the city, at Le Pilon, 1 kilometer West from St. Tropez*

### HOTEL

☆COSTE, Route Nationale, Tel. 0.64. 16 Rooms. Garage free.

## Strasbourg, Alsace

Distance (in kilometers) to: Paris 447; Baden-Baden 58; Colmar 67; Luxembourg 221; Mulhouse 106; Nancy 140. Beach: Baggersee, 3½ kilometers from Strasbourg. Swimming pools: Municipal Baths, Blvd. Victoire. Airport, Entzheim 12, Tel. 207.78 in Strasbourg. 9-hole Golf Course (for information, Tel. 215.79). Tourist Information: 10 Pl. Gutenberg, Tel. 215.79. Pavillon du Tourisme, Pl. de la Gare. Automobile Club d'Alsace, 18 Rue Pontonniers, Tel. 403.05. Touring Club de France, 10 Pl. Gutenberg, Tel. 400.79.

## HOTELS

☆☆☆☆*MAISON ROUGE,* 22 Pl. Kléber, Tel. 306.62. View of Pl. Kléber. Service charge 15%. 120 Rooms. ☆☆☆☆*LE NOUVEL HOTEL* (no restaurant), 4 Rue Francs-Bourgeois, Tel. 300.60. Service charge 15%. 70 Rooms. ☆☆☆*NATIONAL* (no restaurant), 13 Pl. Gare, Tel. 272.22. Service charge 15%. 55 Rooms. ☆☆☆ *CARLTON,* 15 Pl. Gare, Tel. 402.82. 75 Rooms. ☆☆☆*LUTETIA* (no restaurant), 2 bis Rue Gen.-Rapp, Tel. 305.60. Service charge 15%. 40 Rooms. Garage. ☆☆☆*VILLE DE PARIS,* 13 Rue de la Mésange, Tel. 401.03. Service charge 15%. 75 Rooms. ☆☆*MONOPOLE-METRO-POLE* (restaurant closed Mondays), 16 Rue Kuhn, Tel. 210.33. Service charge 15%. 80 Rooms. ☆☆*VOS-GES* (restaurant closed Sundays), 3 Pl. Gare, Tel. 217.23. Service charge 15%. 65 Rooms. ☆☆*BRIS-TOL* (restaurant closed Wednesdays), 4 Pl. Gare, Tel. 200.83. 41 Rooms. ☆☆*RHIN* (no restaurant), 7 Pl. Gare, Tel. 201.78. Service charge 15%. 60 Rooms. ☆☆*HANNONG* (no restaurant), 15 Rue 22-Novembre, Tel. 216.22. Service charge 15%. 80 Rooms. ☆*EUROPE ET VIG-NETTE* (no restaurant), 28-40 Rue Fosse des Tanneurs, Tel. 310.91. Service charge included. 59 Rooms. ☆*BRUXELLES,* 13 Rue Kuhn, Tel. 301.89. 23 Rooms.

## RESTAURANTS

☆☆☆*VALENTIN SORG,* 50 Rue Vieux-Marché-aux-Vins. ☆☆*MAISON KAMMERZELL* (closed Mondays), 16 Pl. Cathédrale, Tel. 418.54. Specialties: Choucroute au Riesling "Kam-merzell," Poularde strasbourgeoise, Crêpes "Kammerzell." Wines: Huna-wihr, Barr. ☆☆*ZIMMER* (closed Mondays), 8 Rue Temple-Neuf. Specialties: Choucroute à l'alsacienne, Coq au Riesling. Wines: Mittelwihr, Hunawihr. ☆☆*AUBETTE* (closed Mondays), 31 Pl. Kléber, Tel. 211.94. A la carte. ☆☆*PALAIS DE LA BIERE,* Pl. Kléber, Tel. 417.56. ☆☆ *MARNE,* 6 Pl. Etudiants, Tel. 202.30. ☆☆*TAVERNE DU GRAND KLEBER* (closed Wednesdays), 47-49 Rue Grandes-Arcades, Tel. 302.77. ☆*CROCODILE* (closed Wednesdays), 10 Rue Outre, Tel. 213.02. ☆*BROG-LIE,* Pl. Broglie, Tel. 310.73. ☆ *TAVERNE GRUBER,* 18 Rue Vieux-Marché-aux-Grains, Tel. 200.70. ☆ *BRASSERIE PITON* (closed Wednesdays), 16 Rue Vieux-Marche-aux-Grains, Tel. 212.01. ☆*BACCARA* (closed Thursdays), 13 Rue Faubourg-Saverne, Tel. 215.09. A la carte.

*Outside of the City: La Wantzenau, 13 kilometers from Strasbourg, Post Office Address: La Wantzenau.*

## RESTAURANTS

☆*AU MOULIN,* Tel. 1 La Wantzenau. ☆*ZIMMER,* Rue Principale, Tel. 5 La Wantzenau.

## Talloires, Alps

Distance (in kilometers) to: Paris 555; Geneva 56. Excursion round the lake of Annecy.

## HOTELS

☆☆☆*LE COTTAGE* (George Bise), (May-October), Route Abbaye, Tel. 10. View of lake; quiet. Specialties: Mousse de foie de volaille a la gelée de porto, Omble chevalier poche à la George Bise, Poularde Braisée à la crême d'estragon. Service charge 15%. 23 Rooms. Garage. ☆☆*ABBAYE* (May to September), Tel. 2 and 37. View of lake; quiet. Service charge 15%. 65 Rooms. Garage. ☆*LAC* (Easter to September), Tel. 8. View of garden. 40 Rooms. Garage free. ☆*BEAU SITE* (Easter to October), Tel. 4. View of lake. 32 Rooms. Garage.

## RESTAURANTS

☆☆☆*CHEZ LE PERE BISE* (Easter to October), on the lake, Tel. 1. View of lake. Specialties: Pâté chaud, gratin de queue d'écrevisses, Poularde de Bresse. Wines: Douvaines, Talloires. 8 Rooms. Garage free. ☆*GARCIN* (Easter to October), Tel. 24. View of mountain. Specialties: Pâté en croute du chef, Omble chevalier braisé aux ecrevisses, Fricassée de volaille Rosemonde. Wines: Talloires, Roussette de Seyssel. 8 Rooms. Garage.

## Toulouse

(Gateway·to the Pyrenees)

Distance (in kilometers) to: Paris 681; Bordeaux 250; Carcassonne 92; Font-Romeu 189; Lourdes 174; Luchon 141. Swimming pools, open-air and indoors. Airport at Blagnac, 7 kilometers, Tel. 381.03. Tourist Information: Maison du Tourisme, Square Ch.-de-Gaulle, Donjon du Capitole, Tel. 229.13. Automobile Club du Midi, 17 Allées Jean-Jaurès, Tel. 259.13. Club Alpin Français, 43 Rue Gambetta, Tel. 256.77. Touring Club de France, 17 Rue Ste. Ursule, Tel. 276.32.

☆☆☆*GRAND HOTEL ET TIVOLLIER*, 31-33 Rue Metz, Tel. 239.93. Service charge 15%. 200 Rooms. Garage. ☆☆☆*CIE DU MIDI*, Gare Matabiau, Tel. 229.93. Service charge 15%. 63 Rooms. ☆☆☆*REGINA* (no restaurant), 73 Rue Bayard, Tel. 254.66. Service charge 15%. 120 Rooms. Garage. ☆☆*CAPOUL*, 13 Pl. Wilson, Tel. 259.95. 150 Rooms. Garage. ☆☆*PARIS*, 66 Rue Gambetta, Tel. 214.97. 57 Rooms. ☆☆*FRANCE* (restaurant closed Saturdays), 5 Rue Austerlitz, Tel. 228.84. Service charge 15%. 50 Rooms. ☆☆*VICTORIA* (no restaurant), 76 Rue Bayard, Tel. 214.90. Service charge 15%. 85 Rooms. ☆☆*GRAND BALCON* (no restaurant), 8 Rue Romiguières, Tel. 208.08. Service charge 15%. 60 Rooms. ☆☆*ARCADES* (no restaurant), 9 Pl. Capitole, Tel. 201.17. Service charge 15%. 41 Rooms. ☆☆*RAYMOND IV* (no restaurant), 16 Rue Raymond IV, Tel. 209.41. Service charge 15%. 30 Rooms. Garage. ☆*OURS BLANC*, 2 Rue Victor-Hugo, Tel. 262.40. Service charge 15%. 32 Rooms. ☆*PRINTANIA* (no restaurant), 55 Rue St. Rome, Tel. 254.05. Service charge 15%. 75 Rooms. Garage free. ☆*DU TAUR* (no restaurant), 2 Rue Taur, Tel. 201.54. Service charge 15%. 30 Rooms. Garage free. ☆*GAMBETTA*, 39 Rue Gambetta, Tel. 244.59. 30 Rooms. ☆*OPERA* (no restaurant), 1 Pl. Capitole, Tel. 222.66. 30 Rooms. Garage free. ☆ *BAINS* (no restaurant), 5 Rue Labeda, Tel. 206.10. Service charge 15%. 75 Rooms. Garage.

## RESTAURANTS

☆☆*LAFAYETTE* (opening date indefinite), 15 Pl. Wilson, Tel. 252.52. ☆☆*LE REGENCE* (closed Mondays), 63 Rue Alsace-Lorraine (2nd floor), Tel. 260.52. Service charge 15%. ☆☆*BRASSERIE REGINA,* 75 Rue Bayard, Tel. 220.76. ☆☆*PAIX,* 7 Pl. Capitole, Tel. 251.56. ☆☆*LA FRE-GATE,* 16 Pl. Wilson (2nd floor), Tel. 259.61. ☆☆*LUCULLUS,* 8 Rue Austerlitz, Tel. 226.12. ☆*BELOSSI,* 3 Blvd. Strasbourg, Tel. 225.79. ☆ *RICHELIEU* (closed in August, and Tuesdays), 9 Rue Constantine, Tel. 218.44. ☆*AUBERGE BASQUE,* 1 Rue Boulbonne (2nd floor), Tel. 231.63.

## Le Touquet, Paris, Plage

Distance (in kilometers) to: Paris 221; Amiens 106; Calais 66. Beach resort. Casino de la Forêt (summer). Sea swimming pool, on the boardwalk. 18-hole Golf Course (for information Tel. 0.74). Tourist Information, Mairie, Tel. 6.05

## HOTELS

☆☆*ALEXANDRA* (Whitsunday to September), Blvd. Daloz, Tel. 0.97. Service charge 15%. 30 Rooms. ☆☆ *BRISTOL* (Easter to October), 17 Grande Rue, Tel. 8.00. ☆☆*BRITAN-NIA* (Easter, open 15 days, and from Whitsunday to September). Service charge 15%. 40 Rooms. Garage free. ☆☆*CENTRE* (March to October), Rue Paris and Rue St-Jean, Tel. 0.05. Service charge 15%. 40 Rooms. ☆☆ *RIVA-BELLA* (Whitsunday to September), 12 Rue Léon-Garet, Tel. 0.21. 27 Rooms. ☆*SELECT HO-TEL,* 63 Rue St-Louis, Tel. 3.50. 36 Rooms. ☆*TOUQUET HOTEL* (Easter to September), 17 Rue Paris, Tel. 2.61. 30 Rooms. ☆*LE RAL-LYE* (Easter to September), 65 Rue Londres, Tel. 3.01. 19 Rooms. ☆*UNIVERSEL,* 10 Rue Bruxelles, Tel. 1.59. 23 Rooms. *ROBERTS HOTEL* (Easter to October), 66 Rue Londres, Tel. 3.47. 28 Rooms. ☆ *RUCHE* (Easter to September), 11-13 Rue St. Amand, Tel. 1.42. 30 Rooms. Garage free. ☆*ARTOIS,* 123 Rue Paris, Tel. 1.57. 22 Rooms.

## RESTAURANT

☆☆*WHITE STAR* (opening date indefinite), 60 Rue Metz, Tel. 1.17. 50 Rooms.

## Outside the City

### HOTEL

☆☆☆☆*WESTMINSTER* (Easter to Whitsuntide, and summer), Av. Verger, Tel. 7.40. View of forest. Service charge 15%. 200 Rooms. Garage.

## Tours, Chateaux de la Loire

Distance (in kilometers) to: Paris 237; Amboise 27; Azay-le-Rideau 25; Blois 60; Caen 232; Chenonceaux 35; Chinon 46; La Flèche 72; Langeais 25; Limoges 202; Loches 40. Swimming pool, open-air, Parc des Sports de Beauregard, 4½ kilometers from the city. 18-hole Golf Course, (for information Tel. 47.85). Tourist Information, for Touraine (closed Sundays and Monday mornings), 98 Rue Nationale, Tel. 50.38. Automobile Club de l'Ouest, 4 Pl. Jean-Jaurès, Tel. 50.19. Touring Club de France, 82 Rue Nationale, Tel. 31.43.

☆☆☆☆*UNIVERS*, 3-5 Blvd. Heurteloup, Tel. 27.12. Service charge 13%. 120 Rooms. Garage. ☆☆☆☆*GRAND HOTEL*, 7 Pl. Gare, Tel. 35.31. Service charge 13%. 132 Rooms. Garage. ☆☆☆*METROPOLE* (restaurant closed from October 16 to Easter), 14 Pl. Palais, Tel. 40.51. Service charge 13%. 80 Rooms. Garage. ☆☆☆*CENTRAL HOTEL* (restaurant closed Wednesdays), 26 Rue Scellerie, Tel. 47.87. Quiet. 50 Rooms. Garage. ☆☆*MODERNE*, 1-3 Rue Victor-Laloux (Marignan), Tel. 51.02. Wines: Montlouis, Chinon. 25 Rooms. Garage. ☆☆*BORDEAUX*, 1 Pl. Gare, Tel. 40.32. Specialties: Perdreau dans son nid, Pied de porc grillé, Sole maison. Wines: Vouvray, Bourgueil. Service charge 15%. 43 Rooms. Garage. ☆☆*ARMOR* (no restaurant), 26 bis Blvd. Heurteloup, Tel. 25.32. 30 Rooms. ☆☆*CYGNE* (no restaurant), 6 Rue Cygne, Tel. 58.67. 25 Rooms. ☆*JACK NOCQUET* (no restaurant), 8 Rue Jules Simon, Tel. 46.98. View of garden; quiet. 18 Rooms. Garage free. ☆*GRAMMONT* (no restaurant), 16 Av. Grammont, Tel. 55.06. 24 Rooms. Garage. ☆*CORMILLOT* (restaurant closed Tuesdays), 2 Pl. François-Sicard, Tel. 46.35. 15 Rooms. Garage free. ☆ *ENTRAIGUES* (no restaurant), 59 Rue Entraigues, Tel. 25.71. 16 Rooms. ☆*TERMINUS*, 7 Rue Nantes, Tel. 51.01. 50 Rooms.

### RESTAURANTS

☆☆*LYONNAIS*, 5 Blvd. Heurteloup, Tel. 48.84. A la carte. Service charge 13%. Specialties (certain days only): Brochet Val de Loire, Rillons de Touraine, Poulet poële tourangelle.

Wines: Vouvray, Chinon. ☆*LE RALLYE*, 38 bis Av. Grammont, Tel. 43.95. ☆*RABELAIS*, 24 Pl. Rabelais, Tel. 31.64. ☆*ALEXANDRE* (closed Fridays), 4 Rue Colbert, Tel. 57.84. ☆*BUFFET GARE*, Pl. Gare, Tel. 46.12. ☆*AU BEC FIN* (closed Mondays), 69 Rue Nericault-Destouches, Tel. 22.10.

*Outside of the City: St. Cyr, Post Office Address, St. Cyr*

### HOTEL

☆*LA MOISANDERIE*, 2 Rue Victor-Hugo, Tel. 34 in St. Cyr. View of park; quiet. 15 Rooms. Garage free.

*St. Symphorien, Post Office Address, St. Symphorien*

### HOTEL

☆*CASTEL FLEURI*, 2 Rue Groison, Tel. 50.99 in Tours. View of garden; quiet. 15 Rooms.

### RESTAURANT

☆*LE NEGRE* (closed Wednesdays), 103 Av. Tranchée, Tel. 5 in St. Symphorien.

*Ste. Radegonde, 3 kilometers from the city, Post Office in Ste. Radegonde*

### HOTEL

☆☆*HERMITAGE*, Rue Jeanne-Wedells, Tel. 19 in Ste. Radegonde. Quiet. 20 Rooms. Garage free.

## Trouville, Calvados, Normandy

Distance (in kilometers) to: Paris 200; Cabourg 18; Caen 42; Le Havre 51. Beach resort. Casino in summer. Saltwater swimming pool, at the beach.

18-hole and 9-hole Golf Course, "New Golf," (Whitsuntide to September), 4½ kilometers from the city (for information Tel. Deauville 29.55). Tourist Information (Easter to Whitsuntide, and Summer), Casino, Tel. 61.19.

### HOTELS

☆☆☆LE FLAUBERT (restaurant Le Topsy in building), Rue Flaubert, Tel. 64.21. View of Beach. Service charge 15%. 25 Rooms. ☆☆☆BELLEVUE (Easter to October), (restaurant La Sole Normande in the same building), 1 Pl. Maréchal-Foch, Tel. 60.85 and 62.13. Service charge 15%. 100 Rooms. ☆☆LE PIGEONNIER (Easter to September), at the beach, Tel. 67.84. 15 Rooms. ☆☆ LE CHATHAM (Easter to September), Pl. Casino, Tel. 66.71. Service charge 15%. 15 Rooms. ☆☆FRANCE (Easter to October), 26 Blvd. F.-Moureaux, Tel. 62.02. Service charge 15%. 50 Rooms. Garage. ☆☆PLAGE (Easter to September), Pl. Maréchal-Foch, Tel. 60.68. 40 Rooms. ☆☆ NOAILLES ET AUBERGE DE LA CORNICHE (Easter to October), 72 Rue Orléans, Tel. 62.90. 28 Rooms. ☆TIVOLI (Easter to September), Carrefour Tivoli, Tel. 60.36. 40 Rooms. Garage. ☆REYNITA (Easter to October), 28 Rue Carnot, Tel. 63.13. 30 Rooms. ☆FLORIAN (opening date indefinite), 30 Rue Plage, Tel. 67.40. 15 Rooms.

### RESTAURANTS

☆☆LA SOLE NORMANDE (Easter to October), 1 Pl. Maréchal-Foch, Tel. 60.85. Service charge 15%. ☆☆ LE TOPSY (Easter to October), Rue Flaubert, Tel. 64.21. A la carte. Service charge 15%. ☆LE REGENCE (February to October), Blvd. F.-Moureaux, Tel. 60.71.

### Versailles, Seine et Oise

Distance (in kilometers) to: Paris (via Porte St. Cloud) 20; (via Porte Neuilly) 23; Chantilly 56; Fontainebleau 68. See the Palace, (Hall of Mirrors); Grand Trianon and Petit Trianon (open afternoons); Musée des Voitures (open afternoons); Musée Lambinet (18th-century; closed Mondays, and holidays from November to March); park, fountain display and celebration, summer evenings. Church, Nôtre-Dame; Salle du Jeu de Paume (closed Sundays and holidays). Tourist Information (Fêtes Versaillaises), Hôtel of Madame de Pompadour, 7 Rue Reservoirs, Tel. Versailles 23.50.

### HOTELS

☆☆VATEL, 36 Rue Reservoirs, Tel. 3.58. Service charge 15%. 50 Rooms. Garage. ☆☆ROYAL, 3 Rue Petigny, Tel. 3.51. Service charge 15%. 50 Rooms. Garage. ☆☆FRANCE (restaurant closed Wednesdays), 5 Rue Colbert, Tel. 2.50. Service charge 15%. 18 Rooms. Garage. ☆CHASSE (restaurant closed Thursdays), 2 Rue Chancellerie (Pl. Chateau), Tel. 0.92. Service charge 15%. Garage. 20 Rooms. ☆ST. LOUIS, 28 Rue St. Louis, Tel. 23.55. 25 Rooms. ☆SABOT D'OR (no restaurant), 23 Rue Maréchal-Foch, Tel. 10.17. 7 Rooms. ☆RICHAUD (no restaurant), 16 Rue Richaud, Tel. 10.42. 29 Rooms. ☆ PALAIS (no restaurant), 6 Pl. Lyautey, Tel. 20.74. 7 Rooms. Garage.

## RESTAURANTS

☆☆*LONDRES* (closed Mondays), 7 Rue Colbert, Tel. 5.79. View of garden. A la carte. ☆☆*VILLA MAINTENON*, Rue Peintre-Lebrun, Tel. 19.01. 10 Rooms. ☆☆*ILE-DE-FRANCE*, 45 Rue Carnot, Tel. 05.28. ☆☆*BRASSERIE MULLER*, 23 bis Av. St. Cloud, Tel. 0.43. ☆*LE CAPITOLE* (closed Tuesdays), 45 bis Rue Maréchal-Foch, Tel. 3.54. ☆*NEPTUNE* (closed Tuesdays), 1 bis Rue Paroisse, Tel. 10.20. A la carte. ☆ *CHAPEAU GRIS* (breakfast only; closed Tuesdays), 7 Rue Hoche, Tel. 10.81. A la carte. ☆*TRIANETTE*, 7 Rue Recollets, Tel. 03.89. ☆*HOSTELLERIE DU ROY*, 16 Rue Chancellerie, Tel. 19.59.

## Vichy, Auvergne, Allier

Distance (in kilometers) to: Paris 341; Clermont-Ferrand 59. Spa (May to October). Casinos: Grand Casino (summer), Elysée Palace (summer). Open-air swimming pools: Sporting, Bellerive. 18-hole Golf Course (for information Tel. 20.66). Tourist Information, 11 Rue Parc, Tel. 21.79, and Automobile Club de Vichy, Tel. 20.66.

## HOTELS

☆☆☆☆*MAJESTIC* (summer), 6 Rue Petit, Tel. 25.51. Service charge 15%. 100 Rooms. ☆☆☆☆*CARLTON* (May to September), 26 Rue Président Wilson, Tel. 25.01. Service charge 15%. 200 Rooms. ☆☆☆☆*AMBASSADEURS* (May to October), 1 Rue Parc, Tel. 25.26. Service charge 15%. 200 Rooms. ☆☆☆☆*BAINS* (May to October), Rue Président Wilson, Tel. 25.81. Service charge 15%. 125 Rooms. ☆☆☆☆*PAVILLON SEVIGNE* (summer), 10-12 Pl. Sévigné, Tel. 25.91. View of garden. 75 Rooms. ☆☆☆☆*ALBERT I* (May to October), Av. Paul Doumer, Tel. 20.93 and 41.01. Specialties: Filets de sole, Poulet au curry. Wine: St. Pourcain. Service charge 15%. 150 Rooms. Garage. ☆☆☆☆*ASTORIA* (May to October), 2 Rue Président Wilson, Tel. 23.20 and 23.36. Service charge 15%. 90 Rooms. ☆☆☆*REGINA* (Easter to October), 4 Av. Thermale, Tel. 20.95 and 52.95. Service charge 15%. 130 Rooms. ☆☆☆*LILAS* (restaurant closed from October to May), 35 Av. Victoria, Tel. 25.71. View of garden; quiet. Service charge 15%. 120 Rooms. Garage. ☆☆☆*QUEEN'S HOTEL* (May to October), 113 Blvd. Etats-Unis, Tel. 21.13. View of park. Service charge 15%. 102 Rooms. ☆☆☆*PRINCES ET PLAZA* (May to September), 15 Rue Parc, Tel. 20.53. 120 Rooms. ☆☆☆*PAIX* (May to October), 17 Rue Parc, Tel. 20.56. Service charge 15%. 90 Rooms. ☆☆☆ *LUTETIA* (closed December to February), 5 Rue Belgique, Tel. 22.17. Service charge 15%. 80 Rooms. ☆☆☆ *AMIRAUTE* (May to October), 20 Rue Président Wilson, Tel. 20.13. Service charge 15%. 90 Rooms. ☆☆☆ *RUSSIE ET MEDITERRANEE* (May to October), 12 Av. A.-Briand, Tel. 26.85. Service charge 15%. 100 Rooms. Garage. ☆☆ *GRIGNAN* (May to October), 7 Pl. Sévigné, Tél. 23.59. Service charge 15%. 90 Rooms. Garage. ☆☆☆*MONTPENSIER* (Easter to October), 48 Blvd. Etats-Unis, Tel. 26.97. Service charge 15%. 59 Rooms. ☆☆☆*GALLIA* (May to October), 14 Av. Paul Doumer,

Tel. 23.90. Service charge 15%. 80 Rooms. ☆☆*ERMITAGE DU PONT-NEUF* (May to September), 5 Square Albert I, Tel. 20.73. Service charge 15%. 90 Rooms. Garage. ☆☆*PORTUGAL ET DE L'INTENDANCE* (May to October) (no restaurant), 121 Blvd. Etats-Unis, Tel. 23.82. Service charge 15%. 63 Rooms. ☆☆*AIX ET CHAMBERY* (along the park), Tel. 21.40. Service charge 15%. 55 Rooms. ☆☆*EUROPE* (May to October), Pl. Victor-Hugo, Tel. 20.34. Service charge 15%. 90 Rooms. ☆☆*FRANCE ET PASTEUR* (May to October), 19-21 Av. A.-Briand, Tel. 27.07. Service charge 15%. 60 Rooms. ☆☆*SPLENDID* (May to October), 28 Rue Maréchal-Foch, Tel. 20.35. Service charge 15%. 115 Rooms. ☆☆*LOUVRE,* 15 Rue Intendance, Tel. 27.71. Service charge 15%. 45 Rooms. ☆☆*MONDIAL* (April to November), 39 Rue Paris, Tel. 32.05. 75 Rooms. Garage. ☆☆*BALMORAL* (April to October), 4 Rue Gallieni, Tel. 21.91. 75 Rooms. ☆☆*RIVOLI* (May to September), 5 Blvd. Russie, Tel. 21.51. 87 Rooms. ☆☆*VICHY* (restaurant closed October 15 to April 15), 6 Blvd. Carnot, Tel. 22.31. Service charge 15%. 55 Rooms. ☆☆*WINDSOR* (May to October), 34 Rue Salignat, Tel. 21.59. 82 Rooms. ☆☆*LAFAYETTE* (May to September), 11 bis Rue Alquie, Tel. 23.48. Service charge 15%. 50 Rooms. ☆☆*FOCH ET CENTRE* (Easter to Christmas), 12 Rue Source-de-l'Hôpital, Tel. 22.46. 69 Rooms. ☆☆*CENTRAL,* 3 Pl. Gare, Tel. 21.24 and 32.54. 100 Rooms. ☆☆*TRIANON* (no restaurant), 9 Rue Desbrest, Tel. 46.88. 28 Rooms. ☆ *BREST ET ST. GEORGES* (April

to October), 27 Rue Paris, Tel. 22.18. 60 Rooms. Garage free. ☆*FLORIDA* (May to September), 5 Rue Source-de-l'Hôpital, Tel. 21.71. 65 Rooms. ☆*GLOBE,* 57 Rue Paris, Tel. 21.35. 10 Rooms. Garage. ☆*ALGERIA,* 22 Blvd. Carnot, Tel. 36.98. 82 Rooms. ☆*MASSENA* (May to October) 4 Square Albert I, Tel. 21.50. 40 Rooms. ☆*POSTE ET NOUVELLE POSTE* (May to September), 33 Rue Paris, Tel. 21.67. 75 Rooms. Garage. ☆*CONCORDIA* (May to September), 15 Rue Roovère, Tel. 29.65. 34 Rooms.

### RESTAURANTS

☆☆*CHANTECLER* (summer), 23 Rue Parc, Tel. 25.51. Service charge 15%. ☆☆*ALHAMBRA* (closed October to March), 5 Rue Sornin, Tel. 21.41. ☆☆*LA RESERVE* (closed Mondays), 3 Pl. Hôtel-de-Ville, Tel. 27.37. Specialties: Escargots farcis, Tripes à la mode de Caen, Moules mariniere. Wine: St. Pourcain. ☆☆ *LE ROYAL BRASSERIE* (April to October), 12 Rue Président Wilson, Tel. 35.20. ☆*RICOUX* (May to October), 26 Quai d'Allier, Tel. 26.90. Service charge 15%. ☆*TAVERNE DES FLEURS* (March to September), 19 Rue Sornin, Tel. 26.77.

*Outside the City: Charmeil, 6 kilometers from Vichy, Post Office Address: St. Rémy-en-Rollat*

### HOTEL

☆☆*CHATEAU DE CHARMEIL* (Easter to October), Tel. 31.31 in Vichy. View of park and valley; quiet. 14 Rooms. Garage free.

## Villeneuve-les-Avignon, Provence

Distance (in kilometers) to: Paris 672; Avignon 3; Orange 22. Tourist Information: 1 Pl. St. Pons, Tel. 44.

### HOTEL

☆*LE PRIEURE,* Pl. du Chapitre, Tel. 20.31 in Avignon. View of park; quiet. 25 Rooms. Garage.

### RESTAURANTS

☆*HOSTELLERIE PROVENCALE DU VIEUX MOULIN,* Tel. 1.64. View of Rhone. A la carte. ☆*MIDI,* 6 and 8 Pl. St. Pons, Tel. 0.52. 8 Rooms.

## Vittel, Vosges-Alsace

Distance (in kilometers) to: Paris 327; Epinal 43; Nancy 71. Spa (open May to September). Casino (summer); swimming pool; bath house (May to September). 18-hole Golf Course (June to September) (for information, Tel. 0.03 and 1.56). Tourist Information (May to September), 1 Av. A.-Bouloumié, Tel. 0.72.

### HOTELS

☆☆☆☆☆*GRAND HOTEL ET CERES* (summer), Tel. 0.83 and 2.37. View of park. Service charge 15%. 450 Rooms. ☆☆☆☆*VITTEL PALACE* (summer), Av. Gérémoy, Tel. 0.05. Service charge 15%. 120 Rooms. ☆☆☆*NOUVEL HOTEL* (summer), Av. A.-Bouloumié, Tel. 0.16. Service charge 15%. 180 Rooms. ☆☆☆ *SOURCES* (summer), 6 Av. A.-Bouloumié, Tel. 0.17. Service charge 15%. 150 Rooms. Garage. ☆☆☆*CONTINENTAL* (opening date indefinite), Av. A. Bouloumié, Tel. 0.07. 250 Rooms. Garage. ☆☆*PROVIDENCE* (summer), Av. Châtillon, Tel. 0.27. Service charge 15%. 70 Rooms. ☆*LORRAINE* (April to September), 40 Rue Verdun, Tel. 0.48. 24 Rooms. ☆*TILLEULS,* Av. P.-Bouloumié, Tel. 1.34. 52 Rooms. ☆*BELLEVUE* (May to September) Av. Châtillon, Tel. 0198. 60 Rooms. Garage. ☆*FRANCE,* Pl. Dames, Tel. 0.29. 20 Rooms. Garage. ☆*BEAUSEJOUR* (summer), Av. P. Bouloumié, Tel. 0.34. Service charge 15%. 45 Rooms. ☆*PARIS* (summer) (no restaurant), 26 Rue Paris, Tel. 0.40. 30 Rooms.

### RESTAURANT

☆☆*JEANNE D'ARC ET POSTE* (summer), 51 Rue Verdun, Tel. 0.61. Service charge 15%. 35 Rooms.

# INDEX